THE IMPERIAL KAISER

A Portrait of William II

BY

LAWRENCE WILSON

DORSET PRESS
New York

Originally published as
The Incredible Kaiser

This edition published by Dorset Press,
a division of Marboro Books Corporation,
by arrangement with
Robert Hale Ltd
1991 Dorset Press

ISBN 0-88029-617-8

Printed in the United States of America

M 9 8 7 6 5 4 3 2 1

Contents

1 THE PROBLEM PRINCE   9

2 HAIL, KAISER, TO THEE!   21

3 DROPPING THE PILOT   34

4 WILLIAM AT SEA   49

5 FISHING IN TROUBLED WATERS   61

6 BÜLOW, BRITAIN, BATTLESHIPS   73

7 "I AM THE BALANCE OF POWER"   82

8 WILLIAM'S MASTER-STROKE   95

9 MOROCCO   101

10 THE NOVEMBER STORM   109

11 THE POWDER BARREL   119

12 THE EXPLOSION   135

13 WORLD WAR   146

14 IN A COLD, GREY DAWN   164

15 EXILE   180

Index   187

CHAPTER ONE

THE PROBLEM PRINCE

THIS is the story of the German Emperor who was Queen Victoria's grandson, of a Prussian who felt half an Englishman, a ruler who could not rule himself, a warlord who was afraid of war, a timorous autocrat, an aggressive dreamer, an actor unconvincing as an emperor and elusive as a man. Some people thought he was mad, others despised him, yet others felt an undying respect. He could certainly inspire devotion; he was a scintillating conversationalist, a charmer when he liked. But he could also offend, outrage and disconcert. To the Germans he was at first affectionately and later, when he failed to grow up, condescendingly known as "the young Kaiser". Others, beyond his country, called him "the mad dog of Europe".

Seldom has there been a ruler who so conspicuously failed to put his good intentions into effect or a man with such a genius for loading hatred and blame upon himself. But today the question of guilt seems irrelevant. A man cannot help his temperament, cannot choose his parents, and though with most people an area of freewill remains to them between the plant of heredity and the pot of environment, in the case of Kaiser William this area seems to have been unusually small. He was always a rudderless ship at the mercy of every gale.

The unfavourable winds first began to blow in his childhood. In 1858, when his father, Frederick William, Prince of Prussia, married Queen Victoria's eldest daughter he was twenty-seven and the young Victoria was eighteen. Though she had blushed when he had picked white heather for her at Balmoral and seemed a demure little bride, she quickly established an ascendancy over her handsome husband which was to last throughout their married life. He was good-natured, easy-going and rather stupid. She never ceased to regret that she had been born a woman. Physically strong and active, mentally alert with wide interests in the arts and, as soon transpired,

9

THE KAISER'S LINKS WITH BRITAIN

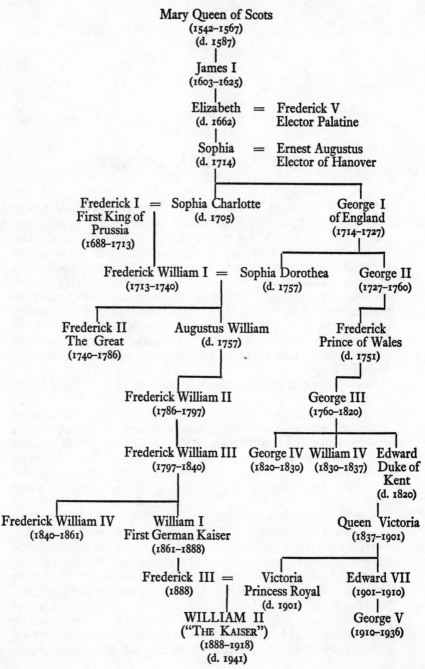

Mary Queen of Scots
(1542–1567)
(d. 1587)

James I
(1603–1625)

Elizabeth   =   Frederick V
(d. 1662)   Elector Palatine

Sophia   =   Ernest Augustus
(d. 1714)   Elector of Hanover

Frederick I   =   Sophia Charlotte   George I
First King of   (d. 1705)   of England
Prussia   (1714–1727)
(1688–1713)

Frederick William I   =   Sophia Dorothea   George II
(1713–1740)   (d. 1757)   (1727–1760)

Frederick II   Augustus William   Frederick
The Great   (d. 1757)   Prince of Wales
(1740–1786)   (d. 1751)

Frederick William II   George III
(1786–1797)   (1760–1820)

Frederick William III   George IV   William IV   Edward
(1797–1840)   (1820–1830) (1830–1837)   Duke of
                                                    Kent
                                                    (d. 1820)

Frederick William IV   William I   Queen Victoria
(1840–1861)   First German Kaiser   (1837–1901)
                        (1861–1888)

Frederick III   =   Victoria   Edward VII
(1888)   Princess Royal   (1901–1910)
                      (d. 1901)

WILLIAM II   George V
("THE KAISER")   (1910–1936)
(1888–1918)
(d. 1941)

in politics, with a tenacious will and restless ambition, Victoria would have been a match for better men than Frederick.

There was not much she liked about her new home. Looking back on an idyllic childhood dominated by an adored father with liberal views and breadth of intellect, she found the Prussians stiff and reactionary, content seemingly to live and die in a rigid hierarchy which made her impatient and contemptuous. But one day things would be different. Frederick's father, soon to be King William, was already sixty-one. When he was gone, the pliant Frederick with Victoria at his side would rule Prussia's destinies. Victoria dreamt of an anglicized country firmly allied to Great Britain. In one of his innumerable letters dealing with the problems of Prussia her father Albert had written: "I will repeat that a great, liberal generous policy is the prerequisite for an alliance with England, for hegemony in Germany and for renown in arms." In due course the Prince Consort clearly expected his daughter and son-in-law to put this policy into effect and when he died in 1861 Victoria swore not to disappoint him. A paternalistic autocracy would never do. Her father had written: "The days are past when a single man could expect millions of educated thoughtful people to trust their entire welfare to the hands of *one* man, be he personally ever so excellent and honourable." Albert had declared: "Prussia claims to stand at the head of Germany, but she does not behave like a German", and he had gone on to speak of "constitutional development". Albert disapproved of the whole Prussian system and had seen no reason why it should not be radically changed—whatever Prussian history had been.

These precepts Victoria swore to keep. Both loyalty to her parents and intellectual conviction demanded it. One day she would put them into effect and the means lay to hand—her husband. With increasing insistence she set to work on him. "A liberal practical constitution"—"orderly and legal means", a replica of her beloved England should be built on the unpropitious Prussian soil, with extended suffrage, a representative parliament, cabinet government and the Sovereign, like her dear Mama, a benign figurehead, consulted and deferred to, of course, but never an autocrat. Frederick was an apt pupil. Soon, under Victoria's tutelage, he was actually pitying his father for his wrong-headed ideas. He was sorry to see him lean on conservatives, sorrier still when he appointed Bismarck his First Minister. "It is a totally erroneous idea," Victoria tartly assured him, "that a man like Bismarck can be of use to our country—he has no principles." Soon, with an eye to the future and the support of liberal politicians, Victoria was urging Frederick to stay away from the State Council, which he had a right

to attend. Frederick had qualms. What about his duty to his father?
"You owe it to your future," Victoria sternly reminded him, "to the
country and to your children to keep aloof from everything which
might lead people to have an erroneous idea of your political
convictions. This is really your duty and in no way conflicts with
that to your father. Please, please, dearest, listen to your little
wife. . . . I am afraid you are too good and think that you are doing
your duty by sacrificing your opinion to that of your dear Papa.
You have other duties which, in my opinion, take first place."

As early as 1862, Victoria was calling Bismarck "my *bête noire*",
and when Frederick, upbraided by his father for parading liberal
views in opposition to himself, declared that he had "howled and
sobbed" all night, she wrote to him: "I am inexpressibly sorry for
your poor father, for sooner or later he will reap what he has sown.
Think of the future and thank God you are as you are and not
deluded and confused and mistaken as your poor Papa is." If
Frederick, she continued, was reduced to tears by speaking out, let
him keep silent in future. As for herself: "I have the example of my
dearest Father before me. . . . He advocated every true, right and
sound principle and therefore was great and wise and happy."

This needed some swallowing, but Frederick performed the feat.
He was so much under Victoria's thumb, so anxious to believe he
enjoyed her tyranny that he noted in his diary: "My little wife is
my most devoted adviser, my whole support, my indefatigable
comforter."

Meanwhile, in deepest mourning for her Albert, Queen Victoria
had resolved to give her last energies to perpetuating his work.
Albert had wished for an alliance between England and a liberalized
Prussia. Albert's will should be done. Fortunately, her daughter
was stationed at the very hub of events in Berlin. For all her tender
age, she was the spearhead of the campaign to turn Prussia, the
"police State" as she called it, into a replica of England. This aim
she pursued as a reckless partisan, utterly intolerant of any opinions
that differed fron her own and seemingly unaware that she was a
traitor to her adopted country. In September, 1862, King William
threatened to abdicate if his desire for a restoration of the three-year
term of military service was thwarted by the Federal Council.
Victoria jumped head-first into the controversy, bringing every
ounce of pressure to bear on Frederick to persuade his father to
carry out the threat. "I consider," she wrote to her husband with
clammy hypocrisy, "that you should make this sacrifice for the
country," and when Frederick wavered she complained to her
mother: "You know how he loves his father . . ., besides he is not
born a free Englishman and all Prussians have not the feeling of

independence and love of justice and constitutional liberty they ought to have."

But the King did not abdicate and Victoria perforce continued her intrigues against him and Bismarck, using her husband as a stalking-horse. At her instigation he openly dissociated himself in 1863 from his father's policy regarding restrictions on the press and wrote to Bismarck protesting against a "breach of the constitution". To achieve this, wrote Victoria to her mother, had been difficult, but she had felt in duty bound to make Fritz place his "political conscience" above his feelings. "Do not think it is easy, dear Mama. It is very disagreeable to me to be thought meddling and intriguing. But I should not be a freeborn English woman and your child if I did not see all those things as minor considerations. I am very ambitious for the country, for Fritz and the children and so I am determined to brave all the rest."

That there was danger in indulging her feelings as a "freeborn English woman", even danger for the dynasty and for her children Victoria failed to realize. There is no evidence that she studied dispassionately the complexities of German politics or tried to understand what Bismarck was trying to achieve. He, of course, was well aware of the vortex of intrigue that centred round her and when Frederick asked to be excused from attending the State Council he expressed his concern to the King. Frederick and Victoria, he said, did not realize that in reigning Houses nearest relatives were not always fellow-countrymen, but in duty bound to represent other interests than those of Prussia. "It is hard when a country's frontier is the boundary of interests between mother and daughter, brother and sister—but to forget that spells danger to the State."

Victoria, however, refused to plant both feet in the Prussian camp. In 1866 she wrote to her mother: "People are always finding fault with me for all I do. It is too stupid. Of course in Germany I always take the part of the Englishman, and in England I try to stick up for the German." The "try" spoke volumes. Already this perverse attitude had aroused doubts about her loyalty to Prussian interests. "Just fancy," she had reported, "rumours are being spread here that I had found out everything about a Council of State and had immediately reported it to Lord Palmerston." But with the future Queen of Prussia positively flaunting the Union Jack, what could she expect? In the very year of Prussia's apotheosis, in 1871 after victory over the French, she wrote to her mother: "The words of our national anthem always fill my eyes with tears. . . . I have never felt the John Bull so strong in me as during these last twelve months."

But the woman in whom the Archduke Albrecht detected such

"contrariness", such "an inordinate lust for power", was doomed to
wait in the wings while the limelight continued to shine with
redoubled brilliance on her husband's father, now the Emperor
William I. Victoria conceded that Bismarck had made Germany
great and feared, but . . . And she could think of several "buts".
"Have our ideas enlarged? Has our social life developed? Have we
become richer?" Her answer was a sorrowful "no". Apart from this,
a powerful Germany made her envious. Only England was entitled
to be strong. "To become a great *Kultur Staat* and not a *Militär
Staat* is what I want for Germany," she wrote to her mother in
1875, and a year later: "Brutal power and strength have never
impressed me, they can destroy like the wild untamed power of
nature, but they can never construct, erect, ennoble." What *did* she
want? She had professed to be a good Prussian, yet she begrudged
a strong united Germany. She wanted *Kultur*, but not the political
security in which culture can thrive. She decried "party machina-
tions, party hatreds, party tactics", yet sneered at the strength
which could bring order out of chaos. Behind her obstinate opposition to the spirit of the times it was impossible not to see a purely
emotional distaste for Germany and Germans and it was no wonder
that as time went on the future Empress and her husband found
themselves increasingly isolated. It was in this atmosphere of
divided loyalties and largely futile obstructionism that her son Willy
grew up.

Prince William was born in 1859. Victoria was not the sort of
mother to brook independence in her offspring, she was the ruler
of the household and Willy realized the fact at an early age. When he
was a month short of three years old, his father stopped eating one
day at luncheon. Anticipating his mother, Willy called out to him:
"Go on eating, darling, your little wife wishes it!" This aroused
great hilarity at the table, but small boys like to admire their fathers
as models of manly strength and in their mothers find the loving
protection they need until they can achieve independence. In
Willy's family the situation was reversed. Thus his biological urge to
be a man was thwarted. Women, as he could see, were strong, but
men were weak. Within the family there was no masculine ideal that
he could imitate. Victoria took advantage of his dependence in order
to subdue him to her will. His father, if he ever felt love for his son,
must have found this turning into the mournful solidarity of the
oppressed.

Moreover, Willy had been born with a withered left arm. It was a
birth trauma which nothing could cure, but to the proud mother a
reproach which she was desperately anxious to remove. She could
not bring herself to believe that medical science was helpless. The

arm was wrapped in red flannel, massaged, wrenched, manipulated —but remained obstinately blue, cold and several inches shorter than the right. The victim of inept experiments, as he grew older Willy realized that he was different from other boys in two conflicting senses: he was crippled and he was born to be ruler of a powerful nation. To judge from the attitude of those around him, headed by his mother, he was singularly ill-equipped for the task. First in the focus of his attention was the useless arm. It was the enemy of the whole household, the slur on his parents' generative efficiency, the defect which, whatever nature or accident decreed, *must* somehow be made good. He was never allowed to forget it. "How does it feel, Willy?" his mother would ask. "Is there any sensation when I touch it here—or here? Try to lift this spoon, exert yourself, be firm, this is a trial which is sent to test you!" The admonitions, the experiments, the sheer terror of having to pretend that he could run and jump and ride a pony, the falls, the tears, and the threats!

But more insidious, even, more undermining to his self-confidence than the withered arm were the continual stabs directed at his mind. Willy should become a credit to her or else—as far as she was concerned—his mother would have no further use for him. A woman of rigid views, a *maîtresse femme* resolved to stamp her personality on those around her, Victoria could not rest till she had her family in step and nothing annoyed her so much as to see the dawn of a genuinely individual temperament in her offspring. "I tremble when I think of our boys growing up—what they will turn out like," she wrote to her mother when Willy was nine. And eighteen months before, though admitting that Willy was "interesting, charming, clever, amusing, engaging", she had confessed that he had his failings: "he is inclined to be selfish, domineering and proud." But for "domineering" no doubt one should read "healthily self-assertive", while "selfish" and "proud" were the very epithets that applied to Victoria herself.

Here, then, was a clash of personalities which nothing could resolve. The child, severely handicapped and burdened with frightening rumours of heavy responsibilities to come—and the mother, seeking to reduce him to the same supine dependence on her as her husband. A small ship struggling to make headway in a Sargasso Sea of tenacious resistance. But as time passed, Willy became increasingly aware that, amidst the great and stirring life of Prussia, his parents lived in an unhealthy backwater of intrigue and moral isolation. Raising his eyes beyond the confines of his home he could see two beacons gleaming from afar—his grandfather and the doughty figure of Bismarck. They were beyond his mother's spell. They spelt freedom. They were alive and active in the real world where troops marched, bands played and cheers came up like wine from an applauding multitude. At home, all was impotence and asperity, but outside it, swords and helmets glittered, there was a swirl of gorgeous uniforms and the great wind of change blew bracingly through the palace corridors. Grandpapa was a man of mettle, challenging, irascible, with an aura about him of god-like authority. His eye gleamed. His head was high. He walked with a tread as sure as Destiny's. Willy loved him with breathless adoration. Papa, on the other hand . . . Papa in his dingy uniforms with one or two little medals lost in a sea of blue, Papa ever hesitant, weary, the mild eyes forever seeking Victoria's approbation, Papa indistinguishable sometimes from the men who drove horse-trams through the streets of Berlin.

In due course Willy revolted. He had not been drilled to overcome his physical deficiencies for nothing. His will was steeled. Through her very severities his mother opened the door of escape. He was made self-reliant to the extent that he could feed and dress himself, ride and fence as well if not better than a normal boy. This was to be his revenge. The physical fear was subdued. The moral anxiety of challenging his mother's rule could also be faced. Willy would strike out and hitch his waggon not to his father's feeble luminary, but to the glittering constellation of Prussia now rising resplendent in the sky.

But this revolt was slow to take place. In his sixth year, noting signs of a wayward and intractable disposition, his parents appointed a Westphalian Calvinist by the name of Hinzpeter as tutor. His technique was simple. The withered arm was to be ignored. Willy was to behave as though it were normal. This involved riding exercises which plunged him into agonies of terror. As no one else had the heart to do it, Hinzpeter lifted him into the saddle and forced him to trot and canter without stirrups until he fell off. Deaf to all entreaties, Hinzpeter then repeated the process. Again would come a fall. Again the child would be put back until, after weeks of this, Willy achieved a precarious balance.

In book-learning Hinzpeter followed the curriculum established by Frederick the Great's father, the caricature of all sadistic parents. The daily time-table covered every minute of the lessons and of the boy's spare time as well. Loathing and envying the opulence of the Court, Hinzpeter set up the word "renunciation" as the guiding principle of Willy's life. He never praised his pupil or even acknowledged his progress—that again as a matter of principle. This "gaunt, dry figure with the parchment face" as William later described him, did his best to dry up the springs of joy in his pupil and it is easy to imagine how William's simmering resentment against this animated fossil gradually turned against his parents, particularly his mother, who subjected him to this régime.

To the sprightly Willy the world seemed hung with grey curtains. Duty, renunciation, toil, self-improvement—a discipline that went on day after day under the censorious gaze of the dyspeptic tutor. No release, no means of escape. From Hinzpeter to Mama and back again without hope of reprieve. For companions, only his younger brother and sisters, but they, too, were swaddled with oppressive solicitude based on the erroneous idea that character can be imposed from without instead of being developed from within. Princes and Princesses of Prussia dying for want of air while their father wove pious phrases round their heads such as these which he penned for William: "May he grow up to be a vigorous and upright man who will rejoice in the Good and the Beautiful."

But there were more solid things to admire than Frederick's conception of the Good and the Beautiful. In 1862 Bismarck had become Prime Minister of Prussia and a new ruthlessness and urgency had come into the movement for German unity. In the previous year his grandfather had ascended the throne on the death of his lunatic elder brother. In 1864, peering over the nursery window-sill, William had watched the regiment "King of Prussia" marching off to Schleswig-Holstein and victory over the Danes. Two years later, Austria was defeated in a lightning war and William watched the troops returning, headed by his grandfather and father crowned with the laurels they had won on the Bohemian battlefield. Then, on 16th June, 1871, when he was twelve, had come a stupendous scene: the Brandenburg Gate entwined with garlands, flags and streamers fluttering in the breeze, dense crowds in their best clothes lining the Unter den Linden, thronging in stands, on roofs, on top of the Gate itself. Then the clash of military bands, a distant cavalcade approaching, plumes, spiked helmets, black and white chargers, and at its head, Grandpapa, the new Emperor, fresh from his triumph over the French, halting to accept the keys of Berlin from a deputation of white-dressed maidens. William was allowed to ride forward on his pony. In his diary that night he wrote: "The Emperor came past, soon after, Papa and waved to me with the Field Marshal's baton he had just received. I galloped up and rode behind him. Later, when the Emperor rode past me, he put his hand on my shoulder and said: 'This is a day you will never forget.' "

Meanwhile, Victoria was making a progress report on Willy to her mother. "He does not possess exactly brilliant abilities nor any other strength of character or talent. . . . I watch over him myself and every smallest detail of his education. . . . He possesses a strong constitution and would be a handsome lad if it were not for this unfortunate left arm which becomes more and more noticeable, affects his facial expression, his stance, his walk and his deportment, makes all his movements clumsy and gives him a feeling of shyness. . . ." Victoria also claimed that there was a bond of love between them which nothing could destroy. But this was not true on either side. From Willy's seventh year, when her younger son Sigismund died, Victoria became increasingly withdrawn and her children found her a cold and censorious parent.

For eight years, until he was fifteen, Willy toiled under the eye of his tutor and in all that time the strongest stimuli were the glimpses of Prussian might, the doting affection of his father's parents and, on the rare occasions when he saw her, of Queen Victoria. In 1874 he and his younger brother were sent to the *Gymnasium* in Cassel, Hinzpeter accompanying them and retaining control of their education. By now Willy's personality was causing serious concern. There was no doubt he was a very peculiar boy. Making every allowance for his infirmity and the stresses of his position, there was a lot that could not be explained. A normal child develops, adjusts himself to life, enjoys the free interplay between his mind and experience. But Willy did not change. His mind seemed to lack the mechanism which sorts impressions and forms them into a picture. They rebounded from him like droplets of water from a duck. He could absorb facts, yes, but in a fundamental sense he could not learn. Looking back in later years, Hinzpeter described him like this: "On 27th January, 1859, a human being was born with an exceptionally strongly marked individuality which has developed according to its own laws, basically unchanged by anything and resistant even to the strongest external influences—a personality of a peculiar crystalline construction which has remained the same through all phases of development and has retained its own character through all the natural metamorphoses. The resistance was most noticeable which any pressure, any attempt to mould the inner personality into a particular form provoked. . . . It was extraordinarily difficult to reach the inner being. . . . This stubborn nature was extremely resistant even to the discipline of thought." What did all this mean, what did it imply? Monsieur Aymé, Willy's French tutor, noted other characteristics: extreme liveliness of temperament, a love of histrionic poses, a determination to model himself on some chosen hero, Frederick the Great or his grandfather.

Willy did moderately well at Cassel, passed his exams just before his eighteenth birthday and then returned home to Potsdam for his coming-of-age ceremony. A remark of his father's dropped like an icicle into this cheerful occasion. A Prussian nobleman congratulated him. "Don't congratulate me, dear Graf," he replied. "My son will never mature, will never come of age."

Prince William was now a very jaunty young man, highly conscious of his position, thirsty for praise, touchy about anything which affected his dignity. He sensed his parents' misgivings and was secretly wounded to the quick by the fact that their hostility, as he interpreted it, was common knowledge. For six months he now plunged into army life as a lieutenant in the 1st Guards Regiment, finding himself thoroughly at home in the arrogant soldierly atmosphere of those times. Here was his link with Frederick the Great and Grandpapa, with the stream of Prussian tradition and recent history, with his destiny as he saw it: the warrior leader of a warlike people. His imagination was now aflame. Hinzpeter with the parchment face had been returned to file and William could construct his own vision of Germany's past and future. Moving for four terms to the University of Bonn to study law and national economy, he could think of nothing finer than a few months spent by the Rhine, the German river encrusted with legend. In Bonn he took a private course in history from a professor who opened his eyes to the splendours of contemporary German history and planted in him a glowing admiration for Bismarck as the founder and protector of the Reich. Hitherto, William had perforce accepted his parents' views on the great statesman. Now, he returned home with a new truculence towards them, born of the realization that if they had their way Germany would still be a weak and possibly a divided country.

Soon after this, he was married to Princess Augusta Victoria of Schleswig-Holstein, a pious girl who in his eyes possessed the one indispensable characteristic: undying admiration for himself. He was back in the army now, sitting at the lieutenants' table in the mess, rejoicing in the hearty comradeship and the atmosphere of beef and bull. His arm was no longer a hindrance to him—he could ride and fence with the best, and anyway the ceaseless adulation he received from colleagues and superiors with an eye to promotion more than made up for feelings of inadequacy and redoubled the conviction that he was a superior being. With this new freedom a certain heartlessness in his dealings with people became apparent, a self-centred view of the world, a desire to shine coupled with an actor's urge to mask a timorous nature with an outward show of self-assertion.

As the years passed and Prince William, with accelerated promotion from Captain to Major and finally to command of the Guard Hussar Regiment, steadily enlarged his sphere of activities, his problematical nature struck many observers. He seemed to respect no one but Bismarck and the Emperor; he was pushful, tactless and perpetually at loggerheads with his parents. Public functions which the Emperor instructed him to attend aroused his father's violent jealousy and at a regimental dinner at which William was present Frederick publicly denounced him as immature and lacking in judgement. His grandfather, meanwhile, continued to foster his military career, distributing dollops of praise which rejoiced William's heart. The rift with his parents was complete; his mother he treated with indifference and his father with contempt. What would happen when the Emperor died and Frederick, now in his sixtieth year, came to the throne, nobody dared to predict. Victoria with Frederick behind her was the sworn enemy of Bismarck. Bismarck was cultivating the young William. From England Queen Victoria was sending wise letters counselling moderation on all sides.

At any rate, in this uneasy situation, there seemed to be one consoling factor: Frederick, it was assumed, would reign for many years and William would have time to acquire that steadiness of judgement and firmness of character which he so conspicuously lacked. But this was not to be.

CHAPTER TWO

HAIL, KAISER, TO THEE!

As the Emperor entered his ninth decade, the animosity between William and his parents was nourished by Bismarck. Facing the task of ruling Germany with the liberal-minded Frederick backed by his Anglophile wife, Bismarck saw danger ahead for his life's work. Neither Victoria nor her husband concealed that their aim would be to introduce constitutional monarchy after the English pattern. This plan Bismarck was determined to frustrate because he considered strong authoritarian government essential for the preservation of German unity. In Prince William he saw a useful ally against his parents and in due course, when he ascended the throne, an indispensable factor in perpetuating the Bismarck dynasty. For Bismarck, now in his seventies, was cherishing plans for his son Herbert to succeed him.

The ambitious William welcomed Bismarck's overtures with open arms. He was eager to learn his part and the role which Bismarck now assigned to him was that of an ultra-patriotic, pro-Russian, anti-British prince of marked autocratic leanings. This, of course, as Bismarck intended, brought him into renewed conflict with his parents. Long and doleful were the letters which his mother wrote to Queen Victoria complaining of her son's disrespect, indifference, lack of consideration, and Frederick, who had now waited almost twenty years to occupy the throne and was in Bismarck's opinion an "extremely vain gentleman", became increasingly touchy at any suggestion that William was treading on his prerogatives.

In 1884 there were pursed lips and tears of mortification in the Crown Prince's household when William was sent to Russia to attend the coming-of-age of the future Tsar Nicolas II. There was horror when, two years later, he met the Emperor Franz Josef in Bad Gastein and even William was alarmed to think what might be his parents' reaction when, barely returned from his latest triumph, he was dispatched once more on a diplomatic mission to Russia. "Such things," Victoria complained to her mother, "are arranged between the Kaiser and William without seeking our advice or informing us." But protest received direct expression when, some weeks later, Bismarck attached William to the Foreign Office to be initiated into the mysteries of external affairs. "In view of the immaturity and inexperience of my eldest son," Frederick wrote to the Chancellor, "and of his tendency to arrogance, I must consider it positively dangerous to bring him in contact with foreign questions so soon." Bismarck replied that the Prince was now twenty-eight and at that age Frederick the Great as well as Frederick's father and Frederick William III had already ascended the throne.

Not that the Chancellor was oblivious of William's defects, he saw these clearly enough, but William, after all, was the day after tomorrow's sun and Bismarck was determined to harness him to his chariot. "He had," as Count Eulenburg remarked, "only one thought at this time: to remove the future young Kaiser for ever from the influence of his intelligent mother. It was therefore, in his eyes, necessary to deepen the already existing gulf by all possible means and this included increasing the young Prince's hostility to England. The Bismarcks systematically goaded Prince William and drove him, always an extremist, to regrettable and extravagant outbursts."

In the chauvinistic military atmosphere of Potsdam, William now convinced himself that his mother was a traitor to her adopted country and was working deliberately for British interests. His fellow-officers reported him as indulging in positively vitriolic outbursts of hatred and in a letter to Queen Victoria his mother no doubt hit the nail on the head when she wrote: "He is so refractory to any kind of control, excepting the Kaiser's, so mistrustful of anyone who does not heap unqualified admiration on Bismarck that it seems pointless to try and make him see reason." The Chancellor had done his work well and for the moment no doubt it seemed of secondary importance that his young pupil was ready enough to glance at the interesting documents in the Foreign Office, but little inclined to devote serious study to them. Frivolity was, after all, the characteristic of youth. Given time, Bismarck was confident he could train William to a sense of responsibility.

But time was the very factor that was lacking. In January 1887, Frederick began to complain of hoarseness. No significance was attributed to this until, a few weeks later, when making a speech on the Emperor's birthday, he completely lost his voice. A rest was prescribed in Ems, but on returning from the holiday in May the patient was no better. Ugly rumours now began to circulate.

Specialists were sent for, an operation was contemplated to remove a slight growth on the vocal chords, but first it was decided to consult a famous laryngologist, the Scottish Dr. Morell Mackenzie. Mackenzie pronounced the growth to be benign and an operation to be unnecessary. But the hoarseness continued.

In Berlin, meanwhile, politicians were adjusting themselves to the possibility that Frederick's reign, when the old Emperor came to die, would be a short one. In the army, in conservative circles, even in the civil service and the government, voices were raised suggesting that as the Crown Prince was fatally ill it would be better to pass him over altogether and for young William to succeed his grandfather, or alternatively for Frederick to abdicate in his favour. As the summer progressed, William found himself the centre of ambitious hopes. Those, including his wife, who struck a warning note and said he was too young for the throne were in a minority. Too many careers were at stake, too many interests involved for men to weigh nicely the interests of the country. To Victoria this callous shift of allegiance was profoundly wounding and she found it difficult not to imagine that it was deliberately provoked by her son. In October, she had moved with the patient, whose condition had deteriorated, to San Remo where cancer was definitely diagnosed. Frederick was given the harrowing choice between removal of the larynx and tracheotomy. When William arrived—on his grandfather's orders— to hear the truth about his father, Victoria received him coldly, fearing, as William reported later with a cynical metaphor, that "the house of cards on which she had built all her hopes must now collapse". She told him that his father's condition gave no cause for concern, but the stony expression on her face belied her words. Ruthlessly William suggested that his father should renounce the throne in his favour and asked to speak to him. Victoria refused, though in fact Frederick was in a calmer frame of mind than herself. He had faced the diagnosis with great courage, asking the doctors straight out, "Is it cancer?", and being told that it was, choosing tracheotomy as offering at least a chance that he might partially recover his voice. He thanked the doctors for the trouble they had taken over him and that night wrote in his diary: "So now the time has come for me to put my house in order."

Little caring that he had mortally offended his mother, William returned impatiently to Berlin. He was girding his loins now for the possibility of kingship at any moment and, half dizzy with flattery, fear and ambition, his main thought was for himself. On 12th November a bulletin was published announcing to the world that Frederick was suffering from cancer and two days later William coldly declared to Eulenburg that "it is questionable whether a man who cannot speak should be allowed to be King of Prussia at all". Shortly afterwards, the aged Emperor empowered William, not his father, to sign State papers when he himself was indisposed and this provoked renewed despair in the Crown Prince's household.

Bismarck's encouragement of the young man now bore unwelcome fruit. "One day," he had told him, "you must be your own Chancellor." This strengthened William's self-confidence to the point of mania and he sent Bismarck the draft of a communication to be addressed to the Federal Princes upon his accession. An accompanying letter seemed to reflect doubt in William's mind whether the Princes would accept him as their Emperor. "The order of succession deriving from the Grace of God," he wrote, "must be explained to them as a natural *fait accompli* and in such a way that they have no time to bother their heads about it. The old uncles must not put a spoke in their dear young nephew's wheel. . . . Once I have shown them what I am made of and the way I mean to do things, they will obey me all the more easily. For obey they must."

Here was the brash young army officer in all his painful arrogance. Did William not realize the difficulties that had been overcome before the Federal Princes would accept an Emperor at all, had he never read the Constitution where the Emperor was declared to be the first among equals? Restraining himself, Bismarck penned a reply pointing out some home-truths which William took extremely badly. He sought balm for well-merited criticism in the words of flatterers. Count Waldersee, who coveted the position of Chancellor and was shortly to succeed the great Moltke as Chief of the General Staff, was at hand to drop the suggestion in his ear: "If Frederick the Great had had such a Chancellor he would never have become the Great."

Meanwhile, the doctors had told William that his father had not six months to live. To Queen Victoria his mother wrote: "It distresses me to see how arrogant he has become and how horribly he poses. . . ." But if William was spending these months fluttering his feathers like a young cock about to climb on the midden, there was one event which sobered him—the death of his ninety-one-year-old grandfather. The old man with the snow-white whiskers and the ruddy complexion who had become the first German Emperor and the adored symbol of a united Germany contrived a dignified end. Lying on a simple camp-bed that had been with him on his campaigns, wearing a white jacket with a red scarf round his neck, he smiled peaceably at his wife, the Chancellor, the court chaplains and William as life ebbed slowly from him. He talked about the French army, the danger of war and much about Russia. Calling William, whom he mistook for his son, he abjured him to hold fast to Russia. Then he drank a little champagne and at half past eight on the morning of 9th March, 1888, he expired. William stood at the foot of the bed, tears streaming down his face.

In San Remo, where Frederick and Victoria received the news of his father's death, they girded themselves for their thankless task. Pride combined with a sense of duty to make Frederick insist that he assume the reins of government at once. Though he was strictly forbidden by his doctors even to speak now and was forced to make his wishes known in writing and with nods and shakes of the head, he was Kaiser and he would rule. His first act, as a patient still in San Remo, was to pin the Star of the Order of the Black Eagle on his wife's breast, and on a slip of paper he wrote: "I thank God for allowing me to live long enough so that I can reward the courage and energy of my wife." Then he sent a message to Bismarck asking him to continue as Chancellor and then he bethought him of William. Suspicion entered his mind. This reign of his would be a pretence, he knew, but it must not be a farce. There must be no unseemly acts on William's part. Had William come to some pact with his aged grandfather on his death-bed? Had they talked of a coup to ease Frederick out of the way? They were thick as thieves, that was certain. And Bismarck had been there, too: all three of them hostile to Frederick's and Victoria's liberal ideas. All three, no doubt, would have liked to see the Prussian tradition continued in an unbroken, steel-linked chain with no parliamentary putty in between. Resentful and suspicious, Frederick wired to his son: "Deeply distressed that it was granted to you, but not to me to be present at my father's death, on ascending the throne I confidently express the hope that you will be an example to all in loyalty and obedience."

When he received this, William grimaced. But Waldersee was at hand to soothe his ruffled feelings. Never mind, he said. It was not a misfortune really that his parents should rule for a while. They would do so many preposterous things, it would prepare the ground admirably for himself. So, with William eyeing them maliciously from Potsdam and the back of every ambitious general, politician and courtier turned towards them, the dying man and his wife made the long, cold journey to Berlin. Exhausted, Frederick was hustled to the Charlottenburg Palace. There he was installed in lofty rooms and with the Empress constantly at his side he applied himself to the duties of Kaiser. A Crown Council was held at which ministers took the oath. The old Emperor was carried in solemn procession to his tomb amidst driving snow and bitter cold—black capes fluttering—a bare-headed populace—William walking behind the coffin—his father watching from behind the palace windows—all colour drained from the world. As the weeks crawled by, everyone

could see that Frederick would not last long and it became apparent
that his reign was merely an interlude between the glorious Kaiser
William I and his ebullient, but problematical grandson. Confined
now to the palace rooms, not allowed even the briefest breath of fresh
air, coughing into the stove, propped with pillows, surrounded by
the mournful accoutrements of the sick-room, Frederick was doing
his duty to the last, receiving endless streams of officials, impressing
them beyond words with his courage and leaving them with an
indelible memory of his patient, suffering eyes.

No new policies were, of course, introduced. Occasionally,
Victoria clashed swords with Bismarck. Sometimes Frederick tried
to take the initiative in some matter, however small, that might
leave an indelible mark on the future. He was anxious to introduce a
new pattern for army caps, but when told they could not be ready
before Whitsun, he was seen to clasp his hands together with a
woeful look, as though certain he would not live to see them.

Meanwhile, William was acting quite the young ruler, distributing
busts and photographs of himself with suitable dedications to all
those athletic gentlemen who were fleeing the dawn of the liberal age
for the reactionary atmosphere of the Potsdam barrack-rooms. In
April, Bismarck celebrated his seventy-third birthday and William
made a speech. Apparently the real life tragedy left him cold. It had
to be transformed into fantasy before his feelings could kindle. The
government, he said, was like a regiment of soldiers advancing to the
attack. The commander—the old Kaiser—had just fallen. "The
second-in-command, though badly wounded, still rides boldly forward." So all eyes were riveted on the standard-bearer—Bismarck.
Understandably, Frederick was much incensed by this speech. He
disliked being compared to a wounded commander, the tribute to
Bismarck was contrary to his political convictions and most of all,
perhaps, he resented this high-flown imagery which underlined
William's lack of true feeling.

How bitter it was for Frederick and his wife to feel that their son
did not want them and that all eyes were concentrated on him. They
were strangers almost in their own palace. It was scandalous, the
British military attaché reported to England, to see how officials
were trimming their sails to the wind and disregarding the most
elementary dictates of honour and duty. Victoria's moral isolation
was complete. She had always been called the "English woman".
Her restless ambition had always provoked sneers and suspicion.
Every act emanating from Frederick or herself was now ascribed
to her sordid motives of self-interest, or worse. In these ninety-nine
days that she was Empress, Victoria could do no right in Germans'
eyes. But Colonel Swaine, the British military attaché, found words

to praise the fortitude of this lonely woman who was doing her duty "faithfully and tenderly" beside her husband in the face of universal hostility.

On 16th April, Frederick's condition grew suddenly worse and rumours reached Potsdam that he only had hours to live. At once, William jumped on his fastest horse and galloped to Charlottenburg, to find on his arrival that his father was better. Meanwhile, forced to work in harness with Victoria whom he detested, Bismarck was applying all his energies to bridging this awkward interlude, courting the Empress like an "infatuated dotard" as he said, giving way in little things the better to keep a grip on the main lines of policy. At the same time as he was driving this chariot, a rogue young stallion—William—kept nosing into the traces. The Crown Prince was now eagerly scanning the diplomatic documents that Bismarck chose to show him and in true Frederican style plunging his pen in the ink and spattering them with comments. On one, reporting the conversation of two General Staff Officers who had recommended a preventive war against Russia in the previous year, he scrawled a big "YES"! On this Bismarck commented with withering irony: "If your Imperial Highness desires war, why not with France?" Oh, yes, replied William in an excited letter, why not? And he proceeded to favour the veteran statesman with a lecture on the integration of strategy with politics.

To Waldersee, William was saying: "You were quite right, it was a good thing that my father reigned before me," when, late in April, his grandmother the Queen of England came on a short visit to Charlottenburg. The two Victorias fell into each other's arms. Willy was summoned. For a few days, thanks to the old lady's authority, the bickering ceased and the dying Frederick saw his family united around him. But with Queen Victoria gone, the poison flooded back. The Empress would not allow William to go near his father for fear that the patient would be upset. Frederick sat by the window, terribly emaciated with a face like wax. In May, the end was seen to be approaching. Frederick expressed the wish to die in his old home, the Neues Palais at Potsdam. But first, there was a duty to perform and one last pleasure to be enjoyed. Encased in uniform, sitting bolt upright in his chair, he attended the marriage of his son Heinrich to the Princess Irene of Hesse. Then, on 29th May, again in uniform with his helmet on his head, he was helped into a carriage and from the stationary vehicle, with William astride his charger by the door, the Emperor watched a brigade of Prussian troops march past—his troops, his first and last military review.

In early June, he was transferred to Potsdam, in a steam yacht as affording an easier passage, along the River Spree. In their old home, where Frederick had been born and he and Victoria had begun their married life, they felt that here at least was something that really belonged to them, and, all too aware that politically their names would be wiped from the record they rechristened the palace, "Friedrichskron". For a fortnight life lingered on. Frederick's horses were brought into the garden and he tried to feed them through the window. On 14th June, Bismarck called. Frederick took the Chancellor's hand and placed it in his wife's, then held them together with a piteous look. On the 15th William called and, most reluctantly, Victoria allowed him to see his father. Frederick, totally exhausted and coughing violently, began to write a last message for William: "Victoria, myself and the children. . . ." But the sentence was never completed. Shortly after eleven in the morning, he died.

An extraordinary scene then took place. Even before Frederick died, unknown army officers, never before seen at the palace, had been arriving in twos and threes demanding quarters and rations. They had been sent, they said, by Prince William. At the same time, a new Master of the Household suddenly appeared and gave instructions that no one, not even a doctor, was to leave the building or communicate with the outside world. At the back of the palace an officer on horseback stationed himself at the exit. Then troops were heard tramping in the courtyard. As soon as death was announced, the horsemen cantered towards them. A cordon was thrown round the palace. Guards were placed on the gates. In a room inside, the new Emperor's aide-de-camp established himself with pens and passes. No one was allowed to leave the palace without written permission. Meanwhile, in his father's study, William was examining the contents of the desk.

It has been suggested that he was looking for a will which he had reason to believe would adversely affect him, by passing on to his mother, for instance, an undue proportion of the large sums which his grandfather had saved, or by cutting him out altogether. It has been suggested that he suspected his mother of passing on State secrets to England and wished to find proof of this. Undoubtedly he wished to give startling demonstration that he was now the master and deliberately planned this callous offence to his mother's feelings. But as he ransacked his father's papers, his original intention—whatever it was—became blurred. He was a small boy again, delving for secrets, searching unconsciously for clues to his parents' hostility. An eye-witness, Major von Normann, recounts how William's eye lighted on a faded telegram from his grandmother sent on the day of his birth—"Is it a fine boy?"—and how his left hand closed convulsively round the hilt of his sword as he read it.

No, not a fine boy. A crippled boy. Was that why his parents hated him?

This neurotic interlude was an unhappy augury for the new reign, but who at that time could look into William's soul? Throughout Germany artists were mixing their paints and poets their metaphors to celebrate the accession of the first young Emperor that Germany had ever had. "Hail, Kaiser, to thee! As though with eagle's pinions, thou treadst with head held high thy lofty path...." Waldersee recorded in his diary: "In the army everyone is rejoicing over the new ruler. The feeling is widespread that we have recovered from a serious illness and are now heading for happier times." The feeling of release was universal. Nowhere in the world had a materially backward country mastered and exploited industrial techniques with such speed as Germany. Population, production, exports were soaring. From a collection of weak, squabbling and reactionary States, Germany had risen in a brief twenty-five years to be the most powerful nation in Europe. Over past struggles had seemed to hover the special protection of Providence. The miracle, Germans were convinced, must have been wrought by the Almighty for a purpose. They were filled with a sense of movement and progress towards a yet mightier future. They were confident. They were energetic. In every mouth was a phrase which summed it all up: they possessed *quellende Volkskraft*, a gushing vitality which could be put to any use, overcome any obstacle, achieve any victory. But they needed a leader. The old Kaiser had been a legend, Frederick a shadow, but now they had William, young, keen-eyed and vigorous. Hail, Kaiser, to thee!

But strutting and assured, only too ready to be the smoke on top of this volcano, William had first some family matters to attend to: his father to bury, his mother to put in her place. On William's orders, the palace of Friedrichskron was restored to its former name: Neues Palais. On the 18th June, Frederick was buried. The populace was screened from the funeral cortège by troops and no foreign envoys were invited to the service. The ex-Empress had been prevented by her son's guards from going into the palace garden to pick roses for her husband's death-bed. Now, to avoid further humiliations, she and her younger daughters left the palace for her country-seat in Bornstedt.

William, meanwhile, had issued three proclamations, first to his army, second to the navy, and in third place only to his people. To the army, he declared that God had placed him at its head. He appealed for loyalty on the basis of history and tradition and concluded: "So we are bound together, I and the army, so we are born for each other, and so we will hold indissolubly together whether, as God wills, we are to have peace or storm." To the German people he declared: "Called to the throne of my fathers, I have taken over the government looking up to the King of all kings and have sworn to God to be to my people a just and mild Prince after the example of my fathers. . . ."

Reading these pious and unexceptionable sentiments, no doubt the German people were well enough pleased. They noted the frequent references to God and took it as a sign of humility in the young Kaiser. The old Emperor had, after all, placed the crown on his own head to signify that he ruled by the Grace of God and not by the permission of popular assemblies and he had interpreted the phrase in a humble sense implying that he was accountable to God and, like all mortals, dependent on His Mercy. But the German people were not in a humble mood. They were very conscious of the increasing envy they were arousing in the world, they liked to be envied and they liked to boast. What they wanted in their Kaiser was *panache*, a cross between Siegfried and the Archangel Gabriel and this image William was ready to supply. It was pleasant to see him with his bristling moustache, with his own monogram planted on his face, and it could be readily excused if—as palace gossips whispered—he had a large W embroidered on his shirts and even on his underpants and it was a stimulating departure from custom, underlining the new spirit of the times when, only a week after his father's funeral, William treated his people—vicariously, through the Press—to a piece of glittering pageantry. Dressing the palace guards in the ceremonial uniform of Frederick the Great's time and himself wearing the scarlet cloak, which he had specially introduced for the purpose, of a Knight of the Order of the Black Eagle, preceded by Bismarck and the Federal Council, by court pages in black knee-breeches, by the Insignia of State and by the Chief of the General Staff, William Imperator Rex opened the Reichstag in person, reading a speech from the throne, very self-consciously majestical, cloak flung back, head high, in a throaty, parade-ground voice. Then he swept down the steps, seized Bismarck's hand and the aged Chancellor kissed his. Very impressive. The audience clapped. And in millions of households next day, Germans knew they had found their symbol.

But William was obliged not only to be the actor, but to some extent the author of the imperial role. There was no body of custom or tradition suggesting how the German Kaiser should act—there was not even a coronation ceremony. There was nothing to prevent William being a figurehead shielded by Bismarck. On the other hand, he possessed almost unlimited power if he chose to use it. Under the Constitution promulgated in April, 1871, the President of the Federation of German States was declared to be the King of

Prussia "who carries the title of German Kaiser". The Kaiser was empowered to represent the Reich in international affairs, declare war and conclude peace, make alliances and other treaties with foreign States, accredit and receive ambassadors, open and prorogue the Federal Council and the Reichstag and—most important of all—appoint and dismiss the Reich Chancellor.

On paper, therefore, William possessed enormous power. The Chancellor's powers were by no means so clearly defined, but in practice were immense. In the legislative sphere Bismarck was assured of the compliance of the Federal Council—where Bills had to be initiated—both because he was Prime Minister of Prussia and chairman of the Council and because voting in the Council was permanently weighted in favour of Prussia. In foreign affairs, where he was the unchallenged master, he had assured himself complete freedom of action. His executive powers were limited only by the Kaiser's right to dismiss and appoint the Chancellor.

The whole constitution was, in a sense, a sham. It introduced adult male suffrage, but gave the people's representatives no power over the executive. Bismarck was not answerable to the Reichstag. The officials whom he chose to assist him were not members of that body and the only considerable power which the deputies possessed was the right to vote or withhold supplies. So, while the Reichstag talked, Bismarck acted and by now, in his seventy-fourth year, after sixteen years of undisputed power as Prime Minister of Prussia, Chancellor of the North German Federation and finally Reich Chancellor, he was not inclined either by temperament or habit to allow anyone, even the young Kaiser himself, to challenge his authority. But the Kaiser was entitled to issue this challenge if he wanted. Here was one sphere in which the Kaiser would have to steer his own course with no precedents to guide him.

But there was another question. The constitution had been designed to suit conditions prevailing in 1871. Since then, German economic and social life had changed enormously and were still rapidly developing. An industrial proletariat had come into being and a prosperous middle class building up strong pressure against the autocratic, reactionary political system. But with the Emperor Frederick a whole generation of liberal-minded politicians had passed into the shade and Bismarck was determined to sacrifice no jot of his authority to democratic clamour. What would the young Kaiser do? Would he sense the needs of the times or would he cling to the constitution and its already outworn provisions as a sheet-anchor amid the storm of change? Would he prove adaptable or inflexible, courageous or timorous, would he swim with the current or against it?

It was important to know this, but the answers in William's case were not simple. First impressions of the young monarch conveyed only a desire to shine and an insatiable urge to express opinions— well-informed and otherwise—on every conceivable subject. The months following his accession were filled with ceaseless activity and one can imagine the joyous autocrat, free at last from his mother's apron-strings, experiencing with a kind of intoxicated incredulity what it meant to be German Kaiser: when he spoke he was listened to, when he lifted a finger there was silence, orders were obeyed, wishes were fulfilled and always, wherever he went, an expectant, adoring, sycophantic multitude. From a Crown Council in July, he hastened to a banquet for the diplomatic corps, thence to an art exhibition in Berlin. A panorama caught his eye. The All-Highest spoke: "Panoramas have an educative value for the less cultivated public, namely for youth. Every large town should have a panorama." Away, then, to Kiel, and hey-presto, William as an admiral—the first Kaiser ever to wear naval uniform—inspecting his fleet. Then a visit to Cronstadt in the royal yacht, to "inform" the Tsar of his accession, then a triumphal entry into beflagged and bedizened Stockholm beside the King of Sweden. Thence to Denmark where the German fleet awaited him, and so back with an ironclad escort to the Fatherland. A swift visit to the Reich Chancellor at his home in Friedrichsruh followed, then William spent two days exercising his troops. Back to Potsdam. A few minutes could be spared for an African explorer just returned: "German colonial enterprise will always find my lively interest." Off now to Frankfurt and a speech, among the first of over fifteen hundred to be delivered during his reign, all to be reported in the press and later to be bound in thick tomes: "*Die Kaiserreden*".

"My father," he said in Frankfurt, "had the same thought as ourselves—that nothing can be surrendered of our achievements during the great and recent past. I believe that in the whole army there can be only one opinion on this: rather than surrender a single stone of what my father achieved, we would rather leave our entire eighteen army corps and forty-two million inhabitants on the battlefield."

Here, in the metaphor of the "stone" and the edifice which Germans must defend was a first glimpse of one of William's permanent characteristics: a fear of change and dynamism, a desire to see Germany as a compact acquisition which could be preserved like a lump of stone, a longing for a secure and static world. First in his eyes as the great bulwark against upheaval came the German army and soon, in September, 1888, he was holding his first great parades and tactical exercises. 1st September: the great autumn march-past of the *Garde du Corps*, the household troops, in the Tempelhof arena. 7th September: training exercises with the 10th Division. 8th September: manœuvres lasting eleven days with two army corps, complete with cavalry, infantry, artillery, baggage trains, pioneers, field kitchens, supply columns and some of the new bicycle detachments. Uhlans with pennons and lances. William on his white charger in the uniform of the Death's Head Hussars, scarlet saddle-cloth with gold embroidery, riding boots topped with silver filigree, harness studded with glittering metal, alternately commanding a corps in defence and attack. In the evenings, colloquies over maps with the General Staff, then dinner in the field mess—"nothing elaborate", the Kaiser would plead, but the best silver would be turned out and the officers would sacrifice half a month's pay to do honour with sucking pig and charlotte russe to their War Lord. Then on Sundays, Divine Service in an enormous marquee, simple and devout—splendid music by a military band— stirring hymns—lusty male voices and William, the crippled Emperor, moved to tears by the vision which surged in his mind: Germany, strong, valiant, peace-loving and progressive, marching stiffly in step towards the future under the protection of the "Great Ally", the "good old German God", and himself as the Lord's anointed.

God was much on William's lips in these early months of his reign. Beneath the confident, arrogant bearing he was very conscious of the enormous task confronting him and of his own inadequacies. At the same time, the recent past and the rise of Prussia convinced him that a special providence ruled the destinies of Germany. He believed and he needed to believe that in a quite literal sense he had been called to the throne by God, and God had indeed given him a fair heritage. The smiling towns, the great forests and rivers of Germany, German music, German soldiers, courtly pomp and martial virtues—all these indiscriminately filled him with quasi-mystical sensations in which the boundaries between the spiritual and the material worlds dissolved and the universe re-formed into one gigantic projection of the Prussian State where all men—the dead and the living—were soldiers, his ancestors smiled down on him from the clouds and over all hovered a benign and almost tangible Deity.

This was the man with whom Bismarck, the man of action, the resolute realist was called upon to work in harness. "It fills me with joy and comfort," William wrote to him at the end of the year, "that you stand faithfully at my side." Could Bismarck reciprocate these feelings?

CHAPTER THREE

DROPPING THE PILOT

T HE small rowing-boat contained distinguished passengers: the Kaiser, the eighty-nine-year-old Field Marshal von Moltke, Count Waldersee, the Chief of the Kaiser's Naval Cabinet Admiral Baron Senden and Count Philipp zu Eulenburg-Hertefeld. The party was heading through choppy seas under grey skies and pouring rain towards the North Sea from the mouth of the River Weser off Bremerhaven. William professed to be very fond of the sea. The Admiral was supposedly in his element. But old Moltke, the Sphinx, "*der grosse Schweiger*" as he was called, sat glumly in the stern-sheets enduring thumps and showers of spray and longing with all his heart for the comfort of the battlefield. Eulenburg, too, was beginning to feel that the trip had been misconceived.

It had been Senden's idea. That morning in the spring of 1889 there had been a banquet in Bremen town hall—William's first visit to the city as Emperor. Throughout the banquet William had worn the Imperial mask, stiff as a poker, unbending as the royal oak. Now he was to have a bit of fun. The liner *Fulda*, one of the splendid North German Lloyd passenger boats, was due to anchor that afternoon in the mouth of the Weser on her return from New York. How would it be, Senden had suggested, if William descended on her from the mists, climbed on board and inspected the astonished ship's company? "*Herrlich! Ha! Ha!*" William had heartily concurred. So after lunch he and his suite had embarked on a paddle-steamer and splashed down the Weser to the open sea, keeping a sharp look-out for the monster liner. It had rained continually. William and his cronies had shut themselves up in the saloon with strong cigars and stronger stories. Their gusty laughter wafted up to where Moltke and Eulenburg, preferring death by drowning to asphyxiation, were sitting on a dripping skylight. Perhaps feeling that his last moment had come, the Sphinx was unusually loquacious. Between squalls he confided into Eulenburg's ear his distress about relations between

Bismarck and the Emperor. The Chancellor's fiery temperament, he said, was a positive disadvantage in dealing with his excitable master. An understanding between them was urgently necessary. . . .

But now Moltke's remarks were interrupted by the captain who, cocooned in oilskins, suddenly announced: "Ship in sight!" Kaiser and companions surged eagerly up from the saloon, trailing tag-ends of funny stories and looking like smoked fish in their glossy coverings. Their eyes swept the gloomy scene. Where was the ship? They could see nothing. But the captain assured them it was there and Senden seemed confident. Anyway, the *Fulda* had been informed and the plan must go through. The party was split up and stowed in two rowing-boats which were then gingerly lowered on to the surging waters.

Now the precious cargo was heading bravely out to sea. After thirty minutes of anxious rowing, patience seemed rewarded. "There seems to be a dark mass in the fog over there," said someone. "Yes, there she is, lads!" cried Senden. "Pull away!" Soon all eyes were gazing up at a blank, barnacled wall—curiously unkempt for a slap-up liner. "*Allo!*" shouted Senden. "*Ist jemand da?*" Silence—no music, no anthem, not a rope was lowered. Then, high above, two figures appeared at the railing, a man in his shirt-sleeves and someone with a coal-black face. They gazed at the boat-load and the boat-load gazed back. Senden became apoplectic. More shouts. Finally a rope ladder was dropped and he clambered up. In a few minutes, the chastened admiral returned: the ship was a collier. . . .

"Well, then," said William in a small voice, "I suppose we had better go home." The God-appointed ruler was pale now from the buffeting of his stomach and curiously detached. This was no time for recrimination. As the row-boat turned, wedges of water doused the occupants. Forlorn drips gathered on their noses. The rain was incessant, the sea seemed awfully rough. The Field Marshal's face was invisible between an upturned collar and the peak of his cap. A gloomy silence prevailed, broken only by the slosh of water and the creak of oars. William looked more like a mouse than a monarch. Something would have to be done. More funny stories? Eulenburg, the jester-cum-confidant, filled the breach. . . .

The boat-load reached shore at last. Meanwhile, the *Fulda* had turned up. That evening William went on board for a banquet and a speech. "Whatever the dark hours and the fog which may be in store for our Fatherland, our navy and our trade, we Germans will succeed in overcoming them, pressing strongly towards our goal on the principle: We Germans fear God, but no one else in the world." A grandiose picture to arise from the afternoon's entertainment. But Eulenburg, at any rate, was not surprised. He knew his William.

Eulenburg, as William said in after years, was the only friend he
ever had. They had first met in 1885, when as a young man of
twenty-six William was still remote from the throne, four years
married with three small boys. Philipp, or Phili as William called
him, saw quickly how much his friend suffered in the feud with his
parents which was fanned by Bismarck for political reasons. He saw
too how William's self-confidence had been undermined by his
unhappy childhood and physical infirmity and knew well that his
temperamental outbursts and callous jibes sprang from pent-up
aggression against his domineering mother and supine father. In his
diary, Eulenburg was soon referring to the "poor" Prince, and the
epithet clung, recurring year after year, long after William had
ascended the throne. Eulenburg saw a lot and understood William
better than anybody. His dominating feeling was compassion. He
himself loved to stand in the wings and watch life with an artist's
detachment. Managing William and acting as a go-between became
his self-appointed task. Imaginative, indolent, gifted with psychological insight and a scintillating mind, he found more satisfaction
in interpreting the monarch to his baffled advisers than in pursuing
a political career himself. If plums came his way he accepted them,
if not, his position as the Emperor's friend fully satisfied his ambition. Two things only exasperated him: dull minds and boorish
manners. Characteristically he had resigned his commission in the
most exclusive of Prussian regiments because he disliked his captain.
Eulenburg was too soft and pliant to enjoy the military atmosphere.
The arts, not artillery, were his passion.

As for William, he was captivated by Phili's personality and
accomplishments. The delicate web of friendship which the older
man spun round him gave him a feeling of security and a narcissistic
sense that he was loved. He could see himself in Phili's eyes. No, his
friend could not come too close. What was wrong with a marriage
of minds? When Phili sang his own ballads at the piano William sat
devoutly by his side and turned the pages. When a formal dinner
was over, "Phili," he would call mysteriously, "follow me," and
they would retire to a private fireside and talk with intimate smiles,
each curiously excited.

Eulenburg foresaw sooner than anyone the conflicts that would
arise between William and Bismarck, for he was a friend of both
families. Bismarck cultivated him as the Emperor's confidant and
welcomed him to his home at Friedrichsruh. The house, the visitor
saw, was as massive as its owner. Everything to do with Bismarck
was more than life-size: furniture of gigantic proportions, plain,
white-papered walls crowded with pictures and photographs, huge
dogs trailing their master in his knee-high cuirassier's boots, tables

groaning with food—pasties, smoked fish, cutlets, vegetables, all served together. Even the pencils which Bismarck used to annotate documents were as thick as walking-sticks. The whole house lay under his brooding spell. To Eulenburg, Bismarck was charm itself, welcoming him with an Olympian smile and powerful outstretched hand, scrutinizing him with his shrewd eyes while two ferocious hounds sniffed the visitor's legs.

At this time, Bismarck was the master of Germany. As Chancellor, Prime Minister of Prussia, President of the Ministry of State and Minister of Trade and Commerce he held all the reins in his hands. For many years not a minister had been appointed in Prussia except on his nomination. By any and every means he made his officials dependent on him, by the power of his intellect, by knowledge of their private affairs and, where necessary, by outright bribes. As a matter of course he offered to pay off the debts of newly appointed ministers and utterly failed to understand their scruples when they refused—but they seldom did. In foreign affairs he was unchallenged. His skill in managing the Reichstag was unrivalled. His prestige was supreme. As long as Bismarck was at the helm there were no officers or even petty-officers in the ship of State, but only anonymous galley-slaves straining every muscle to obey the master.

To this god-like figure William at the beginning of his reign looked up in veneration and gratitude. For some months he was too busy enjoying the trimmings of power to feel irked that it was not he but Bismarck who possessed the solid core. It was very pleasant to go hunting, to spend days reviewing troops and presenting colours, to reap the plaudits of countless thousands in towns never before visited by a German Kaiser, to make speeches declaring that his life and strength belonged to the German people and to declare, as he did in February, 1889, "I believe that with God's help I have succeeded in preserving peace for many years to come," knowing full well that peace, if assured, was Bismarck's achievement and that the dangers which beset the Reich were being mastered by the same Chancellor who had made his grandfather an Emperor.

Bismarck, for his part, did his utmost to keep the Kaiser in the imperial play-pen. Tempering his ruthless manner, he told William what he considered it good for him to know and encouraged his taste for travel and enjoyment. But it was noticed that the old man who had never been known to lose countenance was at times oddly unsure of himself in dealing with his young master as though he, too, detected those defects in his temperament which Hinzpeter had observed. Nevertheless, he hoped for the best and told a friend that to his last breath he would stand by a Sovereign who was "so gifted, so industrious, so conscientious and so zealously active for the

welfare of the Reich, for peace and the prosperity of the country".
William, meanwhile, was expressing the hope that the great Chancellor would live a very long time.

But in May, 1889, this honeymoon was disturbed by serious internal unrest. For fifteen years industrial peace had reigned. Now a coal strike suddenly broke out in Rhineland–Westphalia for higher wages (existing wages were on a bare subsistence level) and an eight-hour instead of a ten-hour shift. The movement spread to Essen and soon the whole of the Krupps works were idle. Miners in Saxony and Upper Silesia then struck in sympathy. Soon bricklayers in Bremerhaven, brewers in Hamburg and workers in the Thuringian leather industry had joined them—in all, over a hundred thousand men. Strike-breakers were manhandled. Train services were interrupted. A shortage of coal began to be felt throughout Germany. At this juncture, the mine-owners appealed for military help. Uhlans and infantry were sent. There were clashes and casualties. Curfews were imposed. Road traffic was entirely halted. Bismarck was in entire sympathy with military suppression of the strikes which in his eyes were synonymous with insurrection.

Not so, William. For the last eleven months he had preached on the theme of peace, progress and unity. He liked to think of himself as the father of his people. Beneath the film of junkers and military men, he saw an untapped pool of loyalty in the simple working-people. On them, he sensed, Germany's future depended. In his youth, his tutor Hinzpeter, who came from industrial Bielefeld, had taken him into miners' homes, expounded their problems to him. From all this had been born in William's mind the strange conviction that only a group of rapacious entrepreneurs stood between him and the love of fifty million subjects.

Bismarck was discussing further emergency measures with the Cabinet when William appeared unannounced in Hussar uniform. The mine-owners, he said, must give way; the workers were his subjects for whom he was responsible. He threatened to withdraw the troops unless an immediate increase of wages was granted. Bismarck suggested that the owners were also the Emperor's subjects, but William swept on: he would withdraw his troops if the millionaires did not give way. They would soon climb down when their villas were set on fire. Anyway, the situation was dangerous. Without coal the navy could not put to sea, without trains the army could not mobilize. If he were the Tsar of Russia he would declare war on Germany at once.

William spoke with great excitement and this coupled with his abrupt incursion into the Cabinet meeting was well calculated to annoy the Chancellor. Bismarck also detected a striving for popular absolutism with which he did not sympathize. On a document recommending stronger military measures William had commented: "One can only proceed against the extremists with a clear conscience when one has the feeling that just and moderate demands have been fulfilled," and to Eulenburg he said: "I want to help those workers who are loyal to me. Afterwards, those who do not accept my hand can expect trouble."

One is inclined to sympathize with William. But the problem was not purely a social one, it had political implications. Bismarck touched on them when he warned: "This first error of the monarch will lead to increased demands by the Social Democrats." In Germany the Socialist movement had grown out of the stimulus to democratic ideals provided by the French Revolution of 1848. In the 1860s the social agitator Ferdinand Lassalle, whose ideas anticipated many of Karl Marx's, took over leadership of the movement and gave it more definite form. The danger the Social Democrats represented to the established order was aggravated by several factors. They alone among political parties could truthfully claim to represent the interests of the working man, yet because the Chancellor was appointed by the Kaiser and the monarchy was backed by the most reactionary elements in the State they could never hope to rule the country. In Germany, therefore, Social Democracy was bound to be a subversive movement. Its danger was enhanced by the prevalence among the German people of the very virtues of discipline and obedience which the existing order, headed by the Kaiser, preached. These virtues, allied to political inexperience and parochialism of outlook, could be exploited equally well for the maintenance or the overthrow of the constitution. Social Democracy drew great strength from this fact. Its leaders were able, over the years, to establish their unchallenged authority over a docile rank-and-file that found security in cohesion, joy in self-sacrifice for a common cause and a kind of para-military pride in the strict organization and discipline of their movement. Social Democracy was so dangerous, it was said, because it was so German. Local associations were formed, stretching up to *Land, Bezirk*, provincial and finally to national level. Party funds were subscribed to promptly and systematically. In the Reichstag elections of 1884, the Social Democrats polled 550,000 votes. Three years later, the figure was 763,000 and in 1890—a year after the coal strike—this was suddenly doubled. Throughout William's reign the party never ceased to grow in size and influence. Social Democracy was the key problem for Germany, second only in importance to national security.

Bismarck was not blind to the social evils which nourished this movement nor insensitive to the needs of a rapidly growing industrial proletariat. In 1871, with the old Kaiser's support, he had passed an Employer's Liability Act. Schemes of social insurance had followed. Ten years later, the Kaiser had issued an Imperial decree drafted by Bismarck promising measures of insurance against sickness, accident, old age and invalidism. These were all put into effect. But the Chancellor was determined that none of these improvements should be granted as sops to Socialist agitation. Social justice was one thing—capitulation to subversive elements another. The Socialist aim was revolution, not concessions to labour wrested from the existing order. This was made clear by the Socialist leader, August Bebel, in the Reichstag: "To your positive measures for their benefit, the workers reply with ringing laughter." Bismarck took up this challenge. With Socialism steadily growing, the Socialist press breathing fire and slaughter, with two attempts on the life of William I in 1878, the Chancellor resolved that Social Democracy must be crushed before further working-class legislation was introduced. In the Reichstag, he painted a dark picture of Socialists' aims. Their programme, he said, consisted in the negation of existing institutions. They set up the Paris Commune as their model for murder and arson. They were "an association of bandits". Under their tyranny, if it was ever established, life would cease to be worth living—and he introduced and passed an anti-Socialist law restricting rights of association, the publication of subversive books and newspapers and empowering the State to imprison and even deport Socialist agitators.

This was the background against which Bismarck listened to William in the coal strike of 1889. The monarch was urging the very course of action which he held to be most dangerous—capitulation to violence. That might not have been so serious if Bismarck had been able to detect any firm convictions behind it, but William's utterances smacked too much of panic and emotionalism and neither word had any place in the Chancellor's vocabulary. William's mind was like a generator that produced volts but no amperes, sparks but no current. "My policy has been conceived as a whole," Bismarck had once said. "I will not suffer amateurs to interfere with it."

But in June the strike was settled, friction between Chancellor and Kaiser abated, and William was free to set off on a round of pleasures—to East Prussia for hunting, a sea trip to Kiel, back to Berlin to receive the Shah of Persia, thence to Dresden, from Dresden to Stuttgart and from Stuttgart to Kiel again to start his Norwegian holiday. This was a very energetic affair performed in the royal yacht *Hohenzollern* stuffed with boon companions, learned professors, adjutants, secretaries and officials whose job it was to keep the Kaiser in touch with home affairs. Ever since as a small boy on a visit to his grandmother he had gazed at the ships in Portsmouth harbour, William had been in love with the sea. But it was not only grandiose nature which inspired him. The narrow confines of a ship gave him a feeling of security. Life on board held plenty of opportunities for the hearty male companionship which William enjoyed. Surrounded with a small, hand-picked company he could laugh and joke at his ease, secure from problems of State and happy in the knowledge that there was not a single Social Democrat within five hundred miles. If he could not be master of Germany, at least he was lord of the *Hohenzollern*. William inspected the crew, visited the galley and chose the menu, made his retinue—preferably the oldest and fattest members—do physical jerks on deck, playfully pushing them over from behind as they were crouched for knees bend, conducted Divine Service on Sundays and preached sermons full of obscure but glittering imagery.

Braced by his holiday, William on his return was eager for a visit to England. He had not seen his revered grandmother since she had come to Berlin during his father's last illness. Since then, William had stirred the family cauldron to boiling point. Queen Victoria represented all that he loved and admired in England, his Uncle Bertie all that he hated. The Prince of Wales had come to Frederick's funeral and in an unguarded moment had asked Herbert Bismarck whether it was true that the late Emperor, had he lived, would have restored Alsace-Lorraine to France. This had reached William's ears and stirred him to frenzy. Feelings of inferiority which always seemed to overcome him in the presence of his uncle, welled up into furious aggression. In the autumn of 1888 he and the Prince of Wales had been due to visit Vienna at the same time. William had let it be known that he did not wish to meet his uncle, so Edward, in a rage, had gone to stay with the King of Rumania, calling on Franz Josef only after William had left. Soon after, the British Prime Minister, Lord Salisbury, had received from Bismarck a formal complaint from his master at the Prince of Wales's behaviour—under two heads: first the talk about Alsace-Lorraine; second, the Prince of Wales treated William as a nephew and forgot that he was now an Emperor. All this had been passed on to Queen Victoria. She pounced on point two. "We have always been very intimate with our grandson and nephew," she wrote to Salisbury, "and to pretend that he is to be treated *in private* as well as in public as 'his Imperial Majesty' is *perfect madness*. . . . *If* he has *such* notions he had better *never* come *here*. . . . He had also said to the Crown Prince [Rudolf of Austria] that if his uncle wrote him a very kind letter, he *might perhaps answer it*. All this shows a very unhealthy and unnatural state of mind; and he must be made to feel that his grandmother and uncle will not stand such insolence." As to the other complaint, the Queen took her son to task, but he convinced her he had committed no crimes. All the wrong therefore seemed to be on William's side and in these circumstances it was intimated to Berlin that he would not be welcome in England in 1888.

But in the following year, after the ex-Empress Frederick had paid a long visit to her mother, Queen Victoria began to see that the German Emperor could not be permanently ostracized and she suggested to her son that the young man who she had previously described as "hot-headed, conceited and wrong-headed" should be invited to Osborne in the summer. Accordingly, in early August, 1889, William came on his first visit to England as German Emperor.

Though monarchs' quarrels might be fierce they possessed means to assuage them. Gall could be banished with gifts. Before leaving Germany, William was told that his grandmother proposed to make him an honorary Admiral of the Fleet. On his Norwegian holiday he had already nosed enviously round a British squadron on a courtesy visit and the appointment delighted him. Honorary or not, a British Admiral had duties to perform, and William sent the Queen unsolicited advice about naval estimates, fleet dispositions and other technical matters. As a seafaring man himself, he set off from Germany escorted by his own fleet—nothing to touch the Royal Navy, of course; there were only twelve units in all, some of them the oldest ships in service of any fleet in Europe. Still, it was a beginning, and according to German sources the sight of this proud navy aroused "the admiring recognition of the Englanders". William stayed a week with his grandmother and throughout this time orders, gifts and appointments never ceased to descend, on all, that is, except the Prince of Wales. William wore his Admiral's uniform and had his photograph taken, looking very truculent now that he had a stake in British sea power, with the belt slightly askew and the hat cocked at a rakish angle. Portraits and busts were exchanged. William inspected the British Fleet at Spithead (not twelve but over one hundred ships), said it was "the finest in the world", attended a mock battle between 29,000 soldiers at Aldershot, told them that they inspired him "with the greatest admiration". Throughout, William behaved impeccably, though after he had gone the Queen noted cautiously in her diary that it was "such a contrast" to be having breakfast alone again in the intimate family circle. William at breakfast tried the strongest stomachs.

Sailing home again with his own obsolete ironclads, William consoled himself with the thoughts he expressed a few days later in a letter to his grandmother: "My warmest thanks for the quite unexampled honour which you conferred on me with the commission as Admiral of the Fleet. It really gave me such an immense pleasure that I am now able to feel and take an interest in your fleet as if it were my own. . . ." Visions hovered before him of the Royal Navy and the German army preserving the peace of the world— "The 'Red Coat' marching to victory with the Pomeranian Grenadier." "The uniform of an Admiral of the Fleet," said Bismarck later, "can be considered the symbol of a whole phase in the foreign policy of the Reich towards England."

But later in the year, after a ceaseless round of triumphal visits— which earned him the nickname of "*Reisekaiser*", "travelling Emperor"—to towns in every corner of Germany, William, restless as ever, set off for Athens via Italy, there to contemplate antique art and to make a speech on a visit to a British warship in Piraeus harbour which revealed that admiration had now changed to a competitive spirit. "I can see," he said, "that Nelson's famous watchword is now no longer necessary. All do their duty and we as a young seafaring nation come to England to learn something from the British Navy."

In November and December of 1889 William continued his merry-go-round—a mere glance at the calendar of his appointments makes one dizzy: to Constantinople, banquet in the Sultan's harem—to Venice, "my stay here has passed off in every respect to my entire satisfaction"—to Corfu, telegram to Bismarck, "weather splendid, visibility so good that all three peaks of the Peloponnese are visible, a very rare occurrence"—to Italy, thence by train back to Germany, swearing in of recruits, receives the adoptive son of the Emperor of Japan—two days' hunting, back to Berlin again—off to Breslau for pheasant shooting—more hunting with the Duke of Anhalt-Dessau—to Darmstadt, torchlight procession of the students —to Worms, a visit to the theatre, a speech to the Burgomaster in the vestibule before the performance—Frankfurt-on-Main: "splendid progress—all this is due to my grandfather"—back to Berlin, calls on the aged Empress Augusta—off to Hanover to inspect cavalry—back to Berlin, Christmas coming on, audiences, receptions, church services, eight new hats chosen by himself as a Christmas present for his wife, distributes largess incognito to the populace, listens to carols sung by the daughters of distressed gentlefolk, distributes presents to the palace staff—and is already pale with boredom and frustration, itching now that his ceaseless travels no longer give him the illusion of activity to do something great and splendid for the welfare of his people, for the glory of the Fatherland. A hint of what this might be came on the last day of the year: a message to the Reich Chancellor Prince von Bismarck in Friedrichs-ruh—best wishes, satisfaction that "we" have preserved peace in the year that is closing, and especial satisfaction at the passing of the Old Age and Sickness Insurance Act "which represents a consider-able step forward in a field which is particularly close to my heart: *the welfare of the working population*".

The New Year came and on 23rd January the Chancellor, who for the last eight months had been running the Reich by remote control from his home in the Sachsenwald, was summoned to a Crown Council to be held next day in Berlin. The agenda was not stated, the reason for the unusual step not explained. Before the Council meeting, William received Bismarck and urged him to drop the deportation clause from the Anti-Socialist law which was shortly due for renewal by the Reichstag. Bismarck refused. When the Council met, William, afire with enthusiasm, ignited a bombshell. Two draft proclamations were produced, one addressed to the Minister of Trade and Industry calling on him to prepare legislation to enforce Sunday rest in factories, exempt women from work during pregnancy, and restrict working hours of women and children. Industrial councils were to be set up, workers' welfare organizations established. The State coal mines were to be developed into model institutions. All this was to be worked out by a special Council of State presided over by the Kaiser in person. The second proclamation called on the Chancellor to convene a meeting of interested Powers in Berlin to discuss the improvement of working conditions in European countries.

William sought to motivate these proposals in words which revealed a mixture of fear and idealism. He wanted to be the *roi des gueux*, he said, the king of the beggars. The workers must know that he cared for their welfare. German industrialists took no interest whatever in their employees. They squeezed them like lemons, then threw them on the rubbish heap. It was they, not the workers, who were responsible for Social Democracy. Unless the workers were given a greater share in the profits they created there would be more strikes, more violent and better organized this time, and then the troops would have to shoot in earnest. It would be terrible, he said, if he had to stain the first years of his reign with the blood of his subjects. His projects were designed to prevent this. They could be looked on as a kind of preventive war. Today, William reminded his audience, was Frederick the Great's birthday. He wished to issue the proclamations on his own birthday in three days' time. What was the opinion of the assembled Ministers?

But the Ministers—and William took note of this—all looked to Bismarck and it was Bismarck who spoke. The project, he said, would have to be carefully considered. He himself did not like it. It would prejudice the forthcoming Reichstag elections, frighten the property-owning classes and encourage the Social Democrats. However, if His Majesty was determined to act, he would advise that the wording of the proclamations be watered down.

William then again raised the question of the deportation clause in the anti-Socialist law. It would be better for the Bill to pass without the clause, he thought, than risk its rejection by the Reichstag. But Bismarck, it seemed, was positively anxious for the Bill to be defeated. The Reichstag would then have to be dissolved. A vacuum would arise. Social unrest might develop. Then it would be necessary to proceed with force and vigour. Bismarck seemed to welcome civil war. William was appalled and spoke again of not wishing to shed the blood of his subjects. Bismarck retorted—and he could not prove this, but it was his opinion—that it would be fatal to capitulate to the Reichstag. It would undermine the royal authority and encourage the Reichstag to improper self-assertion. "If," Bismarck concluded, seeing William hesitate, "Your Majesty attaches no weight to my advice, I do not know whether I can remain at my post. . . ."

So William capitulated to his Chancellor, well aware that Bismarck would do his utmost to water down his social schemes and justifiably depressed by the old man's readiness to contemplate civil war rather than make concessions to the workers. The truth was that after a lifetime of power Bismarck could not bear to be gainsaid or opposed on any count by anyone, neither by the Kaiser nor by the Social Democrats nor by the Reichstag. When opposition arose, his only recipe was to crush it, but at a time when democracy ruled the Western world and was long overdue in Germany, the recipe was a desperate one.

A week after the Crown Council, Bismarck met his Ministers and tried to bury the Kaiser's project. To his amazement he encountered opposition. Finally, he drafted more innocuous versions of the proclamations, showed them to William and advised him to burn them. William refused. The proclamations were issued—without the Chancellor's counter-signature. On 8th February, Bismarck told William that he would wait until after the Reichstag elections and then retire from all his offices, at the latest by June. On 20th February, election results showed that the Social Democrats had gained twenty-four seats in the Reichstag and polled 1,427,000 votes. In the days that followed Bismarck developed his plans for a *coup d'état*. To William he painted a picture of imminent bloodshed, deliberately trying to work him into a panic. The suffrage, he said, must be altered, the Social Democrats disenfranchised. A new and more severe anti-Socialist law must be introduced. If there was an armed uprising, so much the better. "Social Democracy cannot be reformed out of existence, some day it will have to be shot out of existence." What monarch in Christendom could accept this advice?

But soon Bismarck was offering a yet more terrible prospect. If the Social Democrats could be goaded into open rebellion—and he had no doubt that he could manage that—a state of emergency could be declared, the Constitution be repealed and, after the rebellion had been crushed, a new Constitution be introduced abolishing adult male suffrage and strengthening yet further the power of the executive. William was amazed. But Bismarck, with his prestige and his passion half managed to convince him that a Red Spectre overhung the throne. He now proceeded, while the monarch was still in a frightened mood, to isolate him by reviving an old Cabinet Order of 1852 that had never been rescinded to the effect that no Minister of the Crown could report to or receive an audience of the Emperor except in the presence of the Chancellor. William was now cut off from all advice except the Chancellor's. Bismarck told him of his immediate plans: a stringent anti-Socialist Bill coupled with huge military estimates to be introduced into the Reichstag as a fuse which would blow up the powder barrel. This would stir the Socialists to action—and the rest could be left to Bismarck. This plan William emphatically refused. Bismarck then tried unsuccessfully to sabotage the international conference on labour questions by encouraging Switzerland to proceed with a similar conference which had already been planned.

But on 15th March, the international conference met in Berlin and on that same morning William sought out Bismarck in the Reich Chancellor's house. He had learnt that Bismarck had recently received the Catholic leader Windhorst, of the Centrist party in the Reichstag, a man whom William personally detested and of whom the Conservatives, the main prop of the monarchy, were very suspicious. Anxious about the purport of this latest change in the Chancellor's tactics and burning to reassert his authority, William took Bismarck to task for receiving Windhorst without consulting him. This provoked a tirade from the Chancellor. He was entitled to see whom he liked. It was impossible for him to do his work without consulting political leaders. He refused to submit to the Emperor's control over his personal dealings and the people he received at his own house. "Not even if your Sovereign commands you?" No, not even then. Well, it was not a question of a command, said William, but a desire. The Windhorst visit was reported in the papers. It had aroused considerable comment. Surely it was not the Chancellor's intention to increase popular alarm? On the contrary, said Bismarck, it was his intention. Such confusion must prevail in the country that no one would be able to guess what the Kaiser intended with his policy.

This was one of Bismarck's trump cards—playing on William's fears. But this time it was of no avail. William insisted that his policy must be clear to all. He had been in contact with the Conservatives to make sure that the Reichstag would approve of coming legislation. In Bismarck's eyes this was intolerable interference. Completely losing his temper he flung a heavy brief-case on the table so that the inkpots rattled. He could not go on like this. No work could be done. The Ministers were upset. He demanded to be dismissed.

William changed the subject. The Cabinet Order of 1852—he wanted it rescinded. Bismarck claimed it was necessary and refused. . . . Would the Kaiser dismiss him now, dare he? It was win-all or lose-all. To tip the scales Bismarck decided to humiliate William. It was he who changed the subject now, referring suddenly to a projected visit of William's to the Tsar. Bismarck had already advised against it, but William had preened himself on his success in St. Petersburg when he went as a Prince in 1887. Now the Chancellor drew a sheet of paper from a portfolio. It so happened, he said, that the Tsar had let fall some remarks about the German Kaiser which had found their way to London and been passed on by the German ambassador there. William told Bismarck to read them out. Bismarck declined. So William took the sheet and read for himself what the Tsar had said: "*Il est fou. C'est un garçon mal élevé et de mauvaise foi.* . . ."

But this, the ace of trumps, also failed to win the day. William turned to go, holding his helmet so as to avoid shaking hands. Next day he sent his Head of Military Cabinet to Bismarck demanding cancellation of the Cabinet Order. Bismarck refused, but sent a message saying he was submitting his resignation. Throughout 17th March William waited—no word. At the end of the day he sent another message demanding immediate cancellation of the order or Bismarck's resignation. Then, after dinner, he turned to his friend Eulenburg: "Now you must sing," he said. "We will clear our heads and think of other things." Eulenburg went to the piano, William as usual sat down beside him and turned the pages. His pleasure in the music seemed quite natural and unconstrained. "Even in these painful hours," reports Eulenburg, "his strange mercurial temperament did not desert him. Only for a few minutes was the music interrupted by the burning political question. The Kaiser was called out by the duty adjutant. When he returned and had sat down by the piano he whispered to me: 'The resignation has arrived'—then I had to go on singing."

Two days later, after Bismarck's resignation had been announced and he had been received in a farewell audience, William said: "I feel as sorrowful as though I had lost my grandfather all over again. This is God's will and I must bear it, even though it kills me. The duties of officer-of-the-watch in the ship of State have now fallen to me. The course remains the old one: full steam ahead!"

Some historians have dismissed this as the oiliest hypocrisy and admittedly it was not God's will, but William's, which had dismissed the Chancellor. Nor can he have been thinking of the irascible old man in grandfatherly terms when he uttered those words. But their implication that, after the event, William felt that it had been inevitable and was, at the same time, frightened by the action he had taken was true. For how could William, or anyone in his shoes, have kept a Chancellor who flouted his wishes, sabotaged his plans and held up the imminent prospect of civil war?

William, moreover, was very anxious to shine, and not merely as a figurehead. Frederick the Great still hovered before his mind's eye as the model to be imitated: Frederick whose least word was obeyed and who personally managed everything in Prussia from war to the tax on coffee.

But the last straw was the Red Spectre which Bismarck had conjured and the necessity of a *coup d'état*. It is impossible to say whether he would have carried this out if he had remained in power. Undoubtedly he had over-stressed the danger with the intention of intimidating William—with the most unexpected result. Like a frightened rabbit, William had shied away from the thought of a coup, even with Bismarck to manage it, and had found a different bolt-hole: he would get rid of the Chancellor and so seal off the dangers which he foresaw. Thus in a mind overburdened with fear and a sense of insecurity, the reasons for the fear were not faced, but banished, at least for a time. For William could never face the logic of this Red Spectre and everything in his nature howled against Bismarck's remedy. Nor did he ever dare to look at the subject calmly and detect the only alternative to armed suppression of the Socialists—constitutional reform. His mind was like a clenched fist, always closed to uncomfortable realities. Soon he began to think he had been rather clever in dismissing Bismarck, like a sorcerer who waves his wand and fells a giant.

CHAPTER FOUR

WILLIAM AT SEA

WITH Bismarck gone, William was now free to devise his own drama with himself in the leading role and he was doubly eager to give a good performance because his whole nature yearned for love and approval. But not in one single respect was he well equipped to play it. He had none of the soldierly virtues. He was timid, excitable, restless and possessed one disastrous defect: he could not learn from experience. He could not enter into life, or grow beyond himself. He had studied the part—oh, yes, he knew how to imitate his grandfather's stance, and he had read goggle-eyed of the Great Frederick's ruthless, snarling heroism. But it was from the people of this world that William sought approval, people who could answer back—in the Press, in the volume of their cheers, by the modulation of the voice, by the curl of an eyebrow—and the merest hint that they saw through him and allied themselves with that inner voice which told him he was no good could throw him into a panic.

It was this self-rejection that was really the core of the trouble, allied to a temperament of manic excitability. William was like a Dexedrine-addict, all flickering flame, ready to burn, sear and consume—until a puff of wind extinguished it. As he could not fit in with his fellow-men, he had only two choices: to sink below them or rise far above them. He chose to excel, to break through the fear-barrier into the open sky from where the human race looked like pygmies and he could find absolute freedom to set up his own will, his own whims as the supreme law for the German race. The phenomenon of William streaking across the heavens was too startling to be missed. Bismarck in his retirement declared: "William thinks he knows better than anyone. He recognizes no authority but himself. It is difficult to bring home to him any mistake he has committed." His mother wrote to Queen Victoria: "William imagines that he can do everything himself. But a little modesty and self-understanding would teach him that he is neither Frederick the Great nor the genius that he imagines himself to be."

This was the man who now seized the helm and rang for "full steam ahead". There was no statesman approaching Bismarck's calibre to replace him. As Chancellor, William appointed the fifty-nine-year-old General von Caprivi, the commander of the Hanover army corps and a former head of the Admiralty. Caprivi was a hard worker, a sound administrator and an enlightened patriot without personal ambition. Bismarck respected his personal qualities, but thought nothing of his political skill. In Herbert Bismarck's place who had refused to stay after his father's dismissal, Freiherr Marschall von Bieberstein was appointed Secretary of State in the Foreign Office. He was a Conservative lawyer from Baden, well versed in internal affairs, a good debater and though sublimely ignorant of his new task was to prove a better diplomatist than many professional men.

In these two men William possessed solid though inexperienced advisers. Surely they could steer the ship on a steady course? But the Kaiser was seldom on the bridge. Most of his time he spent touring the state-rooms, making speeches from the mast-head, inspecting the crew and holding sing-songs in the first-class lounge. And when he was on the bridge neither Caprivi nor Marschall could approach him directly. They had to stand at the foot of the ladder, call up to Philipp Eulenburg and ask him to act as intermediary. For only Phili could manage the Captain's moods. Only he possessed the art of making suggestions to him in a way which made him feel that the ideas came from himself.

Not only this, but as inexperienced navigating officer Marschall soon found that he was dependent on his experts, and chief among them, on a sinister figure who shunned the limelight and seemed to be answerable to no one. This was Friedrich von Holstein, fifty-three years old, former protégé of Bismarck's, close colleague of Herbert's, a brilliant and trusted subordinate of the Iron Chancellor who held all the secrets of diplomacy at his finger-tips and was now the only man still in office who even knew where the most important files in the Foreign Office were to be found. Holstein was indispensable, not by accident, but by deliberate design. He had never sought the limelight. The Press never mentioned him. It was the reality of power that intoxicated him, not its trappings. Officially, he was Under-Secretary at the Foreign Office, a "*Geheimrat*", a Privy Councillor and never was the adjective more aptly applied.

Holstein, until his death in 1909, was the evil genius of German foreign policy. As a young man in the diplomatic service he had acquired rooted prejudices. In London in 1864, when anti-Prussian feeling was high because of the war with Denmark, he and other members of the German Embassy had been ostracized by fashionable society. He had felt persecuted and ever afterwards hated England. In 1870, when Prussia defeated France, he projected himself into the minds of Frenchmen, felt persecuted on their behalf—and ever afterwards remained convinced of France's incurable hostility to Germany. Thereafter, he worked under Count Arnim in the Paris Embassy. Bismarck suspected Arnim of intriguing for the Chancellorship and determined to ruin him. Holstein was employed to spy on his Ambassador. In due course, Arnim was charged with semi-treasonable activities, Holstein giving evidence at his trial. Arnim was ruined, but Berlin feeling was on his side. Again, Holstein was ostracized, this time by his own countrymen. Again he felt persecuted—and this time his feelings took the form of hatred for his fellow-men. "The Bismarcks," he complained, "have branded me on the forehead like a galley-slave; therewith they hold me fast."

But Holstein did not resign. It was not Bismarck but his own temperament which made him a galley-slave. If people would not respect his character at least they should defer to his brain, and he set about making himself the hub of German foreign policy, the spider at the centre of the web. In this he was utterly unscrupulous, withholding important information from colleagues, showing glaring favouritism, corresponding over the heads of their Ambassadors with individuals in German embassies abroad. Nobody liked him; nobody could get rid of him. Epithets applied to him were legion: "spiteful", "eccentric", "morbid", "a man with the character of a hunchback", "a spider", "a mole", "vain", "suspicious", "dominated by fantasies", "a good hater and therefore dangerous". He carried a pistol with him wherever he went, avoided publicity like the plague, lived only for his work—and heartily despised the Kaiser.

William and Holstein were the key figures in foreign affairs, yet they only met face to face on one occasion. Holstein preferred to cultivate Eulenburg, Eulenburg cultivated William and William eyed everyone with suspicion, even his friend Phili at times because he was, after all, a subject, and William had to be careful not to unbend too far, otherwise he might never get the mask back into place. An uneasy ship's company. And to distract them further, as the "Germania" went to full speed came the voice of Bismarck, the dropped pilot, from the shore, smothering them all with invective and spinning heaven knew what plots with his supporters in the crew in the hope of returning to power.

In the early years after Bismarck's dismissal William heaped reckless abuse on the disruptive elements in the State. He was dominated by terror that the whole edifice might collapse. "There is only one master in the Reich," he thundered, "and that is myself. I will tolerate no other." "I am well aware that attempts are being made at the present time to spread alarm in the public mind. . . . A spirit of disobedience is creeping through the land. But you know that I look on my position as decreed for me by heaven—I am called to act on behalf of a higher power." Where could William be safe? In his capital perhaps? Berlin might be the womb where he could feel warm and secure. There, surely, honoured by his presence, the citizens would rally as one man round the steps of the throne. But the Berliners, sceptical realists, would not surrender their souls. They stood back, eyed their Kaiser quizzically, cracked wounding jokes and sometimes even went on strike against their God-appointed overlords. It was terrible. William's fevered imagination beat a retreat before the rabble howling for blood. If not safe in Berlin, then safe in the palace. Yes, he said, he would barricade himself, have loopholes cut in the walls, watch the Socialists burning and plundering the city till the distracted citizens appealed for his help: then, with his bodyguard, he would make a sortie, rescue them from the terror, restore order, and reap the plaudits of all honest men. Thus William spoke in private, in these pictures, almost in these words—and his courtiers asked themselves: can this be a man of thirty?

The cohesion which William demanded of Germans could not, of course, be imposed from above, but had to be built up organically. But his mind, though longing for peace, was capable only of stirring up strife—such was the paradox. "Recruits!" he snarled at young men just sworn in to the Potsdam guard regiment: "You have now sworn loyalty to me. That means you are now my soldiers, you have committed yourselves to me body and soul. For you there is only one enemy and that is my enemy. In the present Socialist conspiracies it may be that I shall order you to shoot down your own relatives, brothers or even—which God forbid—your parents, but even then you must carry out my orders without complaint."

This speech aroused a howl of indignation throughout Germany. It was never forgotten—except by William. Only those in his immediate entourage, the military men, knew that if it came to the point he would never order the soldiers to shoot. Words, with him, took the place of bullets.

Meanwhile, within weeks of Bismarck's dismissal, an important pledge for future peace had been abandoned. In 1887 Bismarck had concluded a secret agreement with Russia known as the Reinsurance Treaty. Both partners promised benevolent neutrality if the other was involved in war, except in the case of a German attack on France or a Russian attack on Austria. In June 1890 the treaty was due for renewal. Caprivi, Marschall and Holstein now studied it—the first two with mingled admiration and fear at Bismarck's jugglery—and they came to the conclusion that a provision whereby Russia was conceded the right to occupy Bulgaria was incompatible with a treaty signed in 1883 by Germany and Austria with Rumania. The Reinsurance Treaty had not averted serious conflicts with Russia and even Bismarck did not seem to expect it to prevent an ultimate understanding between Russia and France. The three men therefore now decided not to renew it. Though his grandfather on his death-bed had impressed on him the need for friendship with Russia, William reluctantly agreed. Thus the tenuous link between the two strongest military powers in Europe was broken and Russia, already dominated by a Germanophobe nobility, moved rapidly towards France, her only other possible friend. In July, 1891, the French fleet paid a most successful visit to Cronstadt. Enthusiasm on both sides was extraordinary. Tsar Alexander stood for the Marseillaise— a touch which outraged William to the depths of his soul. On the way home, the French fleet visited Portsmouth. Two years later, in October 1893, a Russian Squadron paid a return visit to Toulon. And in December of that year Russia and France signed a secret military convention promising mutual help if either were attacked by a member of the Triple Alliance.

These developments confronted William with his first real test as the arbiter of German foreign policy. He revealed a highly confused and personal attitude. To him, nations were people to be loved or hated. England was his adored but formidable grandmother shadowed by the odious Edward. Russia was the Tsar Alexander who, as William was never likely to forget, had called him *un garçon mal élevé et de mauvaise foi*. Behind him trotted the young Nicolas, soft, pliant, and a likely target for William's brittle charm. France was a bunch of traitorous regicides, damned souls, contemptible *crapauds*, but dangerous because for some obscure reason they refused to rejoice at Germany's death-grip on Alsace-Lorraine.

For Bismarck's caution in international dealings and sternly realistic approach, William substituted the capers of a neurotic youth, longing to make friends, but fearing he might consolidate enemies. Just before the French visit to Cronstadt he had planted himself on his grandmother again, self-invited, unable to resist just one more glimpse of solid, prosperous Britain which, but for the accident that his mother was not a man, would have one day been ruled by himself. How envious that made him. How pleasant it would have been to have strutted in the safe, sea-girt isle, mistress of the seas, centre of a world empire. Instead, there was his Uncle

Edward, the lazy sensualist, heir to this glory, yet so unimaginative he could not savour the romance of the heritage on which William, from distracted Germany, cast such envious eyes. William was both jealous and contemptuous of Edward. The man's poise, his easy assurance enraged him. He interpreted it as condescension. He never missed an opportunity of turning the tables on his uncle and making him look small. An opportunity arose just before his visit. Edward had been involved in an unsavoury libel case brought by a man who, when playing baccarat with him, had been caught cheating. The British public was considerably upset, so was William, or he professed to be. In Berlin, to his fawning adjutants, he depicted his uncle as now beyond the pale. "It's impossible to have further dealings with the fellow." This was greeted with respectful but delighted silence. In private the adjutants nodded their heads and said William was *ein famoser Mensch* who knew his mind and was not afraid to speak it. To Edward the nephew wrote a letter offering advice as to his future behaviour.

This put William in the most genial mood for his visit. It went off to his entire satisfaction. In the Guildhall he declared: "In this delightful country I have always felt at home as the grandson of a Queen who will always be remembered for her noble character and wisdom. Moreover the same blood flows in English and in German veins. I will always preserve the historic friendship between these our two nations."

But soon William's conception of friendship was revealed. With England particularly it had to be an exclusive love affair. The French fleet tracing its ominous curve round Germany from Cronstadt to Portsmouth was a case in point. Dear, trusting Grandmama should beware. In December, 1891, he wrote to her warning her about the Russians who were fatally weakened by financial and agrarian crises and would otherwise be only too prone to fall on their unsuspecting neighbours. The Russian difficulties, thank God, might restrain the Johnny Crapauds—"as your sailors call them"—"and if they keep quiet everybody else is quiet."

But Franco-Russian relations steadily improved and William, to his dismay, could not quite discover where England stood in this game. He hoped and prayed that his grandmother would do nothing treacherous. Personal visits and warning letters, he decided, were the best means of keeping his finger on her pulse and persuading it to beat time with his own. Each year these trips took place. For the hosts it was like entertaining a box of dynamite. William had to be handled with the utmost care. In 1893 he won the Queen's Cup from the Prince of Wales in a yacht race round the Isle of Wight. Next day, his uncle saw him, ceaselessly active, on board his *Meteor*, taking part in more races. There was really a danger, thought Edward, that with that withered arm the poor fellow might fall overboard.

Still, William enjoyed himself, though he could not spend all week racing round the island, making rings round the English. In the evenings he was confronted with his grandmother and what an agonizing business that could be. "It was strange," noted Eulenburg, who was in the Imperial suite, "to see the Kaiser ill at ease and almost tongue-tied in the presence of the little Queen. Otherwise that was never his way. Admittedly, he never felt free in the presence of women, but this had nothing to do with it. In relations with his grandmother, whom he alternately hated and passionately loved, he was dominated by the painful feeling of not being a match for her. He seemed to be afraid. After seeing the Queen he usually expressed himself to me in terms of enthusiastic devotion and love. But . . ."

But confronted with his grandmother William could never decide how he wanted to feel. At times it was pleasant to sit at her feet and remind her how Prince Albert had swung him in a napkin when he was an infant. At others, he wanted to be treated like a colleague, a fellow-monarch. Unfortunately the monarch and the infant fought in his mind. Only Victoria saw and accepted the fact that they were one and the same thing. That was galling, but sometimes it was rather nice. It just depended on who else was present.

Yearly William was drawn back to the scene of this conflict to renew the battle with the Queen whom he loved and feared. He was thirsty for tokens of her affection. Already an Admiral in the British Fleet, he now wanted and obtained a military appointment—the honorary colonelcy of the 1st Royal Dragoons. In this uniform he called on his grandmother in 1894, attended a military review at Aldershot, met "his" regiment, got treated like one of themselves, raced again for the Queen's Cup, spoke at the Royal Yacht Squadron at Cowes: "I hope that Britannia will continue to rule the waves."

But meanwhile it seemed that the future Tsar Nicolas was supplanting William in his grandmother's affections. Nicolas's visit, with his fiancée, the Queen's grandchild, Princess Alix of Hesse, had preceded his own. From Germany William wrote to his grandmother: Russia was a weak and treacherous nation. Cholera was raging in the western provinces. Russian troops were massing on Germany's borders with the object of preventing him, William, from helping anyone that Russia might attack in the East. . . .

Russia, it seemed, was too weak to be a useful ally for Britain, at the same time she was a menace. This contradictory advice at any rate drove home the fact that it was quite impossible to have dealings with her. But Victoria apparently did not think so. In October, 1894, at the Tsarina's request she dispatched the Prince of Wales and his wife to Russia as the Tsar Alexander was dying. Edward arrived in time to attend the new Tsar Nicolas at his coronation and then at his marriage, making him, with the Queen's approval, Colonel-in-Chief of the Scots Greys on his wedding day. William was appalled. Here was another friendship to break up. That should not be difficult. Nicky was a soft and impressionable youth, a bit dim and obviously lonely. William wrote to him, grappling him to his heart with a good dollop of flattery—and a promise to guard Russia's rear "so that nobody shall hamper your action towards the Far East. . . ." This duplicity which he fondly imagined would be known only to himself eventually became common knowledge in London and St. Petersburg and the Queen wrote to Nicolas saying that the things the Kaiser was telling her about Russia she, of course, did not believe, and she hoped that Nicolas would be equally sceptical when he heard, as no doubt he would, outrageous stories about the English. Perhaps both of them then remembered a speech which William had made four years before when opening the Reichstag: "I have succeeded in confirming the confidence of all foreign governments in the reliability of my policy."

While William was undermining this confidence his Chancellor Caprivi had been making solid achievements, but at the same time enemies. A treaty whereby Britain surrendered Heligoland in return for Zanzibar had enraged German colonialists, though the new Kiel Canal which was under construction would in fact be useless in war with the British dominating its western end. A series of commercial treaties with European countries including Russia, though helpful to growing German industry, had alienated the Conservative agrarians. The Bismarck fronde and military circles continued to pour scorn on the cautious Chancellor and work for his fall. Only the Social Democrats had cause for some satisfaction with a man who opposed drastic action against them and declared: "The government can contain and repress, but that does not solve the question. The damage which we may be liable to suffer must be healed from the inside. We must not get into the habit of looking on the workers pessimistically. We must not abandon hope of regaining their support."

But it was this sensible view which now brought about Caprivi's fall. In June, 1894, the French President Carnot was assassinated by an Italian anarchist. Caprivi had allowed the existing laws against the Social Democrats to lapse. The Conservative Press, knowing well that he would oppose the demand, now howled for their revival. Fearing apparently for his personal safety, William added his voice, wiring Caprivi that a draft law against the Socialists was to be prepared and the "present anxious mood of the bourgeoisie" be exploited to push it through the Reichstag. But William was cruising in Norwegian waters and in no position to gauge the mood of the country. His own, however, was clear enough. He had heard that Gerhart Hauptmann's play *The Weavers*, a subversive piece, had just been performed on the Berlin stage. What were the censors doing? Were they in the plot? Now Berlin workers were boycotting watery beer from local breweries: was this the sign for rebellion? Against this insubordination, he wired, "something *must* be done".

Throughout the summer William fumed and fretted. As Caprivi seemed dilatory he would sound the alarm himself. In East Prussia he thundered: "Into battle for religion, morality and order against the parties of revolution. . .! As the ivy clings to the gnarled oak and protects it while storms howl through its topmost branches, so the Prussian nobility gathers round my House. Let us enter this battle together! Forward with God! And dishonourable he who leaves his King in the lurch!"

The fears which Bismarck had implanted in his mind now surged up and in September William insisted that Caprivi abolish the wide suffrage and prepare to suppress opposition by force if it could not be overcome by legal means. Almost the identical prescription which Bismarck had offered, with the only difference that there was no Doctor Bismarck now to force it down the patient's throat. But, flaring in William's mind, fear burnt up caution and good sense. He was in a mood for drastic action. Let no one gainsay him or force him to compromise, for that would impose a yet greater strain. Caprivi, however, did just this. He had received William's instructions by letter from Elbing where he was attending imperial manœuvres. Now the Chancellor had to track him down in the forests of East Prussia where he was slaughtering insubordinate animals. Still, he was lucky to find William at all: in the last year he had spent 199 days abroad. At least he was now in Germany. William listened to Caprivi's doubts about the projected action and got the impression that his Chancellor was trying to intimidate him. It was really too bad of Caprivi to advise caution when William was poised and ready to put an end to it all by plunging over the cliff. No, no. Sound the parties, William urged. My plan must go through. Reluctantly Caprivi agreed, noting that William did not seem to like a Chancellor who thought for himself.

Caprivi consulted the Conservatives. There was an unbridgeable gulf between their points of view. The Chancellor was emphatically against any anti-Socialist measures that could not be applied under the existing law. The Conservatives were toying with the idea of summoning the Federal Princes to abolish the Constitution. The

Chancellor was also under fire from Bismarck's supporters, while William's military entourage continued to pour poison into his heart about the dilettante Chancellor and his failure to work for the glory and expansion of the Reich. Long ago, Bismarck had noted that William listened to everyone, but in the long run went his own way regardless of his advisers. Now the monarch succumbed to a mood of extreme agitation. In a further audience, Caprivi explained his difficulties and sensing that he no longer possessed William's confidence, offered his resignation. This was not accepted. Oh, no. William explained that he too, on reflection, was now against drastic anti-Socialist action.

A few days later he changed his mind again. In a speech to East Prussian landowners in Berlin he spoke of "the battle which disruptive elements impose on us". Less than a week after this a Cologne newspaper came out with a report that the Kaiser agreed with the Chancellor's attitude and gave him his continued confidence. For William this was the last straw. For one thing, he was not so sure now that he did have confidence in Caprivi, and anyway, it was intolerable that the Press, those gutter journalists, should try and force consistency on him. "My intimate conversation with Caprivi is in the newspaper!" he stormed, and at once demanded that the Chancellor should issue a denial. But Caprivi, as it happened, had not informed the Press; it was probably Marschall who had done so, with the object of strengthening the Chancellor's position. So Caprivi refused to deny the article. Why should he? It was true, wasn't it? Oh no, it wasn't: William was now thoroughly tired of the stubborn General. He felt the reins of power, which he fondly imagined he held, slipping from him. There was only one answer to that: dismissal.

Caprivi went with a good grace. He was not ambitious, he was not an intriguer. He was a capable administrator who had learnt after four years in office just how impossible it was to work with Kaiser William. In his memoirs the Kaiser, in Doorn, found words of appreciation for the honest soldier. But, meanwhile, it was a relief to be rid of him. Perhaps he could now find a better man. Turning to Philipp Eulenburg, he said: "I have no idea whom I can call on. Do you know of anyone?"

There was Bismarck, of course. But Philipp knew better than to mention that name. William had come to look on the Iron Chancellor as a traitor because he had dared to oppose him. For years, until late in 1893, William had had no dealings with the fallen demigod. From the Bismarckian Press he had endured continual pinpricks. He had been forever conscious of those glowering eyes resting on him from retirement in the Sachsenwald. The undercurrent of panic which reigned in the Wilhelmstrasse so long as the great man was alive and capable of resuming office had infected him. Occasionally, when things went badly, he had uttered the despairing cry: "It *must* be possible to rule without Bismarck." And so it had been, depending on what was meant by "rule".

But William had come to realize that Bismarck's popularity in Germany was not waning, but increasing. A disastrous intervention by Caprivi in 1892, when Bismarck had gone to Vienna to attend the wedding of his son and had found the German Ambassador's doors closed to him had swelled public affection for the old man to alarming proportions. Stung by the boycott which Caprivi, urged by Holstein, had imposed on him, Bismarck gave an interview to a Vienna newspaper in which he spoke of "men who have come to the front in Germany whom I was careful to relegate to their native obscurity". These remarks were widely applauded. William, on his pinnacle, felt a rival mountain thrusting up to out-top him.

So far, he had been very careful not to cross swords with Bismarck, even indirectly. He knew he would get the worst of the encounter and in matters like this, where he was competing for popular approval, he slipped instinctively into the most suitable role. The time had come, obviously, for a reconciliation with Bismarck. This was not easy. William must not lose dignity or appear to be currying favour with the traitor. The first move must come from him. But Bismarck never stirred. Oblique suggestions conveyed by intermediaries met with blank refusal. "You're only an old cat now," said someone to Bismarck. "You're not a lion any more." "Oh yes, I am," was the reply. "Watch out!" It was only in 1893, when the lion contracted pneumonia, that William cautiously pushed a bait through the bars: a bottle of rare old wine was sent, nursed by an adjutant, to the doors of Friedrichsruh. This was graciously received. An invitation followed to convalesce in one of the Kaiser's country mansions. No, the old man preferred to get better in familiar surroundings, but when he had recovered he said he would come to Berlin.

This news plunged Holstein, Marschall, the Court, the Foreign Office into a frenzy of apprehension. Oh, God, the lion was returning! The scene in Berlin, noted Eulenburg, was like a farmyard in a thunderstorm, hens and roosters scuttering everywhere with loud cries and desperate beady glances. But the visit went off very well. William was careful to receive Bismarck alone in the palace, with only his wife as witness. They had lunch and talked of the old man's health and of military matters. In the afternoon, while Bismarck went to pay his respects to William's mother—What were they discussing there? Nothing good, assuredly—William spent several hours touring the capital in an open carriage. Not even the January cold could keep him from his loving subjects, or stop him reaping the applause that was really intended for Bismarck. The visit, so far as William was concerned, was a complete success. There was really no need to discuss politics with Bismarck, even if he had dared. Caprivi's dismissal lay five months ahead. As Foreign Minister, Marschall, admittedly, was being so successful that William was beginning to feel a tinge of jealousy. But he had a new adviser now, better than all of them: Kapitän-zur-See Tirpitz. For two years he had been Chief of the Naval Staff. He was resolute, he was clever. He and William saw eye-to-eye: Germany needed a large, a very large navy. That would make Britain sit up. One day it might even make William arbiter of the world.

CHAPTER FIVE

FISHING IN TROUBLED WATERS

FROM boyhood William had been fascinated by the sea and ships. His grandmother's fleet had aroused his envious admiration. Since he had become an honorary British admiral he found it difficult to realize that the Royal Navy did not belong to him. It was only on the return journeys from Britain, surrounded by his own few antiquated warships, that the truth of Germany's naval weakness became inescapable. That must be remedied.

In diplomacy and home affairs William's influence on events is not easy to distinguish. In one sphere only his personal initiative was decisive—the creation of a modern battle-fleet. This was not primarily a matter of calculation. To him a row of menacing iron-clads was a psychological necessity: they symbolized his desire to get on equal terms with Britain, and above all they were the expression of aggressive instincts. Nothing in the wide world combined more power in less space than a battleship.

But aggression was one of William's key characteristics. It simmered perpetually at the back of his mind. Almost any incident at home or abroad could release a flood of sanguinary words. Mention by a courtier of increasing violence in the lower classes brought the comment: "Yes, without some proper blood-letting and some shooting it won't be cured." Demonstrations for electoral reform in which the police had wounded thirty citizens drew excited approval, qualified by the remark: "But next time they must strike not with the flat but the sharp edge of the sword." In personal dealings, William was forever tweaking his defenceless subjects by the ear, pummelling them, slapping them on the back, summoning them with an aggressive gesture or dismissing them with a careless wave of the hand. He took pleasure, it was noticed, in making wounding remarks and watching people squirm. "Are you here, you old swine?" he said to a venerable courtier who had turned up unexpectedly on a hunting trip. Noticing a speck of cigarette ash on the floor he brandished his fist in his Court Marshall's face and roared: "I'll teach you to look after my things!" Abroad, he projected his own aggression into other nations and continually suspected them of seeking the destruction of Germany. The urge to fly out and strike down, to end all in a bloody battle was intense and perpetual. When the real world offered no outlet for his nervous tension he sought to relieve it by incessant travel and activity; when it did, or seemed to do, he would release his pent-up feelings in a flood of extravagant threats with an almost audible gasp of relief. Then the Chinese, or the Japanese, or the Social Democrats or his uncle Edward or the "decadent" French would be overwhelmed with foaming language crammed full of warlike metaphors.

This agitated monarch coincided with agitated times. In Africa the scramble for colonies was reaching a climax. In the last twenty years the British and French had established their rule over vast tracts of territory. There were still some blanks on the map, still a partial vacuum and until it was filled international rivalries would remain at fever-pitch. There were signs that the Turkish Empire was wobbling to a fall. When Turkey collapsed another void would open at a neuralgic point where Austrian and Russian interests clashed and there would be almost unlimited opportunities for extensions of power for one side or another into the Balkans, the Mediterranean and the Near East. Further afield a poverty-stricken China was arousing envious glances from Russia and the young, untried Japan. In Europe the new-found friendship between Russia and France confronted Germany with a set of pincers whose jaws were forever ready to close, while the value of her only firm ally, Austria–Hungary, was dependent on how far, if at all, she would be able to reconcile the hostile nationalities within her borders.

All this would have aroused Bismarck's redoubled caution. He would have thought first of Germany's continental security and made colonial adventures dependent on that need. The German colonial empire had been founded in his day, admittedly—German South West Africa, the Cameroons and Togoland in 1884, the north-east part of New Guinea in the same year, the Marshall, Brown and some of the Solomon Islands in 1885, the Bismarck Archipelago and German East Africa shortly after his dismissal in 1890—but in a famous speech to the Reichstag in 1885 he had firmly opposed the view that the State should take the initiative in acquiring colonies and contended that its role should be confined to giving the necessary protection to private enterprise where this had already established itself in overseas territories and had given proof that they could be exploited to advantage.

But now there were new men, headed by the manic Kaiser, who, spurred by Germany's rapidly expanding population and output and infected by the mounting tide of power-worship, agreed wholeheartedly with the historian Treitschke when he wrote: "Through the settlement of distant portions of the globe the history of Europe acquires a rich new content and the nation is fully justified in demanding that Germany should not lag behind in this great contest of the peoples."

Hypersensitive to questions of personal prestige and convinced that he enjoyed God's special protection, William now determined to hoist the Hohenzollern eagle wherever a spare plot of ground would support a flagpole. It made no difference that existing German colonies were attracting the merest trickle of immigrants or that their economies had to be subsidized by the State or, paradoxically, that a policy of grab would inevitably entail friction with England, the one State whose friendship Germany would be best advised to cultivate. The cry was "full steam ahead" for, as William said, "the waves of opportunity are beating against Germany's shores."

At the same time, a fleet consisting of seven ships of the line, two large cruisers and seven small ones seemed pathetically inadequate to support these ambitions. William's heart was set on battleships, but where, in the Reichstag or in the country, was the support necessary to vote the supplies or see the necessity for this new un-German commitment? An organizer was needed, a man who would supply practical arguments to support William's dream. The man was Tirpitz. Already in 1894 he was penning a memorandum: "A State which has oceanic or world interests must be able to uphold them and make its power felt beyond its own territorial waters. National world commerce, world industry, world intercourse and colonies are impossible without a fleet capable of taking the offensive." Therefore a powerful fleet was necessary. The argument was, of course, weak if it was merely a question of "upholding" German interests. The Dutch had colonies, but no large fleet. But William and Tirpitz were not interested in conserving, they were on the make and it was not a European but a world policy that William was anxious to pursue.

Meanwhile, Caprivi had been succeeded as Chancellor by the aged Prince Hohenlohe, a clever and cautious *grand seigneur* with a lifetime of administrative and political experience. But Hohenlohe was a South German and out of sympathy with the filibustering Prussian spirit. Moreover he lacked the vigour and the taste for flattery to control William's capers or impose his views on him. There was an almost ludicrous contrast between this quiet, cultured gentleman and the aggressive foreign policy which the army, the colonialists, the Kaiser and some sections of the Foreign Office were burning to pursue.

The opportunity came with the Sino-Japanese war which broke out in the summer of 1894 and lasted until the spring of 1895. The Japanese achieved sensational successes, driving the Chinese from Korea, occupying the Liaotung Peninsula to the westward with Port Arthur at its tip, and advancing towards Peking. China then sued for peace and Japan announced her terms: a war indemnity, the cession of Formosa, Port Arthur and considerable adjoining areas of Manchuria. Hitherto, William had been full of enthusiasm for Japanese martial efficiency and found the peace terms "in no way excessive". Their announcement, however, induced Russia to suggest a démarche in Tokyo jointly with Germany and France to dissuade the Japanese from claiming any part of the Chinese mainland. Germany agreed to this and William now abruptly changed his tone. Russia, of course, had vital interests to protect in China; Japan might become a terrible menace. A German expert on the Far East painted the Yellow Peril to William in lurid colours. The Japanese were a hard-working people, their competition might damage European industry; in alliance with England they might dominate and exploit the whole of Eastern Asia. One day, they might even match the Mongol invasions and menace Europe directly. Joint resistance to their demands on the part of all European powers was urgently necessary.

William now saw his opportunity. It was clear that if Russia and Germany succeeded in restraining Japan, China would be very much in their debt: compensations in the way of naval bases could be demanded. Russia, too, would be encouraged to expand into the vacuum which Japanese withdrawal would create and thereby her ambitions would be transferred from the West to the East, Germany's eastern frontier would be denuded, France's dreams of revenge would have to be postponed and Germany might emerge more secure at home and more powerful abroad. Nicky must be firmly pushed along this desirable path. In great excitement, William commissioned an allegorical picture to be painted and in April, 1895, he sent it with a letter to his cousin, declaring that "the development of the Far East, especially its danger to Europe and our Christian Faith is a matter which has been greatly on my mind" and explaining that the picture, which was based on an idea of his own, showed "the powers of Europe represented by their respective Genii called together by the Archangel Michael—sent from Heaven —to *unite* in resisting the inroad of Buddhism, heathenism and barbarism for the defence of the Cross". The picture was entitled: "Peoples of Europe, defend your most sacred possessions!" and

William was so pleased with it that he ordered copies to be hung in ships of the Hamburg–America Line travelling to the Far East. Nicky, too, seemed edified and when William heard of this he rubbed his hands with glee, saying: "Good! So it works!"

But though the démarche in Tokyo produced the desired result and Japan renounced all conquests on the mainland of China, in supporting the step Germany incurred the undying enmity of Japan. And though Russia was indeed encouraged to embark on expansionist adventures in China there was no guarantee that they would be successful; a clash between Russia and Japan became in the long run inevitable and if Russia were the loser she would then be thrown back towards Europe with a permanent grudge against Germany as the instigator of her defeat. William's glib encouragement of the Tsar was therefore a gamble which gave hostages to fortune.

In any case it was two years before compensation was obtained from China. William was very eager for some acquisition as the first positive gain of his reign. His gaze first fell upon Amoy opposite Formosa as a possible coaling-station for the fleet. "Amoy must be occupied immediately," he wired Hohenlohe in November, 1896. "Once it has been occupied we can open negotiations with China." But Tirpitz, at that time commanding a squadron in the Far East, now reported that Kiau-chau, some 800 miles to the north, was the only desirable pearl. The Russian fleet was there on a temporary basis by agreement with the Chinese and when approached by William, the Tsar was evasive about allowing German ships to anchor beside his own. Then two German missionaries were murdered in the hinterland. This sanctioned a release of aggression and William declared: "I am now firmly determined to abandon our hyper-cautious policy which is looked on as weakness throughout the Far East and to teach the Chinese with the utmost firmness and, if need be, with the most brutal ruthlessness that the German Kaiser will not allow himself to be joked with. . . ." Excited exchanges now took place with St. Petersburg and finally the Russians agreed to take Port Arthur and evacuate Kiau-chau to the Germans. Soon after, the port was obtained on a ninety-nine-year lease; England—which had wisely refrained from the démarche in Tokyo—leased Wei-hai-Wei and the French occupied Kuang-chow.

It was a diplomatic success for Germany, but hardly a military one, unless thrusting aside a few junks loaded with chickens could be construed as a naval victory. But the dead missionaries aroused William's crusading fervour. Blood and religion was always the medicine which excited him most. Kiau-chau was occupied by his Far Eastern squadron, and further ships—the last, in fact, in the kitty—were dispatched from Kiel under his sailor brother Prince Henry as reinforcements. Bidding farewell to the men in December, 1897, with the utmost pomp and magnificence, William made a turkey-cock speech, coining the first of the phrases which were to provide such plums for Allied propaganda against him in the World War. He boasted of Germany's might, her legitimate interests, of the need to protect churchly brethren "implanting our religion on alien soil", and he called on Prince Henry to "have at the enemy with the mailed fist". Later, in the Reichstag, von Bülow, who had succeeded Marschall as Foreign Minister in that same year, blandly declared: "We do not want to put anyone in the shade, but we, too, demand our place in the sun."

Meanwhile, before the Sino-Japanese war was over, relations with Britain had become strained over events in the Transvaal. The Boer President Kruger had been assured of German friendship and support when he invited conflict with Britain by refusing reasonable rights to the Uitlanders who had been attracted to his country after the discovery of gold in the Witwatersrand. By making trouble for Britain, William hoped to soften her attitude towards German colonial expansion and ultimately draw her into the Triple Alliance with Austria and Italy. These calculations were based on the belief— which was an article of faith in the Wilhelmstrasse—that Britain could never agree with France or Russia and therefore had only one possible ally on the continent, Germany. Germany, as the phrase had it, was the tongue of the scales, she could tip them in either direction. This thought was very flattering to William.

A good chance to operate the see-saw came after William's birthday in January, 1895, when President Kruger made a speech indicating that he expected German help when the time came to assert his sovereign rights against the British. Malet, the British Ambassador, was instructed to warn Germany against coquetting with the Transvaal. But the flirtation continued. Germany supported the construction of a railway from Pretoria to Laurenzo-Marques, the nearest sea-port to the Transvaal in Portuguese East Africa, and in London this was interpreted as a means of giving Kruger military help. The fears were not reduced when in July William sent Kruger a congratulatory telegram on the completion of the railway and, soon after, two German warships appeared in Delagoa Bay.

In the autumn the British Ambassador issued another warning, complaining to the German Foreign Minister that Germany was encouraging Boer stubbornness towards the Uitlanders and inciting Kruger to place impossible tariffs on imports from Cape Colony. A continuation of this policy could lead to serious complications.

Marschall suggested "small colonial concessions" as a price for abandoning it. His report of the conversation aroused William's electric wrath. "Threats!" he stormed. "At a moment when they have such need of us in Europe!" He called Malet's warning an impertinence and to the British military attaché complained that Malet had spoken of war. For the sake of a few square miles of niggers and palm trees Britain had actually threatened war on the grandson of the Queen! Such language, he said, might oblige him to make common cause with Russia and France. . . .

This was one way to soften proud Albion. Another was to embroil her with Russia and the second method was being employed almost concurrently with the first. A revival of periodic Turkish atrocities in Armenia had convinced Lord Salisbury that the nationalities under Turkish rule were proving too refractory for the Sultan to manage and that his Empire was on the point of crumbling. The Wilhelmstrasse was sceptical about these fears and thought that Britain was merely trying to whet appetites for the spoils and so lessen tension with France over Egypt. But in October, 1895, when Salisbury publicly repeated his warning, William became convinced that the break-up of Turkey was inevitable and his only concern was now to forestall Britain in presenting the Dardanelles to Russia in return for compensation, or alternatively, as he told the British military attaché, if "Britain had any go in her, she would force the Dardanelles herself".

This fantastic suggestion raised eyebrows in London and Holstein's furious anger with his master. But worse was to come. Dissatisfaction among the Uitlanders in the Transvaal had reached fever-pitch and a rising against the Boers was planned to coincide with a raid across the border by a few hundred horsemen under Doctor Jameson. The rising failed to mature, but on 29th December, 1895, the raid took place. The British Government was taken completely by surprise. The German Ambassador in London was instructed to speak the severest language and to ask for his passports if the British Government approved the raid. But the raid was condemned and soon after it collapsed.

That, in normal circumstances, would have been the end of the incident, but William was bent on rubbing Britain's nose in the dust. On the morning of 3rd January, 1896, he appeared unannounced at Hohenlohe's residence accompanied by the head of the Admiralty, the naval commander-in-chief and the chief of his naval cabinet. He was in a state of high excitement which had become chronic since the raid took place. He told Hohenlohe of his plan: marines and other troops should be sent to South Africa and an international conference be summoned to give him the protectorate over the

Transvaal. That, the Chancellor objected, would mean war with Britain. William replied: "But only on land." The logic of this was not apparent.

However, Hohenlohe and the Foreign Minister Marschall were in an awkward position. Feeling in Germany was flaming against England. The Press was comparing Jameson to Genghis Khan. William, they had no doubt, was speaking on this day as a typical German. Some gesture was called for. So, instead of William's dangerous project, Marschall suggested a congratulatory telegram to Kruger. The wire was drafted on the spot and after some strengthening of the terms read: "I send you my sincere congratulations that without calling on the help of friendly powers you and your people have succeeded by your own efforts in restoring peace in face of the armed bands which have invaded your country and in preserving its independence against outside attacks." William and Marschall signed the wire. Hohenlohe, though officially responsible for the Kaiser's political deeds, refrained, and it was dispatched. Even after this, Hohenlohe had difficulty in restraining the Kaiser from sending one of his adjutants to Kruger to find out what help he needed.

In Germany the Kruger telegram was hailed with rejoicing as the prelude to further colonial expansion. William's popularity soared. But in Britain it seemed to tear the mask from the Kaiser's face. It was a gratuitous insult, interference in British affairs, a gesture which, coming at a time of temporary British embarrassment, seemed to throw a flood of light on German ambitions and German mentality. The Kruger telegram was never forgotten and as no British government could ride against public opinion it compromised in advance the possibility of any firm Anglo-German understanding in the future.

Typically, it was not this consideration which caused William soon after to beat a hasty retreat, but his grandmother's anger. He was happy enough to bask in his own people's approval and it was not until many years later, when the folly of the telegram was realized by intelligent Germans, that he began to disown responsibility for it and to claim that Hohenlohe and Marschall had thrust it under his nose for signature on—of all places—Potsdam railway station. But a skilful letter from Queen Victoria in early January blotted out all thought of African rivalries from his mind and brought an abject though preposterous apology. He had congratulated Kruger on defeating the raiders, he said, because they were rebels against the Queen. "Now to me, rebels against the will of Her Most Gracious Majesty are the most execrable beings in the world. . . . I was standing up for law, order and obedience to a Sovereign whom I revere and adore. I challenge anybody who is a Gentleman to point out where there is anything hostile to England in this."

Victoria thought these arguments "lame and illogical", but Salisbury advised her to accept them. So William was let off with the mildest of reproofs and soon he was trying other methods to frighten Britain into the German camp. During the Jameson crisis he had written to the Tsar making violent accusations against England and telling him that he had started negotiations with the French "for the joint protection of our threatened interests". This was true, but France was not to be tempted. Now he sought to convince the British that France was nourishing deep plans in Abyssinia where the Italians had just been heavily defeated. Moreover, Russia, he told the British Ambassador, was intending to occupy Massawa on the Red Sea coast after the expulsion of the Italians so as to block the Suez Canal route to the East. France was to receive the Canary Islands and thus dominate the sea-lanes round the Cape to India. At the same time as William was conjuring this spectre, his Foreign Minister was sounding the French about preventing further British expansion in Africa. Did they stop, Holstein, Marschall or William, to ask themselves what view would be taken of Germany's good faith when these cross-currents of intrigue became known?

The fact was that they were barely known to themselves. Like an enraged hornet William, now thoroughly in his stride as the grace-of-Goddist monarch, was administering pricks and stings without consulting his advisers. The government of Germany resembled a madhouse. In 1894 Eulenburg was noting in his diary: "There is a lack of unity of direction because His Majesty lacks unity in himself. The picture as a whole lacks any sort of harmony and this harmony cannot be created. It was only possible under the ideal figure of the old Kaiser, for every horse was *glad* to be pulling his carriage, which was the coach of State. But now? Everyone is biting each other, beating each other, hating each other, lying and cheating each other."

William listened too much to the political advice of his military entourage. To him a soldier was automatically more clever, more sagacious and—an important point for him—more enterprising than a civilian. His military attachés abroad were always sure of their Sovereign's ear. They spied on their own ambassadors as well as on the countries to which they were accredited, played at politics, wrote confidential reports direct to the Kaiser who, whatever their sins or shortcomings, was always ready to leap to their defence as "comrades in arms". The influence of these military men encouraged him to make drastic and over-simplified decisions and to see everything, from the building of a new cathedral to the acquisition of a new colony, as a kind of battle where his will must be imposed and a victory won. The military camarilla was always at loggerheads with the Foreign Office. The Foreign Office was always looking over its shoulder at Bismarck. There was no permanent contact between the Chancellor and the Kaiser, no settled routine of work. The Kaiser, despite extraordinary swiftness of apprehension, a phenomenal memory and unflagging zest, was incapable of methodical work. When the Chancellor did track him down it was never possible to say what his reception would be. William could be charming, William could also be cruel, violent and threatening. It all depended on his mood and what caused the mood no one could say. Matters of vital moment could be dismissed as trivialities; trivialities be built up into matters of earth-shaking import. Yet William could not be by-passed. He was determined to act the ruler, to put his spoke in every wheel, to say what he chose and to be answerable only to God.

Dissatisfaction with this personal rule, so out of keeping with the times, developed rapidly, and one man at least, Philipp Eulenburg, had the courage to warn William. Eulenburg was still acting as a link between the Kaiser and his government. After a period as Prussian Minister in Oldenburg, he accompanied his master to Venice for a meeting with the King of Italy. Amidst extraordinary pomp and a succession of yachting trips, gondola parties, inspections, banquets and games of tennis, Eulenburg had to deal with telegrams from Berlin and obtain decisions and signatures from the Kaiser. Their conversations took place at the gallop between one festivity and another. Clothes had to be constantly changed: black coat for luncheon, reefer jacket for yachting, whites for tennis, dress clothes for dinner. Eulenburg read telegrams while washing his hands and had to find a secluded cabin on the boat trips to do more work. Soon he was exhausted.

But William never felt tired. In Pola he inspected the Austrian fleet, noted with satisfaction that it was smaller than his own, spoke of the heroes of Austrian naval history and assured his audience that the course was still "full steam ahead". From Abbazia he sent Bismarck a cuirass for his birthday—"the hard steel destined to lie against your breast may serve as a symbol of German gratitude". In Vienna on the way home he inspected an Austrian hussar regiment and told them he was extremely pleased with the material, both human and equine. And at Schlitz, still on the way home, a song composed by His Majesty and orchestrated by the royal bandmaster was played at the evening meal.

Eulenburg did his best to control his master, but with little success. Knowing that the appearance of absolutism which William conveyed pleased nobody in Germany, not even the Conservatives, he tried to make him bridle his tongue, travel less and interfere less in the work of government. Tactless speeches like one in 1891, when William had declared that a "spirit of disobedience" was stalking through the land, evoked cautious reproofs to the effect that there was danger in William indulging his undoubted gifts for oratory. In the autumn of the same year, on a visit to Munich, William wrote in the Golden Book of the city: "*Regis voluntas suprema lex.*" Did this saying refer to the mad King Ludwig of Bavaria? If so, his subjects were not edified. If it referred to the Kaiser, on the other hand, they were even less amused. Eulenburg took up his pen, giving first a witty description of a hunting party to soften the Imperial mood and then saying frankly that the Bavarians had been extremely annoyed. Some weeks later, he wrote again, ending with another unvarnished truth: "Through the heavy stress laid on the personal rule, Your Majesty's standing in the Reich has not improved." Behind these letters was the suggestion that William was too unpredictable, too impulsive. "The poor Kaiser," said Eulenburg to a friend, "makes the whole world nervous."

But these warnings had no effect. In 1892, William addressed the people of Brandenburg, speaking as their Margrave. He fumed against pessimists and grousers and advised them to shake the dust of Germany from their feet. Then he turned to the Almighty—"the old ally of Rossbach and Dennewitz"—and said that He must have special plans for Prussia. The Brandenburgers were destined for great things and he was leading them towards a splendid future. . . . This speech aroused contempt in North Germany and rage in the South. "What even greater things?" said the Berliners. "That was certainly a wonderful day when Bismarck was dismissed." And in the South, as Eulenburg now told William, people were beside themselves that he should speak of a great future for Brandenburg when he was supposed to be German Emperor. The Bavarians were not interested in Frederick the Great, either, or his victory of Rossbach; everyone knew that he had called Bavaria "a paradise inhabited by animals".

William now plunged into an abyss of depression. What had he said to cause such offence? He could not remember, he could not understand. When a mood of excitement was on him, the devastating words poured out. He could not stop them. Such moods were unpredictable. They were bound to recur. What he said on these occasions often surprised himself when he read his speeches in the newspaper. Why did his people have to take them so seriously? Eulenburg received an open telegram: "Many thanks for letter which tells me nothing essentially new. I feel very miserable and have got to keep away from all work. Therefore politics mean absolutely nothing to me at the moment."

But the pendulum swung to euphoria again and Eulenburg was soon back at his master's side, clinging to plunging ships and banging balls about the tennis court so as to catch William in a genial mood when he would listen to warnings and requests. The more important they were, the more necessary it was to beard him in these moments of joyous abandon when he would listen to anything, accept anything so long as the matter was settled in thirty seconds. He was determined to enjoy himself. If it were not for the rebellious Reichstag, his boring Ministers and his carping people, life could be very pleasant. Each morning he sprang out of bed, did rowing exercises and then faced a day of limitless possibilities. He could visit one of his seventy-six castles, palaces and country-houses, ride one of his 340 horses, receive the British Ambassador dressed as a British admiral, make a swift dash to Posen by train and alarm the garrison before the astonished citizens were out of their beds, accept dear Phili's invitation to a party at Liebenburg—the guests would be a merry lot, Phili had written: "Graf Hochberg sings, Graf Molke plays cards, Lieutenant von Hülsen does conjuring tricks, Graf Dohna eats, Graf Kalnein cracks bad jokes, Graf Dankelmann shoots swallows with a pistol"—but whatever he did, all must go with a laugh and at hectic speed. "Pessimists," said William, "I will not tolerate."

CHAPTER SIX

BÜLOW, BRITAIN, BATTLESHIPS

I N the autumn of 1897 Bernhard von Bülow succeeded Marschall as Foreign Minister. His friend Eulenburg gave him some heartfelt advice. "You can only be of use to the country," he said, "if you get the Kaiser's psychology right. William II takes everything personally. Only personal arguments impress him. He likes to teach others, not to be taught. He cannot endure boredom. Stiff, ponderous, over-thorough people get on his nerves. He wants to shine and do and decide everything himself. He is ambitious, jealous and thirsty for fame. Never forget that His Majesty needs praise now and then. He is one of those natures who become peevish if they don't receive a tribute occasionally. He is grateful for praise like a good and clever child."

Here was Bülow's most important test in diplomacy. Could he get on with his master? He possessed many qualities needed for the task: wit, charm, psychological insight, a cosmopolitan outlook and, above all, optimism. The mere sight of Bülow, comfortably obese with a dimple on his chin, perfect manners and a confident smile, was calculated to relax William's nerves. Well connected, with a successful career behind him as diplomat in Paris, St. Petersburg, Bucharest and Rome, aged forty-eight, brimming with health, he seemed refreshingly different from those dour advisers whose intellectual horizons did not extend beyond the potato crop in Pomerania, or the state of the finances in Zipfel-Zerbst.

Bülow was summoned to meet his master in Kiel. He was enchanted with him. It was hardly possible, he thought, for a man to be more charming, unassuming and natural. William, for his part, was equally delighted. It was one of those little *tête-à-tête* scenes where, free for a moment from his entourage, he could drop the Emperor and reveal himself as an excited boy flinging his whole soul in the face of a new-found friend.

But before Bülow could be finally accepted there was an acid-test

of suitability. What was his attitude to naval matters, to the ships
and guns of which William dreamt and was determined to have?
Tirpitz was Secretary to the Navy now and had already drafted a
Bill to be submitted to the Reichstag which would more than
double the fleet within seven years, adding twelve new battleships,
ten large cruisers and twenty-three small cruisers to an existing
strength of seven, two and seven. At the same time, with an
organizing ability exceptional even for a German, Tirpitz was
planning a nation-wide campaign, particularly in the schools and
universities to popularize the idea of a navy. This was very necessary. The Germans were not a sea-going people. Much tiresome
opposition could be expected from the Reichstag, though in a recent
speech in Cologne, on the anniversary of the Battle of Waterloo,
William had declared: "The trident belongs in the German fist!"

Bülow realized at once that if he wanted to be Foreign Minister he
would have to support William's naval plans and think up arguments
to persuade the Reichstag that friendship with England was not
inconsistent with rivalry on the seas. He asked for and was granted
a few weeks' leave to Austria before taking up his duties. On his
return William's first words were: "Well, what about my ships?
What have you thought up in the Austrian mountains?" Bülow's
thoughts had undoubtedly not been comforting. Now, at William's
suggestion, he explained them on "a good stiff walk". As they strode
out along sandy paths at Kiel, he traced the development of
German trade and industry, agreed that a strong navy was needed to
protect them, but thought it would not be easy to avoid friction with
England. A quiet, steady and elastic policy would be needed on the
German side. "Well, that's what you're here for!" interrupted
William. Yes, but it would be necessary to have the monarch's
confidence and support. "You've got it!" said William, slapping
Bülow on the shoulder. Yes, but not only positive, negative support
as well. His Majesty must do nothing that might endanger internal
or external peace. "Aha!" laughed the Kaiser, "this is where the
pi-jaw begins! All right, fire away!"

Bülow said that the "trident" speech had been incautious. A
speech earlier in the year, when William had declared his grandfather to have been a saint and Bismarck merely the instrument of
his august will had been badly received. Even firm royalists had been
offended. This disaffected atmosphere would be injurious to the
Navy Bill. Before it could be passed through the Reichstag it would
be necessary to whip up national feeling. "Well, go ahead then! Go
ahead!" cried William joyously.

He then began to speak about colonies. What did Bülow think
about colonies? Bülow said he was not a timorous man. His Majesty

must not think that. Various things might be attempted in Polynesia. In the Far East, too, there was a wide field for German enterprise. Germany must also have her say in Asia Minor. But it would be necessary to proceed cautiously. Yes, the Kaiser heartily agreed. It was necessary to conquer oneself, he said. He who conquers wins. This was a motto which his wife had set up for him over his writing-desk, in blue letters on parchment. He would not forget their conversation. He was very well pleased.

So William took Bülow with him in the *Hohenzollern* on a visit to St. Petersburg. On the way he propounded a brilliant idea. There were said to be gigantic coal deposits on Bear Island north of Spitzbergen. How would it be if Germany quickly occupied the island and then offered it to Russia in exchange for the naval base which Germany needed in the Far East? He, William, had already told his Chief of Naval Cabinet to hold a warship under steam ready to proceed at once. But Bülow did not like the scheme, said it would upset foreign countries. Now William became upset. He had thought they would be able to work together. But Bülow seemed no better than the fat and fretful Marschall. Bülow said he could not accept responsibility. If the Kaiser did not like him he was ready to go back to Rome, or withdraw into private life with no regrets. Would William like to lower a steam pinnace and set him ashore at once? Memel was coming up on the horizon. He would like very much to visit Memel.

William thought of the strange effect it would make in St. Petersburg if he turned up without his new Foreign Minister. That would really make him look foolish. It was better to keep Bernhard and drop Bear Island. He put his arm round Bülow's shoulder. "Don't take it to heart!" he said. "A lover's quarrel! We'll get on all right."

The weather was splendid, the Baltic as smooth as a lake. As they approached St. Petersburg William's excitement visibly mounted. He was like an actor waiting for his cue or a young girl nervously clutching her posy at her first sight of a ball-room. In such moods, William was aquiver to please. He could adapt himself to foreign surroundings like a chameleon. In the warmth of his reception he saw a promise of eternal peace, in smiles and deference a gage of enduring friendship. Illusion and reality swam and merged in his mind and the muted personality of his cousin Nicky convinced him that he, William, was the true arbiter of Russian policy.

While William exchanged toasts and to his boundless joy was made an Admiral in the Russian navy, Bülow did some sharp haggling over Kiau-chau. On the way home William again lectured him on the need for a powerful fleet. He had drawn up a table showing the comparative strengths of the navies of the world and already sent it to the Reichstag. He then gave Bülow some arguments he could use in debate and in stifling heat as they sailed over the smooth waters repeated them, hour after hour.

In Germany, William, Bülow and Tirpitz went over the arguments once more. Tirpitz explained his aims. Bülow saw at once that the proposed increase in the fleet was not a haphazard one, but part of a carefully considered, long-term plan which opened up large horizons. For the first time, the naval estimates were not to be an *ad hoc* grant, but part of a law which would be binding on the Reichstag for seven years. Obviously, this was the beginning of an expansion which would challenge Britannia. Tirpitz explained his Risk Theory: Germany must possess a fleet not equal in strength to the British—which might be impossible—but strong enough to inflict such damage on the Royal Navy that it would then be at the mercy of the next most powerful fleets, the French or the Russian. If this could be achieved Britain would not risk an encounter. But meanwhile there was a danger zone to be traversed: while the German fleet was gaining strength the British might try to "Copenhagen" it, as Nelson had done to the Danish fleet in 1801. For the time being, therefore, it was important to have good relations with Britain.

This was where Bülow came in. He said: "We must neither provoke England nor tie ourselves to England. This is the Scylla and Charybdis, the danger zone which will have to be crossed." An alliance with England would be impossible as a genuine understanding would be incompatible with German naval plans. At the same time, full freedom of action could only be maintained by avoiding unnecessary friction with Britain. This must be the aim. Tirpitz agreed, William agreed, and thus Bülow became the horse ridden by Tirpitz and spurred by the Kaiser.

Meanwhile, Eulenburg had written to William warning him that his Chief of Naval Cabinet, Admiral Senden, an indiscreet and thrustful Anglophobe, had been arousing alarm by talking joyously of his master's "boundless" naval plans which would be pushed through the Reichstag even if it was necessary to dissolve the Chamber ten times over. Eulenburg advised William not to associate himself too openly with the agitation for the fleet "as the coming Navy Bill is looked on more as satisfaction of Your Majesty's sport than as a necessity for Germany".

To this letter William, fresh from his triumph, as he saw it, in St. Petersburg and enraptured by his talks with Tirpitz and Bülow, replied like an excited schoolboy. He showered praise on Tirpitz, he rejoiced that the newspapers were being brought to heel. "Bernhard (splendid fellow!) is clocking Foreign Office and Press on the block." He had instructed Bülow to tell any Minister who disapproved of his policy to pack his bags. "It is high time for this intrigue to stop and for obedience to be shown to the royal will once it has been declared—as Frederick the Great demanded of his generals before the Battle of Leuthen." The visit to Russia had gone off superbly. "I reached agreement with Nicky on all political questions so that the two of us have more or less disposed of the world." All possibility of war between Germany, France and Russia had been excluded, and a "continental blockade" had been agreed on against America and possibly England. "France is to be brought into this whether she likes it or not. It will be up to you to separate London from Vienna" (Eulenburg was at that time Ambassador to Austria). "Nicky and I parted as close and loving friends, relying *absolutely* on one another and at the moment our relations are better than they ever were under Bismarck. Bülow did marvellously and I adore him! *Mein Gott!* What a difference from the South German traitor [Marschall]! Foreign Office is working under high steam, trotting *haute école* and in a blue funk of Bernhard, *tant mieux*. William I.R."

International events kept up this dizzy excitement. In the spring of 1898, just as the Navy Bill was being hotly debated in the Reichstag and William was toying daily with the idea of dissolution, war broke out between Spain and America over Cuba; soon it spread to the Philippines and the possession of the islands became of burning interest. German warships were sent to protect lives and property in Manila—there were twenty-five German citizens there—and soon unrest was reported among the Filipinos in the capital. William wired Bülow: "Tirpitz is convinced that we must have Manila and that it would be of enormous advantage to us. As soon as the revolution has torn Manila from Spain we must occupy it." At the same time, William was confident that the Spanish fleet would beat the American because Spain was a monarchy. When the Spanish fleet was utterly destroyed off Cavita, William was surprised, but rallied quickly: Germany, he told Bülow, must now withdraw from the situation with the minimum of trouble. In the result, the Caroline and Mariana islands were bought from Spain for 17 million marks.

Meanwhile, the Navy Bill had been passed into law by the Reichstag and in the same month of March, 1898, Joseph Chamberlain, Colonial Secretary in Salisbury's government, discussed the settlement of colonial differences with Hatzfeld, the German Ambassador, opening up prospects of a defensive alliance. Anglo-French rivalry in the Sudan was reaching boiling point, Russia had just refused a treaty for the settlement of spheres of interest in the Far East, and Chamberlain was no doubt anticipating war in South Africa. In these circumstances an abandonment of traditional British isolation seemed advisable.

But William could not see it in this light. He believed that the motive for the approach was concern at the German naval law which would one day make his navy, in combination with others, a menace even to England. There was no harm, therefore, in waiting. Germany would continue to enjoy complete freedom to ally herself with either Britain or Russia and there was no danger, if she hesitated too long, of them coming to an understanding without her. The belief was shared by Holstein. A war, he thought, between Britain and Russia was in the long run inevitable. A British understanding with France was conceivable, but never with Russia. Therefore Germany should stand aloof, ready to throw her weight into either scale when the Anglo-Russian conflict occurred in order to reap colonial advantages.

William, meanwhile, hoped to use the British approach to extract benefits from Russia. In April, 1898, he wrote to the Tsar, painting it as an official and most attractive offer and asserting—quite untruthfully—that Japan and the United States were to be drawn into the agreement and that both countries, with Britain, would then join the Triple Alliance. This was indeed a grinning skeleton. "Now," concluded William, "as my old and trusted friend I beg you to tell me what you can offer and will do if I refuse?" But to William's chagrin, no offer came from St. Petersburg, so he returned to the charge, explaining to Nicky this time that the dispatch of the Duke of Connaught to the French army manœuvres was Britain's "latest move to gain France over from you". But this, too, failed to elicit a response.

Faced with reports from Hatzfeld of businesslike offers from Chamberlain, Bülow and Holstein were meanwhile sitting firmly on the fence and an outright suggestion of a defensive alliance—each party to come to the other's help if attacked by two countries—made by the Colonial Secretary in August merely confirmed their view that Germany could wait until Britain became more seriously involved with France in Africa or with Russia in the Far East. Then, they believed, Britain would offer more advantageous terms for German friendship and be ready to make large colonial concessions.

These views seemed to be justified in the autumn of 1898 when British and French interests clashed sharply in the Sudan. Kitchener had destroyed the Mahdi's army at Omdurman and advanced up the Nile until it met a small French force recently installed at Fashoda. This was a key-point both for French expansion eastwards and the extension of British territory to the south and, with both sides refusing to withdraw, it seemed for a time as if war would break out. Immediately, William telegraphed the Tsar asking what his attitude would be in the event of a conflict. He received a cautious reply. In November, after an Anglo-French agreement had been announced whereby the French would evacuate Fashoda in return for compensation on the borders of the Congo, William tried to keep the pot on the boil by writing to Nicky that the French were a "dying nation" and that his ally's prestige would never recover in the Orient. Later, to the British Ambassador, he stated that England, having gained the upper hand, now had an excellent opportunity to hold a final reckoning with France.

These stings had long been accepted by European statesmen as part of William's temperament and they heard, of course, more responsible language from Bülow. All the same, it was impossible for them to know to what precise extent William influenced German foreign policy and it was a fact, as their ambassadors could tell them, that William's reckless, opportunistic moods often reflected those of the German Press. Like the Kaiser, a large part of it was ceaselessly concerned with Germany's prestige and expansion, obsessed with *Realpolitik*, only too ready to blow the nationalistic trumpet with turgid references to Siegfried and the figures of German mythology, and in these years universal suspicion of German aims was planted and rapidly grew.

Was it merely William's wanderlust, for instance, or were there sinister motives behind his visit to Turkey and the Holy Land in the winter of 1898? Ecstatic at his reception by the blood-stained Sultan Abdul Hamid, delighted to meet a fellow-autocrat who wielded even greater power than himself, William had declared in Damascus: "May the Sultan and the 300 million Mohammedans be assured that the German Kaiser will at all times be their friend." What was the world to make of this, and in particular Britain, France and Russia, who counted innumerable Mohammedans among their own subjects? At least they had to reckon with the possibility that it had political implications. If only they had known! In Jerusalem William had been very unfavourably impressed with the Christian shrines. The warring sects, the dirt, the shoddy architecture had convinced him, as he wrote to the Tsar, "that our Saviour's grave quite certainly is *not beneath* that Church of the Holy Sepulchre which in appearance and decoration compares very badly with the Mosque of Omar in its simple and awe-inspiring grandeur". The silent, dignified devotion of the Mohammedans greatly impressed him. There was no doubt, he said, that if he had not been born a Christian, he would have been attracted to their religion.

But this was not all. Bülow accompanied him on the tour of the

Holy Land and noted that in Damascus William's enthusiasm for Islam reached the point of ecstasy. The populace greeted him with a deep, long-drawn-out cry: "Lululu, Lululu, Lululu!" and this sound, like surf on some distant shore, worked on William like hashish. He was already quivering with delight at two Syrian soldiers whom the Sultan had detached to guard his person. These fearsome characters, with flashing eyes and gleaming bayonets, shadowed the Kaiser wherever he went. They had orders, he believed, to strike down anyone who even looked askance at himself, the Sultan's friend—and the friend of 300 million Mohammedans.

Before William set out for the Holy Land, Bismarck had died. He had last visited the old man on Bismarck's eightieth birthday, in 1895. Then, surely, was a chance, perhaps never to be repeated, to consult Bismarck and listen to his advice? The international sky was clouding. William had committed some terrible indiscretions. Turkey seemed on the point of collapse. England was estranged. In the Far East, after the Sino-Japanese war, the great powers were struggling for spoils. But William had spent the lunch cracking barrack-room jokes. He never saw Bismarck again.

When the old man died in June, 1898, William hurriedly returned from his Norwegian cruise to pay homage to his ex-Chancellor. He was very anxious to do the right thing in the eyes of the German people. His wife had not even wanted to put on mourning and Eulenburg noticed that she found it difficult to keep a smile of satisfaction from her face. William upbraided her severely; he knew what was demanded of them both at this moment. On the coffin at Friedrichsruh he carefully deposited an enormous wreath and stood while the pastor delivered a funeral oration.

But in August he was writing in English to his mother complaining bitterly that through the posthumous publication of his memoirs Bismarck was heaping odium on the Dynasty from beyond the grave. William posed before her as the saviour of the Hohenzollerns. When he came to the throne, he wrote, he had faced the terrible task "of rescuing the Crown from the overwhelming shadow of its minister, of saving the honour and the future of our House from the corrupting influence of the Great Stealer of our People's hearts". An appalling task, but God had helped him. "When the strife waxed hot and Bismarck began his most daring tricks against me, not recoiling before even High Treason, I sent a message to him saying: it seemed to me as if he was riding into the lists against the House of Hohenzollern for his *own family*; if it were so I warned him that this was useless as in that case he *must* be the loser. The reply was what I had expected, and I felled him, stretching him in the sand for the sake of my Crown and our House." As a result, wrote William, he

had faced a storm of reproach from the German people and vilifica-
tion from the fallen Chancellor. But: "I bore it quietly, without
flinching, the Royal standard firmly in my hand, the shield with the
Black and White quarterings on my arm and God above. Alone I
bore it for eight long years! Where is he now? The storm has
calmed, the standard waves high in the breeze, comforting every
anxious look cast upward. The Crown sends its rays 'by the Grace
of God' into Palace and hut and—pardon me if I say so—Europe
and the world listen to hear, what does the German Emperor say or
think and not what is the will of his Chancellor. For ever and for
ever there is only one *real Emperor* in the world and that is the
German, regardless of his person and qualities, but by right of a
thousand years tradition. And his Chancellor has to *obey*! . . ."

But William could not entirely deceive himself. Throughout his
reign he was overshadowed by the figure of Bismarck and no amount
of arrogance, wishful thinking and childish defiance could rid his
mind of the knowledge that in the eyes of his people Bismarck had
entered the German heaven and joined the heroic figures of the
German past. Secretly he longed for an opportunity to show that he was
one with them. It came three years later when a Bismarck memorial
was to be unveiled in Berlin. Bülow was now Chancellor. He asked
whether William would attend. Certainly not, was the reply, to do
so would be beneath the Kaiser's dignity. Then William realized that
he would have to be present, if only for the sake of popular feeling.
So he stood, pale and tight-lipped, in unostentatious uniform, while
Bülow made a speech and unveiled the monument. The Chancellor
spoke slowly so that every word could be heard by his master. He
said that admiration and gratitude for the Iron Chancellor would
never cease so long as a German heart was beating. His gigantic
shadow would continue to grow, for he had achieved what had been
the ambition of the noblest German minds for centuries. His heroic
courage, his work for the Dynasty would never be forgotten. And
he closed: "May the name of that great man go before our people
as a pillar of fire, may his spirit be forever with us."

No mean orator himself, William was deeply moved by these
words. Some of the bystanders feared his anger. But he went up to
Bülow after the ceremony and with an expression of real joy on his
face shook his hand again and again. He had been greatly moved, he
said, and deeply impressed: and for a few hours he could look up
with respect and veneration to the Titan who had given him his
throne.

CHAPTER SEVEN

"I AM THE BALANCE OF POWER"

THE Kaiserin Augusta Victoria was a stately woman, impressive in ostrich feathers and huge hats, with a handsome and kindly face. Her contemporaries agreed that she was an excellent mother and a devoted wife. Even William had to admit this, though of course he could never sort out his feelings towards her. But that did not really matter. The fact was, Augusta was good for him and she knew well enough what she thought about William: God had given him to the German people, he was very weak, very clever and very lovable—frightening at times, but only in the way an erratic chicken frightens a mother hen.

Under her capacious wings Augusta had plenty of room for seven children and a husband, though she was not by any means a masterful woman, and not quite the ideal wife for William, either. She was not clever enough. William was an adept at harnessing plausible arguments to his preposterous brainwaves and it needed tougher minds than Augusta's to argue him out of them. Her weapons were emotional and as William's emotions were chaotic they were not always successful. All the same, he was a lucky man to have Augusta's cocoon to flee to when the pace became too hot, how lucky he never seemed to realize.

Selected at an early age by William's parents to be his wife, Augusta had lived until her marriage at the ducal court of Prinkenau in Holstein. In moments of impatience, William was fond of saying: "It's easy to see she never knew the wider air of Windsor." But the German people never noticed this deficiency. Augusta admirably suited their ideal of womanhood: she was pious, she was good-natured, she was dignified, and if William found it exasperating that her mind could never rise beyond thoughts of children, church and kitchen, they could only applaud. Germans did not like clever women.

Through the contemporary memoirs the Kaiserin glides like a

clipper with billowing sails. She trimmed them to William's gusts. Her compass was religion, not William's home-brewed variety, but the orthodox Evangelical faith. She taught her children to believe in the literal truth of the Old Testament, including the story of Jonah and the whale, mistrusted and pitied Catholics and believed that a special providence guided the destinies of the German nation. With her somewhat blinkered mind she did her best to assuage William's anxieties. When he was fretting over the smallness of his navy she wrote to Chancellor Bülow: "I have tried to put him in a happier mood by telling him that it is like David and Goliath—the strength was on David's side because the Lord was with him. And that I hope is the case with us." But this was small comfort to William whose ambition was to be Goliath and persuade the Lord to change sides.

Augusta had no easy time. German to the core, she was obliged to accept the anglicized education of her children. Their clothes, their toys and their nursemaids came from England. They spoke only English until they were five years old. State functions and William's eternal journeys kept her from them until they were old enough to accompany their parents. And there was little enough she could do to impose a more natural way of life on her husband. Even when he was in Berlin his restlessness never abated. He could not bear to spend a quiet evening in her company. There would be billiards with men friends after dinner, songs with Eulenburg at the piano and, in Eulenburg's absence, William might leap up and conduct the band in a rendering of a ballad which his friend had composed for him and he now claimed was his own. Even the marriage bed, which he never dared openly flaunt, was no haven for the restless ruler. He kept a loaded pistol within reach and sometimes managed to escape Augusta's voluminous presence by pleading an early start next morning, repairing bag and baggage to the Wildpark railway station and spending the night in the royal train.

If such bolt-holes were blocked William could be exasperated beyond endurance. When social activities ebbed in the Neues Palais a kind of nervous melancholia would settle on the company. At meals, only the Kaiser would talk. After coffee he escaped to the billiard-room. On one occasion, Augusta with her ladies followed him and began to knit and read newspapers at a table. After puffing a cigarette the Kaiser joined them and himself began to read. Soon the whole company had their noses buried in literature. Total silence prevailed. This went on all evening until William suddenly shot at his Empress:

"Are you proposing to spend the whole night at this?"

"No, William, but I did not want to disturb you, as you were so busy reading."

William: "Well, what else can I do when it is so incredibly boring here!"

William, it is reported, was always fidgety at home. Wealth and absolutism were poison to someone of his nature. He could do too much, too easily. A wave of the hand and a special train would convey him to any point of the compass, followed by another transporting state carriages and stable staff. A word to his friend Albert Ballin, chairman of the Hamburg–America Line, would put a liner at his disposal for Mediterranean trips. There was no one to gainsay him and few who argued. His Court Marshal for twelve years, Graf Zedlitz-Trützschler, writes in pitiable tones of the frenzied changes of plan involving nightmare feats of organization which William carelessly ordained—and all as the result of a whim. One gets the impression of a man desperately quaffing at some life-giving elixir which somehow he cannot digest. The more travel, the more exhaustion: the more exhaustion, the greater the need for powerful stimulants to revive flagging zest. "If only the Kaiser would sit down and read a book for two hours!", his doctor mournfully complained.

The men who struggled for years with this mercurial monarch and recorded their efforts raised an agonized chorus of despair. William's indiscretions were past belief. On a Mediterranean cruise he was overheard talking earnestly about his foreign and home policy, his personal relations with the European sovereigns and his Ministers to a shadowy figure who turned out to be an Italian pilot who had just boarded his yacht to steer it into Corfu. During the war he told his American dentist of his plans to defeat Italy. He criticized the Americans to the British and vice versa, made jocular fun of foreign envoys to their faces, through sheer cussedness mortally offended the King of Italy, his Uncle Edward and the Archduke Franz Ferdinand of Austria. William's megalomania, his vanity, his cruelty to subordinates, his reckless speeches, his unreliability, his moodiness, his total failure to see the world as it was and men as they were, his verbal aggression, his chronic immaturity—these characteristics fairly burst the seams of contemporary memoirs.

Behind her husband, Augusta, or Dohna as he called her, trailed with only her religion and unbounded loyalty to guide her. Unconsciously she slipped into the same subjective view of life as himself. People who upset him were bad. Those who relaxed his nerves and made him laugh were, in moderation, good. She allied herself with his prejudices, echoed his dislikes, but did not by any means share his enthusiasms. A quiet life surrounded by her children with her favourite dish of cold pork and roast potatoes for luncheon, gentle carriage exercise in the afternoons and tea before retiring was her ideal. There was not much to be said from Dohna's point of view for the fantastic outings which took place when William was at home—a boating trip on the Havel, for instance, with a suite of sixty persons followed by a picnic supper at a spot chosen by William for its inaccessibility to the panting cohorts of lackeys carting impedimenta from the palace.

But more upsetting than the changes of scene were William's mental gymnastics. When the Boer War broke out Dohna was badly out of step. She had always suspected his English relations whom she pictured as cynical realists waiting to gobble up the trusting William. Now, with feeling in Germany aflame for the Boers, she thought it safe to join the anti-British chorus. But not only was German policy restrained (partly because of an impending agreement with Britain over Samoa), but William was extremely cautious, realizing that Germany was powerless to intervene until she possessed a stronger fleet. Worse, a month after the outbreak of war he wangled his grandmother's consent to a visit for her eightieth birthday. Dohna was appalled. William, she felt, was flouting public opinion, certainly he was demanding of her an emotional volte-face which strained her to the utmost. Only a few weeks before he himself had been inveighing against English statesmen for treating Germany as though she were "Portugal, Chile or Patagonia".

But agitated letters to Bülow were of no avail. Blood brothers might be dying in South Africa, the Press might be seething with anti-British hysteria, William was bent on his affair of the heart and nothing would keep him from England. Loyally trimming her sails, Dohna swam in his wake.

This time, William was truly delighted with his visit. Bülow, who accompanied the party, gives a glimpse of him at a banquet in Windsor. After the guests had assembled the aged Queen appeared, carried in a costly litter carried by four Indians clad in rich silks and covered with jewels. Beside his grandmother paced William with a devout expression as though he were in church, in an attitude of "heart-felt reverence and deepest respect". Each morning at Windsor he aggravated his military suite by pointing to the round tower and declaring: "From that tower the world is ruled!" To Bülow he enthused: "This is the most inspiring experience of my life. Here, where as a child at my mother's hand I gazed at the splendour, I am staying today as King and Emperor."

Earlier in that summer of 1899 William had been in an extremely agitated frame of mind. A Bill which he had announced would be presented to the Reichstag for the protection of industrial workers against coercion by strikers had aroused strong opposition. William had damaged its prospects from the start by declaring it to be his

Imperial will that anyone, no matter who he was, who attempted to interfere with the German worker's right to go peaceably about his job should be punished with hard labour. The Bill then became popularly known as the *Zuchthausvorlage*—the House of Correction Bill. Feeling in the country ran high against the renewed expression of royal absolutism. It increased in July when, out of the blue from his Norwegian cruise, William sent a telegram to his old tutor Hinzpeter, who lived in Bielefeld, announcing his intention to present a statue of the Great Elector to the town—"as a sign that as in my ancestor so in me there is an unbending determination to continue undeterred by all opposition on the path I consider to be right". Hinzpeter then published the telegram: the noisy threat it contained obviously referred to the *Zuchthausvorlage*. There was an outcry in the Press. On board the *Hohenzollern* as she dipped into the Norwegian fjords Eulenburg took his master to task, advising caution and self-restraint. His Majesty had many enemies, "Bismarckism" was not dead. At this, William got very excited, claimed that he was firmly "established in all German hearts" and anyway, there were elements in the country who did not deserve consideration and whom he had no need to fear. Eulenburg said the German Constitution was a delicate structure, like a work of art, standing in a glass cupboard. If the Kaiser smashed the cupboard, the people would be enraged and an attempt might be made to force the Kaiser's abdication or restrict his powers. "*Oh?*" said William, with a pinched and anxious expression. "*Who* could harbour such thoughts? *How* would they go about it?" Eulenburg took the bull by the horns and said an attempt might be made to declare the Kaiser unfit to rule. . . . Contrary to custom, William did not end the conversation with a verbal slap on the back but remained thoughtful.

A few days later, William reverted to his talk with Eulenburg. It had produced the exact contrary to the desired effect. "Really," he said, "when I look at the behaviour of the people at home I lose all desire to rule. The only course is to pay no attention to them at all." Parliamentarianism had collapsed, was discredited. Public opinion was sick. Someone had to give the people a lead and that someone was himself. "I claim freedom of speech for myself like every other German," he said. "I must *say* what I want, so that the reasonable elements know what they have to do and whom they have to follow." "Deeds," replied Eulenburg, "are better for a ruler than words." "And they shall have deeds!" shouted the Kaiser—and added with a laugh: "I can see you are afraid I shall use force with the Parliament."

Life, however, did not appear to William as a continuous film, but in sections, seen one frame at a time. As soon as he got to Windsor all his truculence vanished. He had just entered his apartments when he summoned Bülow and told him: "This is the most inspiring experience of my life." At that moment a telegram was brought stating that in the Reichstag the "House of Correction" Bill had not even been referred to committee, but had been turned down flat on second reading. Did William expostulate, fly into a rage? Not at all. The news left him cold. He was gazing out of the window now at a splendid half-troop of his grandmother's Horse Guards clip-clopping in the courtyard below. . . .

With his passion for England it might be thought that William would jump at the chance of a political understanding. But it was not in his nature to accept an agreement between equals. His mind thought in terms only of top dogs and under-dogs. In the dim future hovered the prospect of dictating terms to England and that could only be done when his fleet was stronger. Moreover, he had been launched on his English visit hemmed in with cautionary memoranda from Bülow and Holstein. Both thought a war between England and Russia inevitable and it would be best for William to attend the eightieth birthday of Queen Victoria "in complete independence towards both sides as *arbiter mundi*". This dangerous advice played straight into William's hand. There was no role he liked better. So in talks with Balfour (Chancellor of the Exchequer) and Chamberlain he was evasive and after his return to Germany Bülow in the Reichstag poured cold water on a public speech by Chamberlain in which he declared that Germany was the natural ally of England.

Yet Bülow had left England with the impression that anti-German feeling there was much less than anti-British feeling in Germany. An understanding with England was clearly desirable in the long run: why did he not pursue it? Apart from the short-term advantages which he believed could be gained from waiting, the answer was that he was not a free agent. He had been made Foreign Minister on the condition that he supported William's naval plans. These could only be realized with the agreement of the Reichstag because it held the purse-strings. But the Reichstag would only approve them if strong public opinion was aroused in their favour. This entailed widespread propaganda and to be effective that propaganda would have to arouse a bogy. It was not enough to demand a larger fleet for the general protection of German colonies and trade. They would have to be protected *against* a more than hypothetical enemy. That enemy could only be England. So to get Reichstag approval for a still larger fleet, and particularly battleships, it would be necessary to whip up the already runaway horse of anti-British feeling in the country. In this climate, of course, an agreement with England would find a hostile public opinion and strong opposition in the Reichstag. But the Chancellor Hohenlohe was an aged man. Bülow was ambitious. If he became Chancellor he would need not only Liberal but Conservative support in the Reichstag, and the Conservatives were the spear-head of anti-British feeling. Here was another reason why Chamberlain's hand was rejected.

In the autumn of 1899, while the Press was pouring scorn on the "bestial British mercenaries" fighting in South Africa and a cartoon was published showing Queen Victoria presenting the V.C. to an adolescent soldier for raping Boer women, it was announced that a new naval law would shortly be presented to the Reichstag. William was already beating the drum. Launching a new battleship in October he declared: "We are in bitter need of a strong German fleet," and in November he wired Hohenlohe that he would dissolve the Reichstag if it did not accept the estimates. "Compared with this question, which is a matter of life and death for the Reich, all other considerations must fall into the background."

The government, meanwhile, was trailing abjectly in the wake of public opinion, positively welcoming an incident when the Royal Navy searched a German steamer for contraband off Delagoa Bay and demanding its release in such harsh language that Chamberlain told the German Ambassador, no improvement was possible in Anglo-German relations while such a tone continued. The law, which doubled the number of battleships in twenty years and added a huge financial burden to the country, was approved by the Reichstag in January. Tirpitz had eased its passage with an explanatory memorandum raising the bogy of a British naval war against Germany in which the coasts of the Fatherland could be blockaded and vital imports of corn cut off at little risk to the attacker.

William had been watching British reverses in South Africa with malicious satisfaction. He was not sorry to see his proud relatives in trouble. Perhaps he could now draw them into his orbit. At Christmas, 1899, he wrote highly sympathetic letters to his grandmother and uncle, enclosing to the latter a memorandum summarizing German military views on the lessons to be learnt from the fighting. This was followed in the New Year by a table of "aphorisms", salient points to be observed by the British in the future conduct of the war. They needed to train and deploy more forces. That would take time. Meanwhile they would need "absolute safety against foreign powers", in other words, German friendship. Otherwise "it would be better to bring matters to a settlement. Even the best football club, if it is beaten despite the most gallant defence, finally accepts defeat with a good grace."

To make the threat of foreign complications more real, William had already offered to remain passive on the Tsar's western frontier if he cared to attack India—and taken care that this offer should be known in London. Nicolas, however, informed the Queen that he had no intention of moving and Uncle Edward replied that he could not accept the comparison of England making heavy sacrifices for her world position to a football match. Meanwhile, the anti-British fever in Germany continued, fed, no doubt, by the frustrating thought that if only the Prussian army could reach South Africa it could sweep all before it in a fortnight.

The same thought plagued William: he could throw the amateur British or alternatively the Boers straight into the sea. But a chance for military glory came a few months later, in the summer of 1900, when the Nationalist Boxers started slaughtering foreigners in China. In June, they appeared before Peking, cut the telephone wires and attacked the diplomatic quarter. Then news reached Europe that all foreign embassies had been destroyed and the German Minister murdered. Already, without consulting Hohenlohe or Bülow, William had decided to send out an expeditionary force and a squadron of ironclads. China was remote, the cause was just, the danger was small. Aggressive feelings could be harmlessly indulged. "Peking," he wired Bülow, "must be formally attacked and razed to the ground. The German Minister will be avenged by my troops. Peking must be blotted out!"

Already an international force of Russians, French, British, Japanese and Americans was fighting its way to Peking, but William never paused to consider whether they might get there first or thought of political complications. His Minister's murder was a personal insult, his course was justified, he could conduct operations personally like Frederick the Great, without consulting the politicians, "from the saddle".

Never, wrote Bülow in later years, did he see the Kaiser in such a state of excitement as at this time. "Now," he told his Foreign Secretary, "it is a joy to be alive!"—the same joy, no doubt, that a spectator feels when his emotions are purged by a powerful drama. Speeches fell thick and fast. "On the ocean or beyond it," he declared at the launching of a battleship, "no great decision shall henceforth be taken without the German Emperor." On 2nd July, the first expeditionary corps left Wilhelmshaven. Another speech: "The German flag has been insulted and the German Reich has been mocked. That demands exemplary punishment and vengeance."

The dispatch of further reinforcements was planned and William now conceived the idea that a German General should command the international forces in China. Count Waldersee was hauled from semi-retirement, made a Field Marshal, and his candidature canvassed with Tsar Nicolas. Nicolas agreed to his appointment and approval was also obtained from Britain and France by the simple dodge of pretending that the Tsar had suggested him. Waldersee was then dispatched on a triumphal procession of German cities, to reap "advance laurels", as the sceptics said.

But while Waldersee was girding himself, it was already clear that his services would not be needed. The Boxers were scattering into the hills, order was being restored in China. This made William furious. In a dreadful scene with Eulenburg at Kiel he raged against the British and French who had "betrayed" him and demanded that the Foreign Office should be instructed to conclude an immediate offensive alliance with the yellowly perilous Japanese. His thoughts by now had turned to the partition of China and huge indemnities to help finance the enlargement of his fleet.

Then came a truly pathological speech. More troops were leaving from Wilhelmshaven. Summoned there to attend the Imperial farewell, Bülow noticed a tall scaffold erected on the quay. What could be its purpose? A tower for drying fire-hoses? A structure for a gymnastic display? Doubts were settled when the Emperor in person started climbing the ladder. From the top he delivered the most damaging oration he ever made.

"No mercy will be shown. No prisoners will be taken. As a thousand years ago the Huns under King Attila made a name for themselves still powerfully preserved in tradition and legend, so through you may the name 'German' be stamped on China for a thousand years so that never again may a Chinese dare to look askance at a German." Frenzied efforts were made by Bülow and Eulenburg to suppress parts of this speech—in vain. A local journalist sitting on a roof-top had captured the whole text. Fourteen years later, the word "Hun" was pounced on by Allied propaganda.

Slowly Waldersee was set in motion. On 15th August he set sail from Naples for China. By then, British, American and Japanese troops under a Russian commander had entered Peking and released the besieged diplomats. When Waldersee reached the scene in mid-October there was nothing left to do but hold parades, cast a lugubrious eye over the already looted palaces and haggle endlessly with the Chinese over an indemnity. The "World Marshal" the jocular Berliners were calling him.*

By then, of course, William had lost interest, but not before revealing a glimpse into the depths of his soul. In July, at the height of the excitement, he had raged to his friend Eulenburg against the Conservatives in the Reichstag. "I can only say," reported Eulenburg

*In German "*Weltmarschall*", punning with "*Feldmarschall*".

to Bülow, "that I gazed into a bottomless pit of hatred and bitter-
ness." China had raised the lid and this was the view inside. No
more revealing remark was ever made about the mainsprings of
William's temperament. But as he said to Bülow when the latter
upbraided him for the "Hun" speech: "I know that you only wish
the best for me, but I am what I am and I cannot change."

The practical consequences of William's Chinese caper were
comparatively harmless, but in these years the heavy tread of ultimate disaster was approaching. If the encirclement of Germany had
not been a fact in July, 1914, restraint on Austria–Hungary might
have been exercised from Berlin and the world war at least postponed. And if German policy had been more consistent in the early
years of the century and the German Emperor less anxious to operate
his see-saw, the encirclement—or the *cordon sanitaire*—might never
have come about.

But Bülow, who succeeded Hohenlohe as Chancellor in October,
1900, was too indolent and optimistic to look the future in the face
and with half his attention pinned on controlling the vagaries of his
Imperial master he could hardly do so. William, for his part, became
steadily more arbitrary, subjective and cynical. His few personal
friends, like Eulenburg, could not be perpetually at his side and in
any case their advice was a drop compared with the ocean of flattery
which continually lapped him. The hatred in his heart welled up in
contempt for his fellow-men. Everyone was a *Schwein*, and moreover
was not a fellow, but a subject, and William was not a man, but a
god. This mournful delusion carried him ever further from reality
until there was not an incident in his private or public life, in the
domestic sphere or in politics, which he did not look on as a battle
for prestige and a challenge to preserve the all-powerful mask which
he presented to the world.

Hastening to his grandmother's death-bed in January, 1901, for
instance, he found Chamberlain still anxious for an alliance. William
had rightly seen the danger of prevaricating and had declared at
home: "I cannot swing for ever between the Russians and the
English without the danger of falling between two stools." But when
confronted with a new British approach, spiced, this time, with the
threat that if Germany were not forthcoming Britain might turn to
Russia and France, William dismissed this possibility and claimed,
in face of all the facts, that it was not Germany who needed friends,
but Britain, confronted as she was with the unalterable hostility of
France and Russia. "I," he declared, "am the balance of power in
Europe." For his valuable friendship, he implied, a certain price
would have to be paid. Then an Anglo-German alliance could be
formed: "You to keep the seas, while we would be responsible for the

land. With such an alliance, not a mouse could stir in Europe without our permission."

While William was staking on cards which he did not possess, Bülow was also overplaying his hand. He and Holstein agreed that the British threat to reach an understanding with the Dual Alliance was "a complete swindle, a spectre invented to intimidate us". At the same time they were afraid of Russia and if Germany was to protect the British Empire, then Britain, in return, would have to agree to help in the most likely conflict involving Germany, namely a Russian war with Austria–Hungary over the Balkans. In other words, Britain would have to join the Triple Alliance. If not, she could escape her commitments and leave her ally in the lurch in the one conflict Germany most feared.

These, therefore, were Bülow's terms. To demand them of a country not yet emerged from her traditional isolation, still confident of her power to protect herself and her Empire single-handed was to invite rejection. Perhaps he made these big demands out of fear of anti-British feeling in Germany.

William, in any case, was not consulted. As he insisted on going to England, he had, of course, to be briefed. But Bülow gave his advice in general terms, keeping the thread of negotiations in his own hands. William's visit to his dying grandmother was, in any case, politically harmful. It did not please his subjects and when he stayed on for a fortnight they were exasperated. But these thoughts were far from his mind. He was not used to considering his subjects' feelings and in this case they were irrelevant. Grandmama was dying; he must see her before the end. Augusta objected, Bülow advised him to wait, even the Duke of Connaught, then in Berlin, told the Chancellor that William, at this moment, would be in the way at Windsor. He overruled them all. He was going. He had booked his passage—and on arrival he showered Bülow with telegrams relating in happiest mood the aspect of the chalk cliffs of England, the sea scattered with warships and how he had been able to perform one or two little services for his grandmother before she died "more or less in my arms". Not only that, the British people, the Royal Family, everyone was showing the most touching consideration for himself.

But, meanwhile, William's mother was seriously ill in Homburg. Augusta wired him that he should return at once. The reply was emphatic. His advice and moral support were indispensable to the sorrowing family.

In fact, William was enjoying every minute and had no intention of coming home before the funeral—"the King", he told his entourage with dewy eye, "has *asked* me to stay." Even his Adjutant

General, in the intervals of praying that no disaster would occur, had to admit that the Kaiser was being a terrific success, charming the Royal Family with tactful support in their sorrow, touring London in an open carriage—"Thank you, Kaiser!" cried a voice from the cheering crowds—and refusing, despite his hypochondria, to abandon English soil for the *Hohenzollern* when the Duke of York contracted measles in the next room to himself.

Home again and visiting his sick mother in Homburg, he seemed to have brought the English climate with him. At dinner his officers were astonished to find their War Lord in civilian clothes—which he never normally wore—with a tie-pin bearing his grandmother's cipher in diamonds. During the meal William sang a paean in praise of England which stood "high above German manners and customs". Some months later, he presented Field-Marshal Roberts with the Order of the Black Eagle, the highest decoration in his power to bestow—for conquering the Boers.

But, meanwhile, negotiations with England had foundered on Bülow's terms and the rock of mutual distrust. It had been a golden opportunity, but in rejecting it Bülow still thought that England would come running in the end. With a birth-rate soaring above the French, he believed that time was on Germany's side. The outbreak of war between Russia and Japan removed the threat from the East. Therefore the announcement in April, 1904, that France and Britain had come to terms over Egypt and Morocco left him undisturbed. France promised not to obstruct Britain in Egypt by asking for a time-limit to the occupation. Britain conceded France the right to preserve order in Morocco and make administrative, economic and military reforms. The agreement contained no reference to European questions and no promise of mutual aid in case of war. This seemed a harmless arrangement. It was not directed against anyone and Germany's interests in Morocco were purely commercial—so Bülow declared in the Reichstag.

But William reacted differently. He was not an optimist like Bülow and was quicker than his Chancellor to sense danger. News of the treaty filled him with concern. The French had been very clever, he said, in getting good payment for their friendship without loosening their ties with Russia. But now Britain had nothing more to fear from France she would undoubtedly get tougher with Germany. Moreover, Italy was getting cold feet. His Ambassador in Rome had reported: "The mood in the whole peninsula is now such that active warlike support for Germany would be impossible." William was against strong action—he refused Bülow's suggestion of a fleet demonstration off Tangier—and instead he used strong words, calling on his subjects in a cryptic speech in

Karlsruhe to "clear your eyes and steel your courage in case it should be necessary to intervene in world politics".

The basis of his fears was subjective. He had been left out in the cold. An agreement had taken place behind his back. As Edward VII rightly saw: "He very much likes to be talked about. He is disappointed that we have come to an understanding without his permission and help. He feels isolated." But vicariously William was already standing shoulder-to-shoulder with Nicky in his war against the Yellow Peril.

CHAPTER EIGHT

WILLIAM'S MASTER-STROKE

BISMARCK'S Reinsurance Treaty with Russia had bound Germany to neutrality if Austria attacked Russia. At the same time, her alliance with Austria obliged her to go to Austria's aid in the event of Russian aggression. By a secret provision offering Russia a free hand in the Black Sea, the Straits of Marmora and the Bosphorus the Reinsurance Treaty also made a conflict between Austria and Russia more likely. The whole treaty had been kept a secret from the Austrian ally.

This was the jugglery which Caprivi thought too complicated for his skill and he had persuaded William not to renew the treaty in 1890. As a consequence, Russia confronted with Austrian rivalry in the Balkans, with British competition in the Near and Far East and with Germany's equivocal attitude in Europe had found a new friend —France. The age-old prospect of encirclement again faced Germany. There was danger from France where talk of revenge for Alsace-Lorraine kept bubbling to the surface, there was believed to be danger from Britain as a colonial rival and a country traditionally hostile to the strongest military power in Europe and now, owing to the Anglo-French Entente, there was danger that Germany might lose her position as arbiter between Britain on the one hand, France and Russia on the other. How could the deadlock be broken, the wire to St. Petersburg restored? Obviously it could only be done if Russia were in serious difficulties. These arose in the autumn of 1904.

Since February, the Tsar had been involved in a disastrous war with Japan over spheres of influence in Manchuria and Korea. Hoping to involve Russia more deeply in Asia and so divert her attentions from Europe, William had done all in his power to urge Nicky on. Military opinion in Germany favoured a Russian victory, but when war came it brought a series of disasters. The Russian fleet was mauled in Port Arthur and then blockaded in the harbour. An attempt to break out was defeated with heavy loss. A Russian squadron from Vladivostock was also defeated and the Baltic fleet, hastening to Far Eastern waters, met a tragic end in May, 1904, at the Battle of Tsushima. Russian land forces achieved no success in Manchuria. Then, on 21st October, Russian warships fired on some British fishing-vessels near the Dogger Bank in the belief that they were Japanese torpedo-boats. An outcry arose in England and war for a time seemed imminent. Here was William's chance to embroil Russia and France with England, split the recent Anglo-French rapprochement and re-establish his own position as arbiter. He seized it with both hands. To the Tsar he wrote: "If you become involved in war with England, I will put my fleet at your disposal and force France to go along with us." On 27th October he wrote again suggesting joint action. But with French backing the incident was referred to an international commission which met in Paris and the danger of war receded. William was furious: "Far from jumping to the support of the *Russians* as their allies and escorting them with their fleet the *blackguard* Cambon [French Ambassador in London] has induced the *blackguard* Delcassé [French Foreign Minister] to offer *England* his good services. It is doubly necessary that the Gauls should be reminded by the Russians whose allies they are, i.e., they must show their colours for or against England."

Nicolas was cautious, but not inclined to reject William's overtures out of hand. He was facing disaster in the Far East and revolutionary ferment at home. Some sort of understanding with Germany was necessary because ships of his Baltic fleet were being coaled by the Hamburg–America Line and further friction with England was possible. So he asked William for a draft treaty and the Emperor, after consultation with Bülow, supplied it. It provided that if either country were attacked by a European Power the other would come to its aid with all its land and sea forces. But the Tsar's advisers were worried about French reactions. William wanted Russia to sign the treaty first and inform France afterwards. Nicolas, on advice, wanted to associate France from the start. Negotiations dragged on and finally broke down on this point.

But William did not give up hope. From his accession he had cultivated the pliant Nicolas and had no doubt that, once alone with him, he could persuade him to sign almost anything. In the summer of 1905 they planned an informal get-together in the Baltic, each in his yacht, William in the *Hohenzollern*, Nicky in the *Polarstern*. This would be a splendid opportunity to revive the treaty. With some misgivings Bülow and Holstein gave their blessing and so, greatly excited, William sailed for his rendezvous with Nicky with the yellowing draft in his pocket.

They had agreed to meet at the Finnish island of Björkö. Before leaving, William had sent a telegram: "Not a soul has the slightest idea! All my guests think we are bound for Gotland. Have important news for you. My guests' faces will be worth seeing when they suddenly behold your yacht. Tableau! What sort of dress for our meeting? Willy."

As he crossed the Baltic in his gleaming white yacht, he studied the terms: an alliance binding each country to aid the other if attacked in any part of the world. That meant that Germany might have to fight England on the seven seas. William thought ruefully of his navy. That would never do. What he wanted was to banish the spectre of a Franco-Russian attack on Germany. So William found a sheet of blue notepaper and sketched another draft:

"*Article I*. In the event of one of the two Empires being attacked by a European power its ally will assist it *in Europe* with all its forces on land and sea."

Well content with this and four succeeding Articles, William placed his draft in an envelope and gazed expectantly at the horizon.

Two days later, on 24th July, 1905, Bülow received a telegram from the Kaiser: "Treaty just signed by the Tsar and myself." Bülow wired his congratulations, then waited anxiously for the details. They arrived next day in a long and excited letter from William. Normally cold and suspicious, the Tsar had thawed out marvellously on board the *Hohenzollern*. Smarting under his defeat by Japan he had felt in need of friends. William had courted him, made him feel he was *wanted* and soon Nicolas and his suite had been chattering German with their hosts as if they had not a care in the world. The jollity had then continued in the *Polarstern*. The Kaiser had started to talk of the ancient friendship between Russia and Germany. The monarchical principle was the sole guarantee of peace in the world. What was to stop them—Willy and Nicky— sealing their concord in a definitive understanding? "Oh, yes," Nicky had said. "That would be wonderful." Then William referred to the abortive treaty of the previous year. Nicky remembered it, but not the terms. What a pity. Hm, well. . . . Just by chance—a pure coincidence of course—William happened to have the treaty in his pocket. The artless Nicky was delighted.

"He seized me by the arm [wrote William to Bülow] and drew me out of the saloon into his father's cabin, immediately shutting all the doors himself. 'Show it to me, please'—and his dreamy eyes sparkled brightly. . . ."

William unfolded the blue notepaper. The Tsar read the treaty through carefully. Minutes seemed to pass. William made a short and fervent prayer that God might be with them and guide the young ruler.

"It was deathly still [he wrote]. Only the rustle of the sea, and the sun shone bright and cheerful into the homely cabin, and before my eyes lay the *Hohenzollern* gleaming white with high in the air the imperial standard fluttering in the morning breeze. I was just reading on its black cross the letters *Gott mit uns* when the Tsar's voice beside me said: 'That is quite excellent. I quite agree.' My heart was beating so loudly that I could hear it. I pulled myself together and said quite incidentally as it were: 'Should you like to sign it? It would be a very nice souvenir of our entrevue. . . .' "

Nicky signed, William signed, they fetched a German and a Russian as witnesses. Then Nicky folded the Kaiser in his arms. . . .

Next day, on reaching shore at Pillau, William sent his cousin an ecstatic letter, in English, as usual. "The hours I was allowed to spend in your society will be ever graven in my memory, you were like a dear brother to me." He saw the alliance just concluded as "a cornerstone in European Politics . . . a new leaf in the history of the world." A bloc, he believed, had been formed to which all the nations of the world would gravitate. France, of course, would join and there would be a Quintuple Alliance: Russia, Germany, France, Austria, Italy. "In times to come it may not be impossible that even Japan may feel inclined to join it." And, of course, the smaller nations, Holland, Belgium, Denmark, Sweden, Norway, "will be attracted to this new great centre of gravity by quite natural laws of the attraction of smaller bodies by the larger and compacter ones".

This was a splendid vision—the Pax Wilhelmensis. Only one Power remained beyond its reach. But Britain would be humbled. The adherence of Japan "would cool down English self-assertion and impertinence". Despite Anglo-French flirtations—a French naval squadron was about to visit Cowes after a British one had been fêted in Brest—France, whom William chose to call "Marianne", "must remember that she is wedded to you and that she is obliged to lie in bed with you, and eventually give a hug or a kiss now and then to me, but not to sneak into the bedroom of the ever-intriguing *touche-à-tout* on the Island". And as he wrote this William had visions of himself sharing the delectable concubine with Cousin Nicolas while for once the *touche-à-tout*, Uncle Bertie, was left out in the cold.

But William's fantasy soared ahead of the facts. What of Russia's ally, "Marianne"? Article IV stated: "After the entry into force of this treaty the Emperor of all the Russias will take steps to inform France of this agreement and request her to join it as an ally." This was a pious hope and it was very improbable that the Tsar's advisers would accept the treaty at the risk of alienating France. But that was their look-out. From the German point of view, the treaty had at least thrown a tentative bridge to Russia, it did break the ring round Germany and the restriction "in Europe" did not seriously reduce its usefulness. Bülow would have lost nothing in accepting it and awaiting events—nothing except the satisfaction of having engineered the treaty himself.

But Bülow's vanity proved the stumbling-block. He answered William's ebullient letter with a ten-page memorandum rejecting the treaty, ignoring its advantages and dwelling on the insertion "in Europe". This, he claimed, made the agreement positively dangerous. If England attacked Germany, for instance, the Russians could not be expected to attack India. As for the conclusion of William's letter, Bülow ignored it: "So on the morning of 24th July, 1905, at Björkö a turning point in the history of Europe was reached and a great easement of the situation for my beloved Fatherland which at last will be freed from the terrible pincers of France and Russia."

This was too much for Bülow. Here was William claiming to have secured the peace of Europe at a stroke of the pen. This could not be. Bülow knew his Emperor. At the peak of his euphoria William was at his most vulnerable. The bubble was inflated. A prick would burst it and then William would come crawling to heel. Arguments were not necessary, indeed they were dangerous as seeming to imply that there was at least a kernel of value in William's handiwork. Instead of argument, Bülow would deliver an ultimatum. He knew he risked nothing. He knew that a forceful expression of his disapproval would be taken personally by William and plunge him into the nether-pit of despair. So Bülow simply tendered his resignation.

The effect was instantaneous. Gone was the gleaming sunlight, the rustle of the waves, the "*Gott mit uns*". If ever William believed that he had acted for the good of the Fatherland, had used his talents to achieve a lasting peace and the happiness of his peoples, it was at Björkö. He had never doubted it. His naïve letter of triumph showed that. He had exposed his innermost soul. "See, Bernhard, what I've done—rejoice with me!" But instead—Bülow's resignation, a blank wall, total rejection.

William wrote a reply, striving to keep a matter-of-fact tone:

"My dear Bülow, Your letter just received by messenger. After mature reflection I am wholly unable to see that the expression 'in Europe' has so serious or dangerous a bearing on our situation compared with what it was before as to justify the tender of your resignation.

"I have imparted to you two facts which in themselves represent such enormous progress that they must be evaluated highly from our point of view: one, His Majesty solemnly declared that the question of Alsace-Lorraine was a closed incident for Russia; two, he promised me with his handclasp that he would never enter into an agreement or an alliance against us with England."

So far, so good. William was striving to remain objective, to place the cause above personal feelings. But now these welled up:

"If Bismarck [he continued] had succeeded in extracting either of these assurances from Alexander II or Alexander III he would have been beside himself with joy. . . . I thought I had laboured for you and won an exceptional victory, and you send me a few tepid lines and your resignation!!!"

This seemed to William an act of personal spite. What had he done to deserve it? Nothing. He should in fact have earned Bülow's undying gratitude.

"I am completely prostrated," he wrote, "and fear that I am on the verge of a nervous collapse. . . . I appeal to your friendship for me and beg you to let me hear no more of your intention to resign. Just wire me on receipt of this letter: 'All right', then I shall know that you will stay. . . ."

This was a despairing cry from master to servant. Yet William felt it was not strong enough. Surely Bülow would understand his state of mind? What more could he say to make the man *feel* his agony, realize the hurt he had inflicted and hasten to make amends? For William never doubted that Bülow had not intended to hurt him. It was all a horrible mistake and once aware of William's state of mind Bülow would surely realize it. So William, consciously exaggerating, added:

"The morning after the arrival of your resignation would find the Emperor no longer among the living."

Having written that, William paused. An extravagant statement, certainly. He knew that Bülow would never believe it. And of course he had no intention of committing suicide. Still, that was how he felt at the moment. But for a grown man the feeling was ridiculous, he realized that, and with whimsical humour he added:

"Think of my poor wife and children!"

This letter must have delighted Bülow. He had achieved his object. William had been brought to heel. He could now withdraw his resignation. He had never meant it seriously, anyway.

CHAPTER NINE

MOROCCO

IN early 1904, with Britain weakened after the Boer War, the French army and nation split by the Dreyfus case, and Russia on the brink of conflict with Japan, Count Schlieffen, then Chief of the German General Staff, had considered the opportunity uniquely favourable for a reckoning with France. His plan of campaign involving an attack through Belgium had been drawn up before the turn of the century. The plan and his present views were known, of course, to the Kaiser and the Foreign Office. This, as far as the military were concerned, was the moment to strike, crush the French and banish for ever the fear of a war on two fronts.

This prospect acted on William like molten lava. The possibility of a war, particularly of a successful one launched by himself, filled his mind with chaotic violence. In January, 1904, King Leopold II of the Belgians paid a visit to Berlin. The first few days passed off in complete harmony. Then came the last day, when the King was to return home by train after dinner in the evening. All the guests were assembled, only the Kaiser and his guest were missing. They entered the room at last, William in a mood of truculent excitement and Leopold with a horrified expression. During the meal he barely spoke to the Empress who was sitting on his left. Immediately afterwards he left for the station, so agitated that he put his helmet on back to front. Returned from the farewells, William then enlightened his Chancellor. He was beside himself at the "feebleness" of his colleague. In the most courteous fashion he had reminded Leopold of his proud ancestors, the Dukes of Burgundy, told him that if he wished he could rule again over their territories, extend his sceptre to French Flanders, Artois and the Ardennes. But Leopold seemed not to understand. He had "gooped" at the Kaiser and finally remarked with a nervous smile that he could not possibly win over his ministers or the Belgian parliament to such plans. Then William lost patience. He had no respect, he said, for monarchs who felt

101

themselves answerable to ministers and not to the Almighty. He, William, would stand no nonsense. If there was a war, those who were not for him would be treated as enemies. As a soldier he belonged to the school of Frederick the Great, of Napoleon. If Belgium would not go with him, he would have to consider strategic considerations only. . . . When Bülow looked pained, William was very upset. "I expected your praise and approval," he said. "But the opposite seems to be the case."

So Leopold joined the swelling ranks of European monarchs who suspected and disliked the Kaiser. The more important the issues, the more loaded with possibilities good or ill for Germany's future, the more dangerous it was for William to have a hand in them. Politics, because they dealt with human beings and were involved with personal prestige, excited and confused him. Only on emotionally neutral ground could he apply his considerable intelligence with an untroubled mind.

In the field of science and technology William was always an ardent learner, a modern ruler anxious to keep up with the times. He could absorb technical data like a sponge and on many occasions Bülow listened to him discoursing on scientific matters with admiration for his force and clarity. Shipbuilding, turbines, X-rays, motor-cars, agricultural machinery, all aroused his unfeigned enthusiasm. Prominent men from industry and engineering were always being summoned to the palace without regard for rank or origin to inform their master on the latest developments. Slaby, an electro-technician, Intze, a hydraulic engineer, architects, geographers, archaeologists, even literary historians slipped with personal invitations past the astonished palace guards who were otherwise used to admitting only soldiers and aristocrats.

It is refreshing to see William turn his mind to some useful project, the development of Germany's inland waterways, for instance, or the widening of roads for the automobile age which had as yet barely dawned, and at least it was a form of occupational therapy for him to organize army officers' wives into a sewing club to embroider regimental colours—as had been done in Frederick the Great's time. One can even bear with him arguing about the Lost Tribes of Israel so long as it cleared his mind for more important tasks. But this was never the case. Even on technical matters, such as signalling systems for the navy, he could exasperate the experts by clinging to outworn ideas simply because they were his and he refused to abandon them. And when it came to international politics, i.e. family problems, he was always the agitated *enfant terrible*.

In October, 1904, six months after the Anglo-French agreement, King Edward visited Kiel. He and William had last met at the

Empress Frederick's death-bed, two years before. The Kaiser's
mother had asked to be buried naked wrapped in the Union Jack.
This, of course, could not be allowed. But when William came to
die, would he not want the same? Where did his true affections lie,
which was his spiritual home, Germany or England? Throughout
his life his deepest emotions were not concentrated on the Fatherland, but on the sea-girt isle where the wonderful old Queen had
spoilt him as a child.

In Kiel, William made the highest bid ever for Edward's approval
and England's love. The King was coming at his invitation, though
he pretended to Bülow that Edward had invited himself. In the
harbour the entire German fleet, from the largest battleship to the
smallest pinnace, was assembled. A guard of honour consisting of
the German Princes was drawn up on the quay. Behind them, all
William's ministers and Secretaries of State paced in a flurry of
gold. With difficulty he had been dissuaded from welcoming his
uncle at five in the morning at the entrance to the Kiel Canal. When
the august figure stepped on to the landing-stage, William urged his
officials forward with little digs in the ribs.

Next day, William welcomed King Edward on board the *Hohenzollern*. The ship had been transformed into a fairyland. Artificial
fountains squirted and plashed, huge bouquets of flowers regaled
the eye, the after-deck was covered with a vast awning beneath
which 220 persons were to sip afternoon tea with His Majesty.
Forty-five minutes before his arrival, William was pacing nervously
to and fro in gala uniform, eyeing the decorations, the sky, his watch,
like some village Romeo.

Yachting was an unorganized sport in Germany before William
built it up to the status of an English enclave in German life. The
Royal Yacht Squadron and Cowes Week were matched by his own
creations, the Imperial Yacht Squadron and Kiel Week. On board
his *Meteor* the main cabin was stocked with English books, an
English breakfast was prepared by an English cook and two English
skippers took turns at the wheel. Before King Edward left it was
essential for him to cast an eye on all this and some explanation was
required for the mushrooming German fleet which William had
assembled against the strong advice of Tirpitz and Bülow. But was
not it obvious? With tears in his eyes he explained how, as a small
boy, he had been allowed to admire the ships in Portsmouth surrounded by "benevolent aunts and friendly admirals" and how the
wish had then grown in him to build such ships himself and "one
day to possess as fine a fleet as the English". Edward smiled, but
returned home thoughtful. One thing should have been clear to him.
William's fleet was too dear to him to be lightly engaged.

In October, when the Dogger Bank incident occurred, William gave proof of this. In the atmosphere of Schlieffen's now-or-never plea and of talk that if Britain and France came too close together the danger zone for the German fleet would never be passed, William again plunged into warlike conjectures. What would happen, he asked his military and naval advisers, if England blockaded the German coast to prevent further units of the Russian Baltic fleet being coaled by Germany? What should Germany do? The Chief of the General Staff and the admirals produced a plan involving naval action. William rejected it. Germany, he said, should not dream of risking her fleet, but should attack France—the French were already so tied to the English that they could be looked on as allies.

Confronted with William's warlike fantasies and oceans of marginalia couched in blood-thirsty, hysterical language, historians have tried to distinguish between the froth and the underlying intentions. The talk, they say, can largely be discounted, it was merely an expression of temperament. His real influence was always on the side of peace. When it came to the point, he was always cautious, if only through fear. This is right as far as it goes, but it was harder for his contemporaries, particularly abroad, to make this distinction. And though Caprivi, Hohenlohe and Bülow certainly learnt to discount the more explosive outbursts, they would have been more than human if they had remained unaffected by the rashness and inconsistency of the Kaiser whom they were bound to consult and who insisted on having a finger in every pie. Not surprisingly, German foreign policy bears the indelible stamp of his personality, at least between 1895 and 1905. The zigzag course, as it came to be known, the pursuit of small colonial advantages at disproportionate risk, the game of see-saw between the two groups of Powers in the belief that Germany was the permanent arbiter to whom everyone would have to pay court in the end—all this was too exact a projection of William's temperament to admit the possibility of coincidence. Thus he shared responsibility for Germany's downward course. The tragedy was that when his instinct warned him of danger during the Morocco crisis of 1905, he lacked the will and the ability to put the brakes on or control his Chancellor.

William's heated courtship of the Tsar at Björkö came to nothing partly through Bülow's disapproval, but mainly because the Russians were afraid to alienate the French. William's dream of a continental bloc comprising the great Powers of Europe was at an end. Meanwhile, the Anglo-French agreement had developed far beyond Morocco and Egypt and settled all outstanding differences throughout the world. There was a prospect of the understanding becoming even closer if Russia, suffering unbroken defeat against Japan, should appeal to France to mediate and to Britain, since 1902 the ally of Japan. In 1900 Italy had agreed to French plans in Morocco in return for a free hand in Tripoli and was now becoming a luke-warm partner in the Triple Alliance. Everywhere the ring seemed to be closing round Germany. A determined effort would now have to be made to gain friends or split potential enemies.

William, as we have seen, tried to entangle Russia in friendship through the influence he believed he possessed over the Tsar. But at the same time as his Chancellor was giving spasmodic support to his plan, Bülow was pursuing the diametrically opposite and incompatible aim of splitting the Anglo-French Entente, using Morocco as a lever.

The scheme originated with Holstein. In June, 1904, he was telling Bülow that the settlement of the Moroccan question behind Germany's back was a blow to her prestige which, unless countered, would lead to repetitions in other places. German trade would also suffer from the French "prohibitive system". There was an international convention still in force guaranteeing the open door to the major Powers in Morocco. This might be made the basis of German action. But the situation was complicated by the fact that only recently the Kaiser had told King Edward that he was completely disinterested in Morocco—another of those places consisting of "niggers and palm-trees"—and in the spring he had made a similar statement to the King of Spain.

So Bülow, for the time being, merely avoided recognizing directly or indirectly the agreement made between France and Britain and refrained from asking France for guarantees about the open door as this would involve admitting her preferential position in Morocco.

Instead, it was decided to stiffen the Sultan's opposition to French penetration. The aim at this stage, if there was a clear-cut aim, was to frustrate French ambitions for which she had obtained British approval and so weaken the Entente. But this policy broke down. France was determined to press on with the exploitation of Morocco and at the end of 1904 presented the Sultan with a sweeping programme of reforms backed by an ultimatum. In February, 1905, Bülow then turned to direct threats, telling the French that he had never been officially informed of the contents of the Anglo-French treaty and could not be bound by it; in other words he reserved the right to reopen the whole question of Morocco's future.

It was now necessary to convince France that Germany meant business. It so happened that William was about to set off on a Mediterranean cruise. Holstein saw this as a splendid opportunity to build up a vague atmosphere of menace, and through Bülow he persuaded a most reluctant William to land at Tangier and make a speech.

In March, then, the inhabitants of Tangier woke up one morning to see a small pinnace bobbing towards them across choppy seas from the German liner *Hamburg*, in the stern-sheets the spiked helmet and bristling moustaches of none other than Kaiser Wilhelm. The All-Highest clambered ashore, mounted a fettlesome Arab steed and proceeded to the town with its white box-like houses to meet the Sultan of Morocco's uncle. Dusky beauties gazed from roof-tops, carpets were hung from windows, flowers were strewn in his path, while the cortège, slowly moving in broiling heat through the narrow streets, was flanked by a frenzied mob firing rifles into the air and emitting hoarse cries of welcome. Met by the Arab dignitaries, the Kaiser dismounted and made a speech stressing his recognition of the Sultan as the ruler of an independent land subject to no foreign control and open to the peaceful competition of all countries. German policy, he said, was completely disinterested. Then, guarded by officers with drawn swords, he remounted the dashing white horse, clip-clopped gingerly to the harbour amid belatedly exploding carbines, climbed into the pinnace, went lurching back to the liner, scaled a swaying rope ladder with his withered arm—and was safe once more.

This was not William's idea of fun. But, ludicrous though it was, the operatic nonsense set Europe by the ears. The Tangier visit aroused fear in France—in the previous year a German officer had betrayed the Schlieffen plan to the government—and indignation in England. The German Ambassador reported that in England it was not looked on as a step for the protection of German interests, but as a demonstration against the Entente. The mood was one of active support for France, even beyond the terms of the Anglo-French treaty.

But now that William had set foot on African soil, Germany could not retreat. The French Prime Minister Rouvier was in pliant mood. It would have been possible to obtain dazzling compensation in the French Congo or elsewhere for German approval of a French protectorate over Morocco, but this, the most advantageous course for Germany, was blocked by the promises already given to the Sultan and by William's declaration of disinterest in Tangier.

Instead, Bülow pursued the policy of grinding France in the dust. Holstein, always convinced of Britain's perfidy, believed she would abandon her ally. The aim now was to bring about the fall of the French Foreign Minister Delcassé, notoriously hostile to Germany and joint architect of the Anglo-French Entente, and the means employed was to demand an international conference on Morocco.

Delcassé could not accept this without compromising the agreement with Britain. He refused and then, failing to get the support of the French Cabinet, resigned.

As far as William was concerned, Delcassé's fall removed the last barrier to friendship with France and he told a French General in Berlin that relations between their two countries could now move into smoother and happier paths. He wanted no war, he was fed up with the whole affair, he had never set the least value on Morocco, he gladly made a present of it to France.

This sell-out filled Holstein with burning indignation. To him the Delcassé incident was merely a step towards the complete humiliation of France even at the risk of war, the break-up of the Entente and the prevention of the threatened encirclement of Germany.

But when it eventually met the Algeciras Conference tightened rather than loosened the ring. Only Austria supported the Germans. Italy was only persuaded to attend under threat of terminating the Triple Alliance. She was already an uneasy partner, with plans of her own in North Africa which depended on French support. The Peace of Portsmouth signed between Russia and Japan in October, 1905, had meant the end of expansion in the Far East which Russia had been pursuing for a decade and a renewal of interest in the Balkans in conflict with Austria-Hungary. In Russia feeling was strong against Germany whose Kaiser had for so long been encouraging Far Eastern adventures. France was bullied into accepting the conference and this merely drew her closer to England.

At Algeciras weeks passed in what William called "odious bickering" over matters of police, customs, finance and taxation in Morocco. Pinned to practical subjects it was impossible for Germany to achieve her real object against France. In any case, she was on the defensive. Her sole desire was to avoid complete isolation. The gulf grew ever wider between Germany's aims and the tedious negotiations she had insisted on. Bülow fainted in the Reichstag, Holstein had a haemorrhage, William was feeling persecuted. He accused his Court Marshal of trying to poison him, blamed King Edward for the Algeciras "encirclement" and was suddenly seeing the French army as a formidable fighting force. In public speeches he growled about "sharpening the sword and discerning the goal"—how he wished he could!—but in private he was saying that his Chancellor, though an excellent man, was driving the coach too near the abyss.

In early March, 1906, Bülow had to realize that this was true. At the conference Germany was out-voted on a procedural matter. After months, years of strenuous effort, her isolation now seemed complete. But this was Holstein's policy. His whole career depended on it. A lifetime of masochistic toil and now failure. Germany should abandon the conference, he said, break off diplomatic relations with France and be prepared for the final, the ultimate argument—force of arms. At long last, Bülow said no. William's dearest wish, he knew, was to be known as the Peace Kaiser. William had not liked his Morocco policy from the start. His own instincts were averse to war. So Bülow took the whole matter out of Holstein's hands and the ageing man was left with just one sheet of paper—on which he offered to resign. To his utter amazement, his resignation was accepted.

With the mainspring gone, the German time-bomb stopped ticking. William worked on his Chancellor. This was a highly unfavourable moment for war, he said. Germany could not contemplate war. Nobody wanted war. And with Holstein gone, this was true. So the conference was wound up, with paramount French interests assured in Morocco and Germany left to contemplate a new world situation. At the height of the crisis Britain and France had held military discussions. Russia was now moving into their orbit. In Britain no one now believed that the German fleet was merely the Kaiser's toy, it was an instrument of aggressive policy. In France a new ministry had come to power which included the formidable Clemenceau. Nationalist feeling had been aroused. Self-confidence had been strengthened. As a member of the Triple Alliance, Italy had revealed her weakness. Everywhere, suspicion of Germany had increased and fear of her diminished. Who was responsible? "The miserable degenerate Latin peoples," wrote William, "—instruments in England's hands, a race of eunuchs . . . Roman scoundrels . . . lazy, lying Russians. . . ."

But this was not the answer. As a Chancellor managing both home and foreign affairs, Bülow could not dispense with the expert Holstein. The suit made for Bismarck was several sizes too big for him. And the Kaiser's erratic interference in foreign affairs made Holstein doubly indispensable. Bülow himself was not the ideal choice for Chancellor, but he was the only politician who could manage William and the only one acceptable to William's military entourage. Finally, William: quick to sense danger and with his natural timidity a valuable counterweight to aggressive advisers, but too excitable to be consulted in times of crisis and too subject to changes of mood. He himself had contributed to the encirclement which Holstein had tried to break. He was a master at tying knots, but inept at resolving them. Soon he was to be involved in a tangle from which he could not escape.

CHAPTER TEN

THE NOVEMBER STORM

OCTOBER, 1908. For the last two years, Great Britain had been building Dreadnoughts, a type of battleship of greatly superior speed, armament and protection. The introduction of these monsters, of which the first had been launched in February, 1906, had not been entirely to Britain's advantage. The new ships made all existing battleships obsolete and of these, in 1906, Britain possessed many more than Germany and soon Germany began to build Dreadnoughts herself.

The race in naval armaments therefore began again, from a fresh start, at a more desperate tempo and on both sides with a much greater capital expenditure. Moreover, the construction of Dreadnoughts on both sides of the North Sea underlined the fact that the challenge to British naval supremacy came from Germany and Germany alone. No other nations possessed Dreadnoughts and neither country could claim that it was building from a policy of general security. The Entente between Britain and France made the British and French fleets potential allies and the Russian fleet, after its defeats by the Japanese, had ceased to exist. Japan herself was an ally of Britain. Thus if Germany built, she could only be building against perfidious Albion and if Britain built it could only be in response to this challenge.

In the last two years, therefore, the naval issue had become increasingly clear-cut and urgent, and British feeling against Germany had deepened from distrust to exasperation. The feeling was mutual.

In 1908, further events intensified suspicion between the two countries. In January, Aehrenthal, the Austrian Foreign Minister, suddenly revealed that he had obtained Turkish consent to the construction of a railway through a strip of territory linking Serbia and Montenegro. To Britain, France and Russia this seemed to herald a revival of Austrian ambitions in the Balkans where they had lain dormant for years and they immediately suspected Germany as the instigator of the move. In fact, William and Bülow had barely been consulted.

Soon it was William's turn to suspect Britain. In June, accompanied by the Under-Secretary at the Foreign Office, Sir Charles Hardinge, King Edward paid a visit to Tsar Nicolas at Reval. Concerned at the rate of German naval construction, Britain was seeking closer ties with Russia. William was deeply alarmed. A plot was being hatched. Germany must be on her guard. In Döberitz he harangued some army officers, spoke of encirclement and conjured the spirit of Frederick the Great who, assailed on all sides in the Seven Years' War, had beaten his enemies one by one.

In July, William heard from Metternich, his Ambassador in London. The British, said Metternich, were putting out feelers for a slackening of tempo in Germany's fleet-building programme. They claimed that this would do more than anything to reduce tension between the two countries. With a surge of manly vigour, William stamped on this hope of peace. The British suggestion was "impertinent", he commented. "Metternich must be told that good relations with England are not desired by me at the price of the development of the German fleet. The building programme will be carried out to the last jot, regardless of whether it suits the British. If they want war, let them start it. We are not afraid."

William was still in this truculent mood when, in August, Uncle Edward and Sir Charles Hardinge came to visit him in Cronberg. The King had no intention of squabbling with his nephew over his toys, as he had once called the German fleet, and he left the talking to his adviser. The latter's theme was a reduction in building tempo, a détente and then a review of all outstanding problems. Alone in Cronberg without his Chancellor and determined in advance not to yield one inch of ground, William treated the encounter as a duel to the death. With his perfect English he had no need of interpreters: it was cut and thrust, parry and pounce between him and the Englishman. For two days he clashed rapiers, then, lo and behold, his opponent was overwhelmed. Three long telegrams to Bülow followed, describing in world-historical terms how William had rejected all advances and categorically refused to discuss naval armaments.

The Press of both countries had been full of conjecture about King Edward's visits to Reval and Cronberg and extreme nervousness prevailed in London and Berlin. It was increased in October when the Austrian annexation of Bosnia and Herzegovina provoked a crisis in the Balkans and considerable international tension.

In this atmosphere Englishmen opened their *Daily Telegraph* on

28th October to find the German Emperor addressing them in these words: "You English are mad, mad as March hares. . . ." Reading on, they found that William was trying to express friendship. It was an article headed: "The German Emperor and England. Personal Interview. Frank Statement of World Policy" and was written by an anonymous author who claimed that it was his duty to make known the substance of a conversation he had had with the Emperor, for "moments sometimes occur in the history of nations when a calculated indiscretion proves of the highest public service". William was quoted as saying: "What has come over you that you are so completely given over to suspicions unworthy of a great nation?" He claimed he had always been the friend of England and cited as proof his refusal, during the Boer War, to receive Boer delegates who were touring Europe in the hope of enlisting support. Again, he stated that when the struggle was at its height he had refused an invitation from France and Russia to join with them in calling on England to put an end to the war and thus "to humiliate England to the dust". "Posterity," he said, "will one day read the exact terms of the telegram—now in the archives at Windsor Castle—in which I informed the Sovereign of England of the answer I had returned to the Powers which then sought to compass her fall."

When they read this article, Englishmen were not likely to forget the Kruger telegram. And there had been no joint approach by Russia and France, but only a suggestion of a continental coalition against England by the Russian Minister Muraviev when passing through Berlin, not at the height of the struggle, but in the first weeks of the war. As for the French, they have always maintained that it was William and not they who suggested joint action. There is no evidence that they ever did. The fat therefore was truly in the fire: the English informed of a Franco-Russian plot which never existed. The French and the Russians would, of course, be delighted at William's mendacity and the English would be sceptical: how easy for them to check on his story about the archives. When they did they found no trace of the telegram. As for the Germans: here was William who had been only too ready to cash in on his popularity after the Kruger telegram in a Germany boiling with rage against the British now revealed as the true son of his English mother betraying the interests of Germany for the sake of a pat from his doting grandmama and openly boasting of the fact. An indiscretion indeed, but was this man capable of calculation?

Blithely the article continued to the effect that William had gone even further in his sympathy for his "revered grandmother". He had personally worked out a plan of campaign for defeating the Boers and sent it to England. He now claimed that the plan ultimately adopted and successfully carried out by Lord Roberts was almost identical with it. "That document, likewise, is among the State papers at Windsor Castle, awaiting the serenely impartial verdict of history." Finally, said William, there was the fleet question. Here again the British were needlessly suspicious. The German fleet was not intended for use against England, but for the protection of German trade and one day perhaps for influencing events in the Far East where the rise of Japan had been accomplished and the national awakening of China was possible. "It may even be that England herself will be glad that Germany has a fleet when they speak together on the same side in the great debates of the future."

If William had deliberately set out to affront the Germans, the British, the French, the Boers, the Japanese, the Chinese, and the Russians he could hardly have concocted more explosive statements than these. The Windsor archives revealed no plan of campaign against the Boers, presumably he meant the "aphorisms" he had sent his Uncle Edward. As for the German fleet, the suggestion that it might be used against Britain's ally Japan was almost as offensive as the obvious fact that it was being built in competition with the Royal Navy.

But in Britain it was possible to see the funny side of the article. Not so in Germany. When it was published in the official *Norddeutsche Allgemeine Zeitung* on 29th October it provoked a nation-wide howl of protest and dismay. At first it was assumed that William had approved the article without consulting his advisers, but the reverse proved to be true. It was based on conversations with a retired army officer, Colonel Stuart-Wortley, at Highcliffe Castle near Milford-on-Sea in the summer of 1907. Much impressed by the Kaiser's remarks, the Colonel had made a note of them and when visiting Germany in September, 1908, had obtained his agreement to publish them in the British Press. But first he had sent the article to William for his approval. William had thought it splendid and sent it on to Bülow who was at his country estate.

At this point began a series of calamitous omissions, shortcomings and misunderstandings. Bülow, whether long since bored with William's effusions, or over-burdened with work or simply lazy, did not bother to read the article, but sent it on to the Secretary of State at the Foreign Office, asking him to check the facts and seeming to imply that it had already been decided in principle to publish it. But the Secretary of State was on holiday in Berchtesgaden, likewise the Head of the Press Section was away, so the Under-Secretary of State, Stemrich, had to deal with the matter. Being over-burdened with work (Austria had just annexed Bosnia), he did not read the article either, but passed it down to the final long-stop, a conscientious official named Klehmet. Klehmet worked fast. Combed the facts. Corrected one or two. Then sent the All-Highest article back to Bülow with comments cautiously indicating that publication might be inopportune. But Bülow was in no mood to interpret the innuendos of a junior official. So back the article went, still unread, to William: "checked and approved".

On 29th October, therefore, when Bülow's attention was drawn to the German translation in the *Allgemeine Zeitung*, he got a nasty shock. "Does this agree with the draft that was checked by the Foreign Office?" Yes, indeed it did. Bülow then descended on the luckless Klehmet. Klehmet said he thought His Majesty expressly desired publication. "Haven't you yet realized," stormed the Chancellor, "that His Majesty's personal wishes are often the purest nonsense?"

The German Press, meanwhile, was running hot with indignation against Kaiser and Chancellor. William's "personal rule" was condemned, Bülow's resignation demanded. If Bülow had approved the article, he was unfit to be Chancellor; if he had not, William's personal interference in international affairs must cease. But William believed that Bülow had approved the article. His own constitutional position was intact, he had acted with the utmost propriety. In face of the Press attacks, he now demanded that Bülow should cover him and announce the truth. But the truth was, so Bülow now confessed to his Sovereign, that he had approved the article without reading it. . . .

To William, this seemed a minor matter. After all, the article was a good one. The Press did not understand the British like he did. Their attacks on the views he had expressed left him completely indifferent. What, kow-tow to ignorant journalists, he a monarch of twenty years' political experience! Unthinkable! But poor Bernhard, it was *he* who was in trouble, over this little matter of constitutional responsibility. How could William help him? By agreeing to the publication of an official statement, said the Chancellor, to be issued to the Press implying that the Foreign Office was responsible for publication of the article, that he, Bülow, had not read it and that, if he had, he would not have approved it. William must have looked surprised at this and inquired: "Oh, why not?" and Bülow, with his customary charm and tact, no doubt wrapped up the truth of William's indiscretion with some shimmering flattery so that it looked quite an acceptable parcel. Anyway, he and William obviously agreed to differ on their opinions of the article and William approved the statement. It was issued on 31st October, with the addendum that the Chancellor had tendered his resignation, but the monarch had refused to accept it.

It is curious in the after-light to see the two principal figures in the drama fussing over technical responsibility for publication of the article when it was obviously not this, but its contents, which were the real cause of offence. But at the moment Press and public opinion were concerned to get an answer to the question: who passed these horrible statements, and neither William nor Bülow was anxious to open up the wider issue—William because it would involve heart-searching criticism of himself and Bülow because he did not relish the prospect of bringing to a head the whole question of William's fitness to rule. So in his audience of the monarch, the Chancellor skated daintily past the hole in the ice and pinned his hopes on the soothing effect of the public statement.

William, certainly, was well content and though anxiety was already flickering at the back of his mind, his skill in shirking the truth enabled him to concentrate on the superficial aspect of public criticism and ignore the cause. This was his mood when the Secretary of State, von Schoen, called on him to tender his resignation. Poor chap! Here was another fellow in trouble. And as William saw no reason why the article should not have been approved, there was no question, of course, of accepting von Schoen's offer. Not at all! The man had not sinned. Sacrifice him to the vulpine journalists? Out of the question. The monarch could be very charming when he liked. He clapped the good Schoen on the shoulder and told him: "The affair will turn out to be more harmless than at first appeared." Harmless? Schoen, it seems, ventured to mention the effect that the contents of the article had produced. But William was not worried by this. His statements, he said, had in part been incorrectly reported. Had he not read the article either?

Meanwhile, an interpellation had been tabled in the Reichstag for 11th November, that is, the order of the day was to be interrupted so that an explanation of the whole affair could be demanded of the Chancellor. Bülow was not expecting more than a little mild witch-hunting and William assumed that the public statement had already covered him and that he himself would be left out of the discussion. So he now set off, with Bülow's blessing, for a round of pleasures, first to the Archduke Franz Ferdinand in Austria for hunting and then to his old friend, Prince von Fürstenberg in Donaueschingen for more hunting and ribald entertainment. Distance helped him to dissociate himself from Bülow's pending ordeal in the Reichstag and from Vienna he sent him a wire of facile encouragement: "I always remember you in my morning and evening prayers. . . . There is a silver lining to every cloud. God be with you! Your old friend, William." He added that he was having a wonderful time and had shot large numbers of stags.

But in Berlin an ugly mood was brewing. Contrary to Bülow's hopes, the statement of 31st October had done nothing to allay disquiet. It had cleared the ground merely for the concerted attack which now took place on William's personal rule as such. The Press, the public, even the pillars of the monarchy, the Conservative Party, considered the article pernicious, inept, and totally lacking in political judgement. Moreover, from twenty years' experience of the Kaiser's utterances, every adult in Germany knew that those bombastic and tactless statements did not represent merely a passing aberration on the part of a ruler normally discreet—they were typical of the everyday William; year-in, year-out, he had wooed the Germans themselves in just such tones of mingled pleading and aggression: he had bragged, strutted, lied, contradicted himself and, worst of all in the eyes of a proud and sensitive people, he had made himself and the Imperial Crown ridiculous in the process. So twenty years of sullen resentment at the "personal rule" now suddenly boiled up and overflowed. Germans, in their graphic phrase, had *die Nase voll*, they were fed up, and the Press gave forceful expression to their feelings. One influential organ stated: "If William II continues to pursue a personal policy he will have no one to blame but himself if a shadow is cast over the evening of his life", while another spoke openly of abdication.

To Bülow these thoughts were nothing new. He had often discussed William with Holstein and as long ago as 1897 Holstein had told Eulenburg: "His Majesty must be treated as the child or the fool he is." But Bülow now faced an awkward session with the Reichstag. In the first days of November, the Federal Council met and there was talk of revolution if the personal rule was not ended. In her diary, the Princess Marie Radziwill was noting: "The public feels itself exposed to the whims of a Sovereign in whom from now on no one can place the slightest trust." The Press was sustaining its furious tone. Cartoons were appearing in *Simplicissimus* and other comics: William as a little boy smearing himself with ink while Germania admonished him: "Didn't I tell you you weren't to play at letter-writing any more?"—William's grandfather pleading with the Almighty: "After all, he is 'by the Grace of God' "; and the Almighty replying: "Now you want to put the blame on me!"

In the midst of all this, another appalling gaffe of William's became known. During Kiel Week in the previous summer he had talked to an American clergyman. His remarks were to be published in the *Century Magazine*. They were highly compromising. The German Foreign Office got wind of them and managed to suppress publication, but only in part. The filtrate now appeared in the New York *World*. There the Kaiser was reported as speaking of a passionate aversion to England whose supremacy at sea was to be shattered by a German-American alliance in combination with the Chinese. ...

William, meanwhile, was with his cronies at Donaueschingen, shooting foxes and enjoying the atmosphere of a perpetual Army mess-night where subalterns get debagged in the ante-room and someone pours wine into the piano. His Austrian host, Prince Fürstenberg, was exceedingly wealthy and the festivities lacked nothing in splendour or variety. Between whiles, William managed to glance at the newspapers. Noting talk of a conflict between the Kaiser and his people, he remarked: "Doesn't disturb me in the least."

On 11th November, a stormy debate started in the Reichstag. From the Social Democrats came variants on the theme "I told you so". The Kaiser had always been a thorn in their flesh. As long as William was on the throne, they implied, these crises would recur. But the strongest criticism came from the Conservatives. They were appalled to see the revered institution of the monarchy undermined by the monarch himself. From all parts of the chamber came demands that some effective restraint must be placed in future on the Kaiser's personal rule.

But the violence of the deputies' feelings sprang in part from their impotence. They could not table a vote of censure on William or on the Chancellor. To muzzle the Kaiser effectively would have involved reforming the Constitution, abolishing his right to appoint and dismiss the Chancellor and making the latter responsible not to him, but to the Reichstag. That would have meant Cabinet government after the English pattern and, to base it on a working parliamentary majority, revision of the electoral system and a complete recasting of the reactionary Federal Council which at present held the right to initiate legislation. Thus the whole federal structure of Germany would have to be reorganized and in the process of setting up a democratic régime, the pillars on which the country at present rested—the Crown, the Prussian army and the Prussian bureaucracy—would have been weakened and chaos might well have supervened. Germany was an authoritarian State. This Kaiser crisis revealed its weak spot, but short of a revolution there was nothing to put in its place. Bülow knew this well enough and contented himself with a vague statement which the Reichstag had perforce to accept. Realizing that the *Daily Telegraph* interview had disturbed feeling both at home and abroad, the Kaiser, he said, would undoubtedly exercise greater restraint in future. "Were this not so, neither I nor any of my successors could assume responsibility."

It was now 13th November. Still in Donaueschingen, William

read newspaper reports of the Reichstag debate. They plunged him into the blackest depression. For twenty years, surrounded with flattery, he had talked, travelled, exhorted and patronized. In all that time he had managed to shrug off criticism. Each day was a plum to be chewed and swallowed. The cheering crowds, the deferential courtiers, the workers cap in hand—they loved their Kaiser, or so he had thought. And now? Graf Czernin, among the guests at Donaueschingen, tells in his memoirs: "I had the feeling that I saw in William II a man who, wide-eyed with terror, sees the world as it is for the first time in his life."

But this brief insight was only a flash. Soon William was clinging to the formal aspects of the case. All the criticism loaded on himself he transferred to Bülow. To his friends he kept saying that he had acted constitutionally in the whole affair. He had sent the article to Bülow. Bülow had approved it. Why had he not made this clear? A few days later, William received his hated Chancellor in Berlin. Bülow extracted from him a public statement approving the Chancellor's remarks in the Reichstag.

From this time on, William was inwardly changed. He never recovered his old self-confidence, he had lost faith in his star, and he never forgave Bülow for failing to accept full responsibility for the fatal article. But for the time being he kept his Chancellor because to dismiss him would have put himself in the wrong. On 21st November, William appeared at a public function in Berlin and it was noticed that he read a speech which Bülow handed to him. Two days later, he suffered a mental collapse and was confined to bed. Looking years older, he sent for the Crown Prince and spoke of abdication.

Throughout that winter, William was the ghost of his former self. Self-justification was his only thought. His fantasy got busy. He began to think that he had kept Bülow fully informed of the talks at Highcliffe Castle and Bülow had approved them, had wanted them to be published. Proof? A series of telegrams dispatched to the Chancellor from England. The Kaiser then ordered a search to be made—but no telegrams came to light. Very well. This meant that Bülow had burnt them. . . .

Later, William began to think that he had not sent telegrams, but a letter. Bülow could not remember a letter, neither could his wife who managed his correspondence. "Well, then," said William, "if I did not write to him, I spoke to him. I can show you the tree in your garden where I told him of the conversations."

So Kaiser and Chancellor continued in an uneasy truce until in March, 1909, Bülow felt his support in the Reichstag wavering, and with financial reforms to push through decided it was time to assure himself of William's confidence in case they were defeated. In an audience, he did not retract his disapproval of the *Daily Telegraph* article, but simply asked his Sovereign to forgive him for having caused him distress. At once, William unpacked his reproaches. Bülow had approved every word of his conversations in England, yet he had not defended him in the Reichstag—why? William had told Bülow of his conversation with Stuart-Wortley practically in the same words as it had been printed—remember? In the garden of the Reich Chancellery—remember? And Bülow had *thanked* him for furthering his policy—*remember?* Bülow did not remember, but of course if William said so, it must be true. Renewed apologies. Gracious acceptance. And William in the seventh heaven of triumph and relief. Saved at last.

CHAPTER ELEVEN

THE POWDER BARREL

THE tactless, provocative speeches, the disastrous Kruger telegram, the Waldersee fiasco, the *Daily Telegraph* affair—surely all this should have convinced William by now that it was better to drop discreetly into the background, let others do the ruling and confine himself to symbolic functions? Surely his efforts were self-defeating? For a man who yearned for security it was an extraordinary paradox that he should place himself in the very forefront of political controversy, and by every possible means project an image of himself as the absolute autocrat. What a pretence, what a ridiculous fiction, and what needless distress it caused him! Frightened rabbits bolt for their holes, frightened people gravitate by instinct to the backwaters of life, frightened Emperors can take shelter behind their advisers.

In William's case, admittedly, this would have been difficult. The constitution made him supreme in politics, supreme in war. The German people wanted a glittering figure-head. But these factors would not have been as strong as the realization that he was unfitted to rule if ever it had fully dawned on him. If for a single moment he had possessed insight, seized the full folly of his words and actions, he would surely have recoiled with terror, clamped a padlock on his mouth and if only for egocentric reasons resolved to be more cautious in the future.

But this was William's key characteristic: he could never see that he was wrong, or foolish, or reckless. There was an element missing in his make-up that is common to all normal human beings, the capacity to learn from experience. He would never mature because he could not, he was locked in his own tight little world. He was perpetually afraid, but unaware when he was acting dangerously. That was partly the cause of the fear. So, after the November storm, he picked himself up, brushed himself down, swore at all those who had betrayed him and carried on, a martyr now to the ingratitude and incomprehension of his subjects.

Outwardly he was the same as ever, but inwardly he despaired of
fitting in with reality. It was like a thicket that tripped and clawed at
him, endless and impenetrable. From now on, he shut his eyes to the
brambles and took comfort more and more in his private world of
fantasy. He no longer expected the Chancellor to pay attention to his
marginalia, hardly cared whether his courtiers listened in the
evenings when he read aloud to them, hour by hour, from newspapers, journals and books. But relax he could not. His manic
temperament drove him on. Boredom was an abyss which he feared
almost as much as rejection. In the mornings when they first met
him, his adjutants had standing orders to engage him at once in
conversation so that the All-Highest could start the day with an
illusion of activity. Ministers making verbal reports found that he
barely listened to them, but took the first chance to start a monologue
of his own, often on some subject miles from the point at issue. The
annual round of amusement had become a ritual. April in Corfu;
May at the Wiesbaden festival; June in Hanover, Hamburg, sailing
on the Lower Elbe and Kiel Week; July, the Norwegian cruise—the
same people, the same practical jokes, except that the backs he
slapped were permanently bent now and belonged to Excellencies
and Professors; August in Wilhemshöhe, then, to the end of
October, hunting in East Prussia. From all these entertainments
Phili Eulenburg was excluded. He had been ruined by a homosexual
scandal in 1908.

The Kaiser whistling in the dark, isolated indeed, yet there was
not one of his conflicting emotions which did not extend to his
people. His dreams of power, for instance—not world conquest but
German supremacy. Germany's central position made a strong army
necessary, this strength aroused ambitions in the country which
ignored the defensive purpose for which the strength had been
created. Here was one widespread ambivalent attitude. Another was
pride in the feats of arms which had forged German unity. But the
pride was mingled with fear. As Bismarck had fought three aggressive wars to build the German Empire, so other nations might fight
to destroy it. Bismarck had brought guilt into the German |soul;
that guilt now turned to feelings of persecution. So there was a
nation stewed in hysteria, caught in the emotions of aggression and
fear. As with William, so with the German people their very
dynamism sharpened this conflict and because it was insoluble it
produced a fatalistic feeling that Germany was the victim of forces
beyond her control. The Pan-Germans, the industrialists, the
colonial enthusiasts cried "forward". The agrarian Junkers cried
"back". As their duty bade them, the General Staff dwelt beyond
the sphere of morality on questions of preventive war or defensive

war in which Germany would have to strike first. The politicians saw the world constellation turning against them, but still used Germany's strength for the muddled purpose of preserving peace and extending German influence. The symbol of all this was the fleet, the power allegedly for defence but potent for attack, the brain-child of William hovering between visions of glory and ultimate disaster.

In this chiaroscuro William clung to religion, but here again he groped for reality and failed to find it. His spiritual urges were strong. His mind was constantly suffused with a mystical glow. He was always reaching out for the fourth dimension, yearning for that vision which would bring life into perspective, fill it with meaning, show light and darkness, good and evil as different aspects of the same golden coin. But he could never get away from himself and so nothing was added to him except a mirror-image of what he wanted to find: a benevolent deity surrounded by his Hohenzollern ancestors smiling down from the clouds. This picture possessed the clarity of an hallucination. He cherished it as a substitute for reality. Its authenticity was confirmed when life was kind; when troubles came it was life that was wrong. One can only surmise the anguish of this man, clinging heaven by the hems, at a time when Europe was staggering towards disaster.

The alignment of the Powers in the Triple Entente now left Germany with Austria as her sole surviving ally. Italy could be discounted. But Austria-Hungary, the multi-racial State, might disintegrate. The South Slavs within her borders looked across the frontier to their blood-brothers who dreamed of a greater Serbia. This ambition, if achieved, would wreck the Dual Monarchy. There were various ways to prevent it, some practicable, others less so, but all, in their desperation, were considered by the Austrian statesmen. Serbia could be annexed. She could be partitioned between the other Balkan States. She could be forced to disarm and kept in permanent economic bondage. Or she could be isolated by a league of Balkan States allied to Austria. But none of these courses offered a permanent solution because Slav nationalism could not be abolished. At any rate, Austrian statesmen were agreed that Serbian independence must be destroyed and, backed by the General Staff, they considered war to be inevitable sooner or later. In Berlin this view was deplored. But what could be done? Serbia, it was held, was an Austrian problem. The Austrians must be allowed to deal with it in their own way. The alternative was to impose a German solution at the risk of losing Austria as an ally and possibly destroying the Dual Monarchy. This was the opinion in Berlin and the conclusion seemed clear: Austria must be supported through thick and thin, whatever the consequences, whatever the risk.

The risk, of course, came from Russia. Russia was the traditional friend of Serbia and with a powerful pan-Slav movement bearing on the government had her own plans for Balkan hegemony. These could be realized if the Turkish Empire, which still nominally extended over part of the Balkans, collapsed. Then not only might the Dardanelles be opened to the Black Sea fleet and Russian influence spread over the Near East, but the expansionist dreams of the Balkan countries could be realized and perhaps reconciled at Turkish expense and the map of South-East Europe be redrawn under Russian aegis. The collapse of Turkish power was considered imminent and a vacuum would then be created into which the Great Powers would inevitably be drawn. From the Russian point of view it was merely a question of whether the new constellation in South-East Europe enhanced Russian influence or diminished it. Whatever happened, the situation was bound to change and with revolution simmering at home it was thought essential to profit from it.

As early as 1908, therefore, the ingredients for world war were already in place, awaiting the spark. Europe was divided into two camps, between them an area of turmoil where the vital interests of Austria and Russia were involved. But fatalism was dangerous. It is probable that world war would have come in any case. But it need not necessarily have come at the time it did. There was one factor in the situation which could be changed: Austria's method of dealing with the Serbian problem. It seems clear that Austrian statesmen would never have contemplated crushing Serbia if they had not assumed that a war could be localized. Granted Russia's temporary weakness, Austria could not be sure of surviving a clash with her giant neighbour or of avoiding one without German backing. Thus Germany was the key to the situation. Without unqualified German support, Austrian policy would have been very different. Why, then, did Germany give it? Was there really a danger of losing her ally? Alone Austria would have been far more vulnerable than Germany without Austria.

This question leads back to the personality of the Kaiser. To call a halt to Austria would have required courage and resolution. But men of character did not prosper in William's company and in Bülow he had a Chancellor who, whether or not he fully realized the dangers of the Balkan situation, was impelled by temperament and self-interest to minimize them and pursue a policy which did not confront his master with drastic decisions. As early as 1907, Bülow had written: "For our attitude in all Balkan questions the needs, interests and wishes of Austria-Hungary are decisive."

Soon, Bülow was obliged to honour this blank cheque. In July, 1908, revolution had broken out in Constantinople and the Sultan

had been forced to grant a constitution to his subjects. This extended
to the inhabitants of the Turkish provinces in the Balkans which
were now entitled to elect representatives to a parliament—with the
exception of Bosnia and Herzegovina which for the last thirty years
had been administered by Austria under the Berlin Treaty of 1878 as
a semi-autonomous area.

In October, 1908, the Turkish revolution was used by the Austrian
Foreign Minister, Aehrenthal, as a pretext to annex Bosnia and
Herzegovina, with the ultimate aim perhaps of including Serbia in
the Austro-Hungarian Empire and establishing a form of trialism.
The ground was prepared, at any rate to Aehrenthal's satisfaction, by
obtaining Russian agreement in return for the promise of diplomatic
support for her aim to open the Dardanelles to Russian warships. But
the Berlin ally was not consulted and the coup was launched before
Russia could make effective progress regarding the Straits.

As a result, Aehrenthal's action was universally condemned. The
Serbs were furious at Austria swallowing their fellow-Slavs in
Bosnia, the British were indignant at the abrogation of an international treaty, the Russians were convinced they had been duped,
and William was seething with wounded vanity because he had not
been consulted. Bülow's written request for an audience was
blackened in the Kaiser's angular writing. He was deeply wounded
in his feelings as an ally. He was the last in Europe to hear of this
coup—nice thanks for his former loyalty. The Turks, William's
friends, would be incensed. If the Sultan declared a holy war, he
would not be particularly surprised. "But of course we can do
nothing against the annexation."

The last sentence was all that mattered to Bülow and, realizing that
Russia was not ready for war and could do nothing against the
annexation either, he was already giving pledges. The basis of his
policy, he declared, was *la loyauté sans phrase*. "The more difficult
the situation in which the [Austrian] Minister finds himself, the
more must Aehrenthal be impressed by our fidelity." In this
question, he wrote to the Kaiser, a disapproving, even a hesitant
attitude on Germany's part would never be forgiven by Austria.

In practice this meant that Germany had to pull Aehrenthal's
chestnuts out of the fire. Short of a European war, which no one was
anxious to start, Serbia was the only country which could disturb
the annexation of Bosnia and Herzegovina and strong protests were
coming from Belgrade. Britain and Russia demanded an international conference to discuss the Bosnian question, but before
Serbia was brought into line Aehrenthal and Bülow refused to agree.
The key to the Serbian attitude lay in Russia: if Russia advised
Serbia to accept the *fait accompli* she would do so. In extremely

harsh terms which amounted almost to an ultimatum Bülow therefore demanded unqualified Russian acceptance of the annexation. Aehrenthal meanwhile was threatening to use force against Serbia. The combined pressure brought Russian agreement: Serbia was isolated and obliged to submit. International agreement to the annexation was obtained in March, 1909.

The settlement was hailed in Germany as a triumph for the Chancellor and William was happy to share in the plaudits descending on his Chancellor. He himself had disliked the dependency on Austria-Hungary: that was now forgotten and he joyfully declared that he had stood by his ally "in shining armour"—a phrase, incidentally, which was not relished in Vienna. Certain facts, however, had been overlooked in the euphoria prevailing in Berlin. There had been no war because Russia was not ready for war. In St. Petersburg, an eventual conflict with Germany was now considered inevitable. Austria-Hungary had not been strengthened. World suspicion of Germany had been increased. The Bosnian crisis bore all the characteristics that later led to war: arbitrary Austrian action, unqualified support from Germany, provocation of Russia, and German attempts to localize the crisis. They succeeded once but they might not succeed again.

For the time being, however, William felt reassured. Bülow had brought the ship into smooth waters again—William could now get rid of him. He had never forgotten the *Daily Telegraph* humiliation and time had merely hardened his belief in his own innocence and Bülow's treason. Bülow soon discovered that, behind a mask of goodwill, the Kaiser was turning against him and after losing Reichstag support over financial reforms he offered his resignation. This was accepted and he was summoned to Kiel to discuss his successor. He found the Kaiser on board the *Hohenzollern* surrounded by his warships. Nervous, impatient, with a touch of embarrassment, the Kaiser met him on deck. "Dear Bülow," he said, "you don't need to bother me with a long discourse about your successor. I have decided to take Bethmann. He is as true as gold, a colossal worker, very forceful, he will clear up the Reichstag for me. Besides, I shot my first roebuck at his home in Hohenfinow. . . ." Bülow pulled a long face, said that Bethmann knew nothing of foreign affairs. "Leave foreign affairs to me!" said William with a gay laugh. "I have learnt something in your school. It will be all right." Bülow then tried to advise his master to reach a naval agreement with England. "Haven't I told you often enough," said William, very annoyed and glancing at his wrist-watch, "that I will allow no one to interfere in my shipbuilding? Any such proposal is a humiliation for me and my navy." Bülow asked how German honour could suffer through a voluntary agreement with England which reduced the danger of war. "I don't believe in such a danger!" retorted William emphatically and, glancing at the massive warships around him, raised his head and with a proud look declared: "I am entitled to a certain feeling of satisfaction when I look at these fruits of my endeavours." Bülow added other warnings, including, if he is to be believed, advice to be careful in the Balkans. But William was now hopping with impatience, he was due to have luncheon with the Prince of Monaco. "All right, all right. I won't forget what you say. You can be quite happy. But now I must go. I must not keep Monaco waiting. . . ."

A few days later, no longer Chancellor, Bülow had a farewell audience in the Berlin palace. William's conflicting emotions were pitiful to see. He could barely restrain his hostility; at the same time, feelings of guilt seemed to be swimming in the background. He told Bülow he was very busy and much annoyed that the change of Chancellor had upset his Norwegian cruise. When Bülow had gone, he received the representatives of the Federal Princes and told them he had been obliged to allow his Chancellor to retire into private life because the poor man was losing his memory, had become almost an imbecile, no doubt owing to pressure of work. Soon after, he wrote Bülow a charming letter, praising him for his services, and then received a visit from the King of Württemberg. Pointing out the exact spot in the palace where Bülow had taken his farewell, he drew himself up like a victorious commander surveying a battle-field and declared: "This is where I gave that piece of carrion the sack."

The next victim, Theobald von Bethmann-Hollweg, aged fifty-three, was an experienced administrator of a kind not uncommon in Germany: conscientious, hard-working, utterly honest and painfully aware of the responsibilities of high office. He had been Prussian Minister of the Interior and for the last two years Secretary of State for Home Affairs. Unlike Bülow he possessed humility, perhaps too much. How little he knew, how much there was to learn. But he never despaired. Ultimate truth, he was convinced, existed and could be winkled out of its shell by a mind sufficiently persevering and acute. He was a thinker, a philosopher and something of a Hamlet, much given to larding his speech with qualifications: "on the other hand this" . . . "but we must not forget that". To reach a decision was an agonizing process. Kant and Schopenhauer helped sometimes, at others, the members of his family went on tip-toe, while Papa with furrowed brow twisted his head to and fro struggling for clarity. Of foreign affairs he was as ignorant as a new-born babe. But William was happy. He would show the good fellow the ropes and there was no danger here, none at all, that the faintest gleam of popularity would ever touch Bethmann's head.

His appointment was fateful. There were only two resolute men in the government, Tirpitz and the ruthless Foreign Secretary, Kiderlen-Wächter. Both knew what they wanted—an increase of German power. The Kaiser knew what he did not want—war. And Bethmann, learning as he went, tried to steer a course between the two. The pattern soon established itself: a zig to fall in with the Kaiser's wishes, a zag to take account of Tirpitz's or Kiderlen's forceful opinions and as a result a wobbling course which consolidated the encirclement of Germany while the Press continued to scream "Forward! Forward!" without knowing precisely in what direction.

Tirpitz and William were, however, agreed on one point: Germany's growing fleet was an essential instrument of policy, it must continue to grow and no foreign power must be allowed to "dictate" its size. William looked down with boundless scorn on mere civilians, including the Chancellor and the members of the Foreign Office, who dared to express an opinion on naval matters. Their job was simply to obtain the necessary credits from the Reichstag and explain to Britain in particular that the fleet was not directed against anyone, it was laughable to think of it as a menace, and anyway the British, of all people, had no right to begrudge Germany the means of defence which they possessed in such overwhelming strength themselves.

For some time, indeed, the British had watched German shipbuilding with something like indifference. After King Edward's visit to Kiel in 1904 their attitude began to change until now, in 1909, they looked on the race in naval armaments with serious concern, firstly because it forced them to spend vast sums on maintaining their superiority, money which the Liberal government would have preferred to spend on social schemes, secondly because it was poisoning Anglo-German relations and exciting the public of both countries and thirdly because Britain had already gone far enough from her traditional isolation and had no desire to be forced too firmly into the Franco-Russian camp.

This feeling of alarm was duly reported by Metternich, the German Ambassador in London. The British, he said, were anxious for some sort of agreement. William was delighted. The British, he thought, must be seriously embarrassed. No doubt they were running short of money. It would be foolish, in that case, to agree to a reduction in the rate of German shipbuilding. The pressure must be maintained. Then glittering prizes could be won. What, he wondered, had the British got to offer?

When, thinking the moment favourable, Bethmann took up negotiations it was the Kaiser backed by Tirpitz who introduced this atmosphere of unreality into the proceedings. The British were perfectly well able to sustain the armaments race, if need be indefinitely. They were not arguing from weakness, but from strength and though they sincerely desired friendship with Germany they had no intention of binding themselves in a way which would alienate France. Why should they? They had no need to fear the German fleet at its present strength, or for many years to come now that the French, Russian and Japanese fleets were friendly. It was ultimate German intentions which worried them.

But this was never understood in Berlin and the Germans over-played their hand from the start. Bethmann was sincerely anxious for an agreement on political grounds and realized that a reduction in naval building alone, without any political strings, would help to reduce tension. But he knew that the Kaiser and Tirpitz, forget-ting that the saving of money and material would be of equal advantage to both sides, would never agree to the smallest reduction in the German tempo without striking "compensation", and he allowed himself to make impossible political demands. At Tirpitz's insistence these were attached to an offer of minimal reductions in the rate of German building, but this left open the ultimate size of the German fleet and it was this which really interested Britain.

In 1909–1910, negotiations broke down because of the wide difference between the British and German view-points. If there was to be any political arrangement at all, Britain wanted it to follow the naval agreement. But before talking ships, the Germans wanted to talk politics, and in terms which left no doubt that their aim was to ensure British neutrality in a continental war. This would have wrecked the Entente, but Grey, the British Foreign Secretary, was clear: "I want a good understanding with Germany, but it must be one which will not imperil those we have with France and Russia."

Six months later, in September, 1910, negotiations were resumed. The British wanted the Germans to state their target for battleships. Again Bethmann said that a political agreement must come before naval discussions, again William had visions of an accord at the pistol-point. Germany, he said, must be included in the British entente with France and Russia, parallel policies must be pursued throughout the world. If Britain asked for a guarantee of her Indian possessions, Germany must demand the guarantee of Alsace-Lorraine. He was surprised, no doubt, when the British refused to consider these fantasies and he drew the conclusion that the approach had been a trap to reduce German shipbuilding without any equivalent concessions and that therefore it must be increased until the British were frightened into the German orbit.

The third and last attempt to reach naval understanding took place a year later, in 1911–1912, by which time Anglo-German relations had been further inflamed by events in Morocco. Though the independent sovereignty of the country was guaranteed under the Act of Algeciras French penetration and exclusion of foreign competitors was continuing. William, who was secretly intimidated by perennial French agitation for revenge over Alsace-Lorraine, positively welcomed the diversion of French troops and resources to Morocco and wanted to wash his hands of the whole affair. In 1909, on his initiative, a treaty had been signed with France recognizing her special position in Morocco in return for guarantees of commercial equality. Now, in 1911, when disorders broke out and the French grip tightened on the country, he saw no reason to protest and maintained his attitude of disinterest.

Kiderlen, however, who dominated Bethmann in foreign affairs, had a plan reeking of sulphur and bombast. Germany's last intervention in Morocco had resulted in diplomatic defeat. This could be made good if Germany now declared the Act of Algeciras unrealistic and demanded compensations from France in return for allowing her a free hand in Morocco. If need be, German warships should occupy Agadir on the West coast and not be withdrawn until the compensation was forthcoming. Discussions were started with France. William's cupidity was aroused by a tale that they were ready to cede the whole of the French Congo. This was untrue. Negotiations dragged on. The whole affair now became a matter of prestige: France must give way, Germany could not retreat, her honour was at stake. The fires of patriotism were alight, ardently fanned by the Press. In this atmosphere it was easy to persuade William that one warship dispatched to Morocco would teach the French that Germany meant business. The All-Highest, pausing for a moment in East Prussia where he was slaughtering animals, gave his assent and the nearest ship to the scene, the gunboat *Panther* with a crew of nineteen, was sent to Agadir to "protect German lives and property".

In Germany "the leap of the Panther" as the newspapers called it was hailed with rejoicing. *Westmarokko Deutsch!* was the cry. Elsewhere there was deep indignation. France concerted policy with Britain, stiffened her attitude and refused to cede "the sizeable morsel" of territory which Kiderlen required. Kiderlen was seriously fearing that his bluff would fail. Bethmann, deep in thought, was trying to build a new and more logical case on the Act of Algeciras. William, his perceptions sharpened by fear, was scrawling: "What

the devil is to be done now? This is a pure farce! Negotiations go on
and on and nothing comes of it. If we lose our valuable time like
this, the British and Russians will stiffen the backs of the Gauls and
dictate to them what they should graciously concede to us."

By now, Britain was fearing that the *Panther* symbolized Germany's intention to stay in Morocco. In the Mansion House Lloyd
George made a speech warning Germany not to ignore British
interests. This drew an assurance that no claims were being made
in Morocco itself and this in turn pacified the French. Four months
after the *Panther*'s "leap", during which time the Entente Powers
ruminated on this latest exhibition of the mailed fist, France and
Germany agreed on an exchange of territory: a large slice of the
French Congo for a small slice of the German Cameroons, and a
completely free hand for France in Morocco. On paper it seemed a
good bargain for Germany, but the French were ceding sand cake in
return for rich Dundee. The German colonial secretary—whose
advice had been ignored—resigned in protest and a storm of indignation was raised in the Press. This was national humiliation, national
dishonour, a "defeat worse than Jena" and why, some papers wanted
to know, had such large sums been spent on the German army if it
was not to be used on an occasion like this?

The babel of voices which spoke in German foreign policy was
even more apparent when naval discussions were resumed at the
end of 1911. Conflicting arguments were reaching the Kaiser from
London. Metternich reported that the British were ripe for an
agreement with Germany. Though angry over Morocco, they were
most anxious not to see Europe split into two opposing camps. On
the other hand, the German naval attaché was talking of British
desires to "Copenhagen" the German fleet. To this siren song
William lent a readier ear because it came from a military man. From
the events of the summer he had already concluded that "a better
tone towards Germany can only be achieved by a yet stronger fleet".
Tirpitz was at hand with fresh plans: estimates which would increase
the rate of building by one super-battleship a year, greatly increase
the sea-going personnel and add twenty or more submarines to the
existing fleet. All this William approved, without consulting Bethmann or Kiderlen. When they heard of it they were indignant.
Bethmann protested. William threatened to find another Chancellor.
Finally, in despair, Bethmann instructed Metternich to try and
extract some concession from the British, for instance a neutrality
agreement, large enough to persuade the Kaiser to modify the new
estimates.

No such offer was forthcoming and Metternich doubted whether
the British would enter any agreement which weakened the Entente,

particularly under the threat of yet further increases in the German
fleet. Was it really worth sacrificing good relations with Britain, he
asked, for the sake of one more battleship a year? This line of
argument aroused William's indignation. He would not allow a
foreign power to interfere in his naval policy. As Emperor and
supreme war-lord he refused to permit it. "It would be a humiliation
for our people. The estimates must stand!" This truculent mood,
always uppermost in dealings with England, lasted throughout
November and December. When the British offered not to oppose
German colonial ambitions William declared that he wanted no
colonies through England's kind offices, he had enough, alternatively
he could take or buy them without England's permission. In any
case, if Germany acquired more colonies she would need a fleet of
double the size to protect them. . . .

But in January, 1912, a dramatic incident took place which
plunged William into the highest excitement. The British financier
Sir Ernest Cassel came to Berlin to sound the possibility of personal
discussions between a British Minister and the German Government. Wide prospects of a colonial, naval and general agreement
were opened. Years later in Doorn, when his proud fleet lay at the
bottom of Scapa Flow, William wrote of this moment in words
which showed that even in retrospect he had no conception of the
responsibility that had weighed on him. A British approach!
Ah-ha! One more stage in the tit-for-tat with England. "An intimate
friend of Edward VII was appearing before the German Kaiser
without any previous announcement through diplomatic channels
with a verbal note inspired by the British Government. And this
from England, the motherland of constitutionalism! Summoned by
telephone, Bethmann was quickly on the spot. It was interesting to
watch his play of features when he was informed." Tirpitz was also
summoned. It was decided to draft a reply at once, which should be
in English to avoid misunderstanding. This was a happy moment
for William. He was the best English-speaker. "So now," as he wrote
as a man of over sixty in exile, "there was this picture: I sat at a
desk, the gentlemen stood round me. I read out a sentence of the
note and drafted a reply, which I also read out. Then criticism
started from left and right. To one, it was too conciliatory, to another
too abrupt. It was trimmed, shaped, improved. . . . It gave me many
a grammatical and stylistic headache. After hours of work, the note
was finally cast. . . ." Oh, clever William.

Germany welcomed discussions and in February Haldane, the
British War Minister, arrived in Berlin, empowered to negotiate *ad
referendum* to the British Cabinet. He found himself talking to two
separate governments, Bethmann on the one hand, the Kaiser and

Tirpitz on the other. Kiderlen-Wächter, the Foreign Secretary, was not even consulted. Bethmann did not know what Tirpitz wanted and had only the vaguest idea why there was a German navy at all: he presumed it was "for the general purposes of Germany's greatness". But William and Tirpitz were determined to sacrifice no jot or tittle unless Bethmann could extract a sweeping neutrality agreement. Instead, Haldane offered a harmless political formula plus British concurrence to the purchase by Germany of colonial territories from Portugal and Belgium—all this in return for the curtailment of the new naval estimates. Tirpitz was ready to make some concession, but when British naval experts studied the estimates they found them more far-reaching than expected and the concession ludicrously small. The Cabinet then modified Haldane's offer. The Germans were highly indignant. William's temper was not improved by a British statement that, whether or not an agreement was reached, they were confident that Bethmann wanted peace. "It is obvious," he snarled, "that they have no idea who is the master here." To reinforce this, the master sent direct instructions to Metternich demanding an offensive and defensive alliance. The British refused to go beyond Haldane's original formula. Negotiations collapsed—and William drew the conclusion that his diplomats would do well to consider his wishes in future. He knew "better than they how to handle the British".

These negotiations were almost the last instance of William's direct intervention in affairs. Their failure resulted in the exact opposite of Germany's aim to ensure British neutrality in the event of a European war. British squadrons previously stationed in the Mediterranean were moved to the North Sea and French ships were sent South to replace them. Britain was now under an obligation to defend the French Channel coast. Though there were still no written commitments, she could not fail to support her neighbour. William spluttered about mobilization against this "threat of war" but had perforce to accept the situation.

These were not the only events which he was powerless to influence. In the Balkans, Serbia, Bulgaria and Greece had formed an offensive alliance under Russian patronage in anticipation of Turkey's collapse. All the Balkan countries were itching to drive out the Turk and the object of the agreement was to concert action and an equitable division of the spoils. The prospect of upheaval filled the Great Powers with alarm. Russia was worried lest Bulgaria should seize Constantinople thereby dominating the exit from the Black Sea, and her encouragement of the alliance aimed at controlling the conflagration when it came. Austria feared the expansion of Serbia, and Germany feared the prospect of having to support desperate Austrian action to prevent this at the risk of a European war. The Balkan countries were therefore told that, whatever happened, no revision would be permitted of Turkey's European possessions. Ineffectually, William protested at this démarche. He was rightly sceptical of its value and extremely frightened lest, when war came, the Great Powers should be induced to intervene. Typically, his fear prompted violent language. "Let there be war! *Es komme ruhig zum Krieg!*" The Bulgarians, he said, were the people of the future. The Balkan States wanted an increase of territory. This could only be obtained at the expense of Turkey. "If they smash the Turks, then they are in the right and are entitled to reward. The Great Powers must keep a ring round the battlefield. There must be no interference in the name of so-called peace. The eternal stress on peace . . . has produced a eunuch-like attitude on the part of European statesmen. . . . The Eastern Question must be solved with blood and iron!"

But blood and iron solved nothing, just the reverse. In October, 1912, Montenegro, followed by Bulgaria, Serbia and Greece, declared war on Turkey. The forces of Islam were quickly routed. The Greeks occupied Salonica and southern Macedonia, the Serbs western Macedonia spilling over into Albania and the Bulgars surged in a ferocious horde towards Adrianople, inflicting a shattering defeat on the Turks and incidentally seizing northern Macedonia. The aggressors then paused, breathless, none of them satisfied, each eyeing the others' spoils. In November, Turkey invited the mediation of the Great Powers. At once, William's simple formula broke down. It was impossible, though he still urged this, for Germany to wash her hands of the new situation because Austria was deeply involved.

Serbia wanted a port on the Adriatic and part of North Albania. Russia supported the demand, Austria refused to concede it. Here at once was a possibility of world conflict, made more urgent by the fact that, without waiting for anyone's permission, Serbia marched to the coast and occupied Durazzo. Was she to be thrown out and, if so, by whom? If not, what of the effect on Austria's seven million Slavs? It was impossible for Germany to stand aside. Russia would have to give way and Kiderlen considered this might be achieved if German support was offered to prevent Bulgaria reaching Constantinople. Already, therefore, Kiderlen was sliding into a position which only two months before he and Bethmann had been emphatic in condemning: Germany as "satellite" of Austria.

At this moment with horrid clarity William saw the writing on the wall. Why, he asked the Foreign Office, should Austria not let the Serbs have their Adriatic harbour. He refused to undertake a war against Russia and France for this question. "Certainly many of the changes brought about by the war in the Balkans are highly uncomfortable for Vienna, but none is so drastic that we should expose ourselves to the risk of war because of it. I could not justify that to my people or my conscience." What did this mean? A sudden abandonment of Austria? That was what William implied. Bethmann thought hard and decided he could not risk it. He hurried to Letzlingen, where the Kaiser was once again hunting, to remonstrate—only to meet the same argument in a more emphatic form. A war on two fronts, said William, in which England would probably fight on the opposite side was an undertaking "in which everything would be at stake and Germany might possibly go down in ruin". It was impossible for Germany to risk such a war for the sake of Albania or Durazzo. The alliance with Austria said nothing about the German army and people being placed at the service of another country and the moods of its foreign policy.

What arguments Bethmann used are not known. He must have stressed the implications of this attitude: Austria at the mercy of Russia, possible break-up of the monarchy, chaos in southern Europe. At any rate, William was soon agreeing that Austria must not be left in the lurch, but must be made to negotiate so that, if it came to the worst, Russia would be put in the wrong. With great relief Bethmann wired to Kiderlen: "Right basis found again today."

Meanwhile the Austrians did not know what they wanted. Agreement to Serbian expansion in return for political guarantees? The setting up of an independent Albanian state? Immediate war against Serbia? Some sort of diplomatic success seemed necessary, but what? Russia was mobilizing and with heavy heart the aged Franz Josef gave orders to mobilize on the Galician front. Time was running short. The Austrian Chief of Staff came to Berlin to concert war plans and in fatalistic mood William now gave orders that the German public must be enlightened about the issues at stake, otherwise no one would know "for what interests Germany has to fight in this war".

But war was, for the time being, avoided. Russia dropped her support for Serbia, largely because she could not be sure of Britain if it came to a European conflict, and the Serbs had to be content with a railway linking them with an internationalized harbour on the Adriatic. At the same time, an independent Albania was set up. This meant that neither Greece nor Serbia could retain all their Macedonian spoils; they cast envious eyes on Bulgaria which retained the lion's share and in June, 1913, the second Balkan war broke out. It ended in August with the Peace of Bucharest from which Serbia and Greece emerged greatly enlarged and Bulgaria severely weakened.

Except for the south-east tip, Turkey had been driven from Europe.

But Serbia was still not satisfied and secretly Russia was promising her yet further territory when the Austro-Hungarian Empire collapsed. The Austrians were still undecided how to deal with the Serbian problem. Russia was spending vast sums on developing her army and building strategic railways to her western frontier. The money was provided by France. After her defeat in Europe it seemed probable that even Asiatic Turkey might crumble into revolution and chaos. In Berlin the Kaiser, backed by his military advisers, now saw war with Russia as inevitable, and that meant with France. After a visit an English bishop reported: "The Kaiser spoke with a note that was new to me. I felt that he was under the influence of a great fear."

CHAPTER TWELVE

THE EXPLOSION

THERE was a cartoon by Daumier called "The European Balance", showing a top spinning on the edge of a naked sword. This was the situation in 1914. The Triple Entente faced the Triple Alliance. Russia was seeking to promote an alliance between Rumania, where the pan-Slav current was strong, Serbia and Greece. Austria was trying to form a counterweight to Serbia consisting of Rumania, Greece and Bulgaria. Thus Austria and Russia had contradictory designs concerning Serbia and each was competing for the favour of Rumania. To this confusion another factor was added: German ambitions in the Near East. The Berlin–Baghdad railway was under construction and in early 1914 Turkey was coming increasingly under German economic and military influence. There was the possibility of an alliance between the Central Powers, Bulgaria and Turkey. If this came about and Serbian ambitions could be brought under control, a wall would be raised against Russian expansion and the Central Powers would, at least temporarily, be secure. On the other hand, Russia, already weakened by internal dissension and permanently handicapped in the event of war by a slow rate of mobilization, would face a formidable coalition led by a country which, owing to her geographical position, was notoriously trigger-happy.

Already in the Bosnian crisis and again in the Balkan wars Europe had gazed into the abyss and in Vienna, Berlin and St. Petersburg statesmen were beginning to feel the truth of the German saying: "Better a terrible end than terror without end." Of all the actors in the drama, it was William, of course, who was least able to stand the protracted tension. Bethmann had converted him to unqualified support for Austria and already in the autumn of 1913, on hearing of plans to eject the Serbs from Albania, he had assured the Austrian Chief of Staff: "I'll go with you. You must be in Belgrade in a couple of days. I have always been a supporter of the peace, but that has its limits. Finally there comes a situation where a Great Power cannot stand by any longer and *must* draw the sword." To Count Berchtold, the Austrian Foreign Minister, he spoke in similar terms. The only possible relationship between Austria and Serbia was the dependence of the smaller upon the greater, "according to the planet system". If this dependence could not be brought about by economic means, then Belgrade would have to be occupied. "In that case," said William, "you can be sure that I will stand behind you".

But William did not believe that Austrian action against Serbia would bring in Russia. Russia had not stirred in 1908 or 1912 and William trusted heavily in his friendship with the Tsar on whom he continued to lavish letters, gifts and advice.

But into this dream there burst, in May, 1914, the strident voice of a Russian professor. Writing to a former teacher in Germany who then published the letter in a periodical, the Russian reviewed developments in the Balkans and the Near East, blamed Germany for Russian reverses in recent years and called Germany "the principle enemy of Russia". "The Russia of today," he went on, "demands respect for its honour and consideration for its interests. . . . War with Germany would be a misfortune, but we shall not shrink from the bitter necessity if it becomes really necessary."

Before the sensation caused in Germany by these words had subsided, an article—equally cynical or realistic—appeared in a Russian newspaper. Russia, said the writer, "has done everything to anticipate the enemy when mobilization comes and concentrate the army as quickly as possible in the first days of war". France should do the same. "The greater the number of soldiers she maintains in peace, the sooner she will be ready in war. . . . Russia is ready and hopes that France will be ready." This article did not escape William. "Well!" he commented. "At last the Russians have shown their hand! Whoever in Germany still refuses to believe that in Russo-Gaul they are working at high pressure for an early war with us deserves to be sent to the mad-house!" This view was fully shared by Chancellor Bethmann-Hollweg.

Thus even before a shot fired by a Serbian assassin on 28th June rang out in Sarajevo, killing the Archduke Franz Ferdinand, the heir to the Austrian throne, the alarm-bells were shrilling in William's mind. He was on board his yacht at the Kiel regatta when news of the crime was brought to him. At once the regatta was cancelled. William disembarked, moved, as he wired to his Chancellor "to the depths of my soul"; "completely overwhelmed", he told the bereaved father. Franz Ferdinand had been his hunting companion, he had been with him only a fortnight before. Assassins had killed the President of the French Republic in 1894, the Empress of Austria in 1898, the King of Italy in 1900, the King of Portugal in 1908, the King of Greece in 1913. It was like the French Revolution all over again. Chaos was rearing its head. The monarchical principle was threatened. From Vienna the German Ambassador reported that "even among serious people there is a wish that a thorough reckoning must be had with the Serbs once for all". William's comment was drastic: "Now or never."

It was possible though not certain that the Archduke's assassin, an Austro-Hungarian citizen of Serb nationality, had been an agent of the Serbian Government. But that was not the point. One week after the murder William received a memorandum from the Austrian Government that had been drawn up before 28th June and made it clear that Austria had desired war with Serbia even before the murder took place.

With the memorandum came a letter from Franz Josef written after the murder. Even if the Serbian Government's complicity could not be proved, he said, the fact remained that Serbia sought the union of all South Slavs under her flag and this was a permanent danger to Austria-Hungary. Serbia was the pivot of pan-Slav agitation and her elimination as a political power was essential. The letter ended with an appeal to William who would now, it was said, be convinced that "a reconciliation of the antagonism that separates us from Serbia can no longer be thought of".

The appeal was well calculated to stir William's heart. The aged Franz Josef had already lost his eldest son, his wife, and now his second heir—all by a violent death. Political, personal and not least religious considerations combined to sway William to support drastic action. Years before, when preaching a Sunday sermon on board the *Hohenzollern* he had cried:

"Yes, the old God still lives! The great ally still rules—the holy God who cannot allow sin and crime to triumph, but who will lead his holy cause against an unholy people, the all-powerful God who can strike through the strongest walls as though they were cobwebs and scatter the mightiest hosts as the sand—God the Merciful, the Faithful, who bears the joy and the woes of his children on his father's heart, who hears every sigh and succours every need. . . ."

Now, if ever, there was a cause which the Great Ally could make his own. Was it not true that foul murder had been committed, true that a Christian people would be fighting against anarchy and evil, true that survival was at stake? Neither William nor Franz Josef had sought this quarrel. Their conscience was clear. There must and there would be an end to terrorism. The godless Serbs must be punished.

On that same day—5th July, 1914—that he read the letter and the memorandum, William in exalted mood sent Franz Josef a personal message. Without asking if there was proof of official Serbian complicity in the assassination, without consulting his Chancellor, without imposing any restrictions on the proposed Austrian action or asking for any details of its scope, William pledged his full support. Franz Josef must strike quickly, act at once. The moment was favourable. Russia, William believed, would not move. But if she did, Germany would accept the consequences. It was the green light. Here, at last, after so many years, was a tangible enemy, a concrete case, proving to William that the dim sense of persecution that had haunted him all his life was justified. What a relief to have a tangible foe, to be no longer fighting shadows, to have all conflicts reduced to this one clear-cut issue! The German Ambassador in Vienna had already received a severe rap on the knuckles for advising moderation. "Who authorized him to act thus?" scolded William. "It is very stupid. It is absolutely none of his business. It is solely Austria's affair what she means to do in this matter. The Serbs must be disposed of, and that right *soon!*"

After dispatch of the message, still on 5th July, William informed his Chancellor. Bethmann-Hollweg approved. Realizing that he had written a blank cheque, William asked what form the Austrian action should take. "Leave it to them," he was told. Then William summoned the Minister of War, General von Falkenhayn. Was the army ready for all emergencies? It was. And finally, how about William's annual cruise to Norway? He was ready to start. Should he cancel it? No, said Bethmann. He had better go. It would help to keep the pot from the boil.

From now on, William was the victim of events and of his advisers, chief among them, Bethmann and Moltke, the German Chief of Staff. They knew their master, knew there was trouble coming and knew he would never stick to his guns. Bethmann was determined that the Serbian thorn should be excised. He pinned his hopes on persuading the world that this was an operation of local concern. But both men, Bethmann and Moltke, accepted the possibility of a world war. If it came, the Chancellor's concern was to present Germany in the most favourable light, as the victim of aggression, Moltke's to choose the right moment to mobilize before Russia was ready, strike France to her knees, then turn on the Bear. He believed that moment was at hand. Meanwhile, William should enjoy the sea breezes and be encouraged to relax.

While William was leading the crew of the *Hohenzollern* in their physical jerks, Austria was girding herself for battle. It took eighteen days to reach agreement on the political and military plan of attack. Then, on 23rd July, an ultimatum was fired at Serbia containing impossible demands which no independent country could accept.

Germany was not consulted either about the timing or the terms. Knowing only that stiff demands were to be made, Bethmann nevertheless circularized the Entente capitals on that same day, calling the Austrian terms "equitable and moderate", asserting that the conflict was solely a matter between Austria and Serbia and calling on all concerned to stand passively on the touch-line while the battle raged.

Back now from his cruise, William could take comfort from the fact that his people seemed to be behind him. On the following day, after the terms of the ultimatum had been published, a Berlin newspaper declared that the time for goodwill or negotiation was past. "Serbia must make her choice quickly and without reserve. The German people are relieved to feel that the Balkan situation is at last to be cleared up." Meanwhile, Austria-Hungary was seeking to justify her action by telling the Powers that the Serbian "incendiary movement" threatened the survival of the Monarchy.

Austria intended to declare war the moment Serbia rejected the ultimatum, but to the world's surprise she accepted it with minor reservations and within the time-limit of forty-eight hours. This meant that Serbia surrendered control of her affairs to an extent that virtually destroyed her sovereignty. But having resolved on war, the Austrian statesmen were in no mood to revert to peaceful solutions. Giesl, their Ambassador in Belgrade, was packed and ready to leave and thirty minutes after receiving the Serbian reply he asked for his passports. That same evening in Vienna the mobilization of eight army corps and three cavalry divisions was ordered.

Meanwhile, having given Austria unqualified support, William was beginning to fear the consequences. Austrian intransigence filled him with alarm. He was beginning to doubt whether the conflict could be localized and on hearing of the Serbian reply he declared with admirable good sense: "A great moral victory for Vienna, but with it every reason for war disappears. Giesl might have remained quietly in Belgrade." To his Foreign Minister, Jagow, he wrote: "I am convinced that on the whole the wishes of the Dual Monarchy have been fulfilled. The few reservations which Serbia makes on individual points can, in my opinion, be settled by negotiation. The Serbs have announced *urbi et orbi* a capitulation of the most humiliating kind." But he thought that, having gone so far, for prestige reasons the Austrians must at least be allowed to brandish the sword on Serbian territory. They should be told that, though grounds for war no longer existed, guarantees were necessary for the fulfilment of Serbian promises and these could be obtained by a temporary occupation of Belgrade. "On this basis," wrote William, "I am ready to mediate for peace."

But William's words fell on stony ground. Prompted by the

General Staff, his Chancellor was urging Vienna to hasten action. It was not Serbian promises which Bethmann wanted to see fulfilled, but Austrian demands, the same demands whose severity had aroused the consternation of the world and Russian anger. He knew that Austria had mobilized, not to apply pressure but to make war and that war was imminent. In the swift occupation of all Serbia he saw the best chance of presenting Russia and the world with a *fait accompli*. So news that might weaken William's determination was concealed from him, in particular a British proposal to mediate between Austria-Hungary and Russia, and his own suggestion was not transmitted to Vienna until twelve hours after he had made it. By that time, war on Serbia had been declared. In sending the proposal Bethmann instructed the German Ambassador in Vienna: "You will have very carefully to avoid giving the impression that we wish to hold Austria back. It is simply a question of finding means to realize Austria's aim of cutting the vital cord of Greater Serbian propaganda without entailing a world war, and if this cannot finally be avoided, of improving as far as possible the conditions under which it will have to be fought."

Bethmann's deception of William went even further. Believing that his proposal had been conveyed immediately and accurately to Vienna, William was persuaded by his Chancellor to wire the Tsar saying: "I am exerting my utmost influence to induce the Austrians to arrive at a satisfactory understanding with you." If it came to a world war, said Bethmann, this telegram would place Russia's responsibility in the clearest light. But at the same time, Bethmann, without informing William, was sending threatening messages to St. Petersburg. Following the Austrian mobilization against Serbia, Russia had ordered partial mobilization, but only on the Austro-Hungarian frontier and this, the Germans had promised, would not lead them to mobilize against Russia. But now, on 29th July, after the Austrians had started to bombard Belgrade, Bethmann warned the Russians that "a further continuation of Russia's measures of mobilization" would force Germany to do the same—"and a European war could then scarcely be avoided".

Meanwhile, in blissful ignorance, William was exchanging conciliatory telegrams with the Tsar. "An ignoble war," Nicky had wired, "has been declared on a weak country." Indignation in Russia was intense. He was under heavy pressure to take extreme measures. "In the name of our old friendship," he pleaded, "I beg you to do what you can to stop your allies from going too far." This was precisely what William wanted to do, and what he thought he was doing. Unaware that his own Government was using threatening language to the Russians, he replied, calling on Nicky to refrain from military measures as these would "precipitate a calamity which we both wish to avoid and endanger my position as mediator which I willingly accepted on your appeal to my friendship and help".

But the time for mediation was almost past. There was a dynamism in the situation which no one, however good his intentions, could halt. Austria believed she was fighting for the existence of the Dual Monarchy. But if her efforts succeeded, Russian ambitions in the Balkans and the Near East would be blocked and an intolerable humiliation inflicted on a country already riven with internal strife. Russia, too, saw this as a life-and-death struggle. Deceived by his own Chancellor and dependent on fragile bonds of friendship with the vacillating Nicky there was not much that William could do.

In this state of helplessness he received ominous news from London. Up to now he had not dared to think of possible British action. On 28th July, King George had been reported—it seems incorrectly—as saying: "We shall try all we can to keep out of this and remain neutral." "That is enough for me," William commented to Tirpitz. "I have the word of a King." But on the 30th, Lichnovsky, the German Ambassador in London, reported a conversation with the Foreign Secretary. Sir Edward Grey had deplored Austrian intransigence and speaking of a serious situation in which the British Cabinet could not ignore public opinion had said that if Germany and France were drawn into the conflict, Britain might not be able to stand aside.

This was a shock to Bethmann, but to William it was a traumatic experience stirring up all his resentment, envy, love and hatred of Britain. With trembling pen he spattered the telegram with comments almost as long as the text itself: "The crassest deception!"— "English pharisaism!"—"A common crew of shopkeepers"— "Grey proves the King a liar!"—"His words to Lichnovsky spring from a guilty conscience"—"He knows well enough that if he were to utter a single serious sharp and warning word in Paris and Petersburg advising them to remain neutral both would become quiet at once"—"But instead, he threatens us!"—"Common cur!" —"England alone bears the responsibility for war and peace, not we any longer"—And pathetically he added: "That must be made clear to the world."

But Britain could not possibly be disinterested in a war which might put Europe under the heel of a single Power and it is clear that a combination of recklessness and fatalism on the part of William and his advisers hastened the coming of Armageddon. William had given Austria a promise of unqualified support. Bethmann backed him, cherishing with purblind fatalism the hope that

the conflict could be localized. Now, on 30th July—the very day that
Nemesis began to rear its head—the Chancellor surrendered to the
military men and the chariot went plunging towards the abyss. Considering the moment "extraordinarily favourable" for Germany to
fight a war, Moltke sent a message to the Austrian Chief of Staff
urging full mobilization and promising that Germany would do the
same. Austria took the advice. That same night general mobilization
was decided on in Vienna. Next day—before this decision was
known in St. Petersburg—general mobilization was ordered in
Russia.

The world was now on the brink. The forces were aligned and
for Germany the time-factor became all-important. With Russia
mobilized, France would mobilize. In her central position, Germany
could not delay, but would have to strike first. It was not a matter of
weeks, but of days, even hours. It was still not too late, perhaps,
on that 30th July to try and put a brake on Austria, insist on the halt
in Belgrade and at least attempt negotiation. But this was the very
last moment. Another day and it would be too late. William had
always been proud of taking the initiative into his own hands. He
had always leapt at the chance to shine. Here was his opportunity.
But he did not seize it or even see it. He was busy with other things,
still scribbling on that telegram from London, still deep in the mire
of neurotic fantasy: "I have no doubt that England, Russia and
France have *agreed* among themselves—after arranging to have the
casus foederis arise for us through Austria—to use the Austro-Serbian
conflict as an excuse to wage a war of annihilation against us."

Yes, it was a plot. Who had contrived it? Uncle Bertie, of course.
Yes, "woven by Edward VII", continued by the Powers of the Triple
Entente, "and now brought to completion by George V". The
diabolical cleverness of these unscrupulous enemies! The encirclement of Germany, William believed, had now been accomplished,
"and England sneeringly reaps the most brilliant success from the
purely *anti-German world policy* which she has persistently pursued
and against which we have shown ourselves helpless, while she
twists the noose of our political and economic destruction out of our
loyalty to Austria and we squirm *isolated* in the net. . . . Edward VII
is stronger after his death than I who am still alive".

Stretched by the tensions of the real world, William's mind had
suddenly snapped and he was a child again, struggling impotently
against the tyranny of his elders. But the child now wielded enormous power, he had a sword, he could strike back. While the sands
of peace ran out, his pen scratched on: "This whole business must
now be ruthlessly disclosed, the mask of Christian peacefulness
publicly and abruptly torn from England's face, its pharisaical

hypocrisy exposed on the pillory. Our Consuls in Turkey and India, agents, etcetera, must inflame the whole Mohammedan world to fierce rebellion against this hateful, lying, unscrupulous nation of shopkeepers. . . . If we are to bleed to death, then at least England shall lose India."

Forty-eight hours later, William met his Chancellor, Falkenhayn, Tirpitz and Moltke. At 5 p.m., on their advice, he ordered mobilization. They stood round him while he signed the order. Then he looked at them, a frightened man. "Gentlemen," he said, "you will live to rue the day when you made me do this." On that same day, Germany declared war on Russia. Guarantees of French neutrality were then demanded in the knowledge that they could not be forthcoming. It was intended to crush France and then turn against Russia. The General Staff was confident. Germany had the finest army, interior lines, the best railway system in the world.

But William was sunk in black foreboding. Where in war could he escape from harsh reality? The Great Ally, the shining sword, those speeches where he had talked of battles, banners and bravely storming troops, where were they now compared with the drab prospect of field-grey columns weaving their way methodically across the western plains amid blood, screams and the chatter of machine-guns? There was no room for heroics here. This was the moment of truth. And despite glib remarks in the past that in war he would be his own commander-in-chief, he realized that he was not a soldier, he never had been. He possessed an aggressive spirit, but not a warrior's soul. Those imperial manoeuvres where he had commanded one side and invariably been allowed to win had been a sham. The troops he defeated had stood up after the battle and no harm done, still in their splendid uniforms, their glittering helmets, ready to receive his laughing congratulations: "A tough enemy! You gave me some trouble! Better luck next time!" But now this was in earnest. There was a real enemy. Statistics, ballistics, food, fodder and reinforcements ruled the day. The pageantry had gone. There would be no banquet after the battle, no speeches. It was kill or be killed. To the depths of his soul William shuddered and longed to escape.

In this mood William received a report from London—incorrect, as it happened—that Grey had promised British neutrality if Germany did not attack France. At once William sent for Moltke. Let the plan be changed, he suggested, the troops be sent East instead of West. . . . One can well imagine Moltke's feelings. There must have been a very long pause. Did William not realize that years of planning had gone into these preparations, that a vast and fully equipped army could not simply be told "right-about turn" and be sent marching to Russia? Apparently he did not. "In that case," said Moltke, "Your Majesty would no longer command an army, but a disorderly rabble." But still William did not understand. He thought of the famous Moltke, the General who had defeated France in 1870, and truculently he retorted: "Your uncle would have given me a different answer."

But Moltke had his way. The button was pressed. On 2nd August, the German armies started to pour through Belgium while Bethmann, in a never-to-be-forgotten phrase, called the German guarantee of Belgian neutrality a "scrap of paper". This scrap of paper brought British public opinion solidly behind the Government and two days later, after an ultimatum to Germany had expired, Britain declared war. In London, on that 4th August, the German Ambassador took leave of Sir Edward Grey. Lichnovsky had long foreseen that in a continental war England could not remain neutral at the risk of French defeat. But his warnings had been suavely dismissed. Long ago, the Foreign Secretary had stated the core of British anxiety at German naval armaments: if the Royal Navy were defeated at sea the German Army could have Britain for the asking. But his words had gone unheeded, and William with Tirpitz was planning to build forty-one battleships by 1920. Now, overwhelmed with futility, Grey and Lichnovsky wept in each other's arms. There was a last message from Grey. He explained again why Britain could not stand aside, but added that any intention of crushing Germany lay far from him. But William was terrified and amazed. He had never believed that Britain would actually draw the sword. Surely the ties of kinship were paramount? Surely they could realize, over there, that his battleships were only a symbol, that his dearest wish was merely to sail them over the Channel to some peace-time review, reap the envious plaudits of his cousins and then raise his bubbling glass to peace under the protection of the German Kaiser?

It was all a mistake. "Could I ever have dreamt," he told his friends, "that Nicolas and Georgie would deceive me? If my grandmother had been alive, *she* would never have allowed this!" On Grey's last message he scribbled: "Slippery as an eel! Hypocritical liar!" He surrendered his titles of British Field-Marshal and Admiral of the Fleet and then ominously, but with a hint of pride in his British blood, spoke to the American Ambassador: "The British alter the whole situation. A stubborn nation. They will keep the war going."

But in those first days of the war there was one consolation. For the time being his people stood behind him as never before. "I know no longer any parties," he cried, "but only Germans!" This matched the popular mood. Dissension, criticism, the memory of his past follies which the Press had not forgotten—all dissolved. The slate was clean. This was a new start. The unity which he had failed to create was now forged—overnight—in the crucible of war. William could not lead in the field, admittedly, but he could harangue the troops, study the maps, shuttle in the royal train between East and West with boxes of decorations and cigarettes for the soldiers. He could urge his commanders on: "Forward! Forward!"—and so for a time perhaps silence that inner voice which told him that the last shreds of his personal power were being scattered in the gale of the world.

CHAPTER THIRTEEN

WORLD WAR

THE German people entered war with feelings of absolute confidence. They had the best army in the world and the army had a plan of robust and brutal simplicity. It would all be over in six weeks. While a thin screen held the Russians, the bulk of the German forces, outnumbering the French by 350,000 men, would sweep through Belgium and on towards Paris. In the South, unsuitable country for wide deployment, the enemy would be contained. Northwards, four armies would press forward like a giant windscreen-wiper pivoting on Metz. On the right flank the First Army under von Kluck would move anti-clockwise round Paris and then turn East to encircle the main French forces and drive them to their destruction. With France prostrate, the German juggernaut would then be transferred eastwards to deal at leisure with the Russian Bear.

This was the Schlieffen Plan, evolved in 1905, officially adopted in 1912 and applied with modifications by Moltke in August, 1914. It worked with terrifying precision. While the French were struggling to get an army into Belgium, believing that the fortress of Namur would survive for a fortnight, the line which they proposed to hold was crumbling under the German tide. Liège fell, and Namur after a bombardment of four days. The first British troops, regular soldiers fresh from their transports, met the Germans at Mons, fell back, again at Le Cateau, the French were defeated at Charleroi, then the places fell thick and fast: Douai, Cambrai, St. Quentin, Amiens—names which were to burn in men's minds for a generation. The British were cut off from the Channel ports. The French were still retreating. The Germans crossed the Aisne, took Rheims, reached the Marne, crossed the Marne, their advance guards could already see the Eiffel Tower, while cavalry patrols were groping towards the forest of Fontainebleau south of Paris.

In Berlin, meanwhile, at his palace by the banks of the Spree,

Kaiser William was feeling impotent in the widest sense of the word, the victim of forces beyond his control. These victories in the West were very fine, they filled him with exultant glee: on the other hand, they had been planned and were now being won without him. That hurt his feelings as War Lord, though he well knew he could never command in the field. His agitation would be too great, his nerves would play tricks, the bloodshed would excite and exhaust him. Even the victories, therefore, were tinged with melancholy, until the moment came—surely not long distant?—when Germany's laurels could be laid at *his* feet and he could congratulate Moltke on having carried out *his* orders.

Meanwhile, the news from the East was bad. The Russians had entered East Prussia. Though this was not his fault, William could not help feeling guilty. Out there, facing the barbarian hordes, his commander's name was von Prittwitz—a key to memory. Captain Prittwitz it was who had saved Frederick the Great at Kunersdorf, a hundred years before William was born, another battle against the Russians where the heroic King had struck with inferior numbers, led his troops into battle, had two horses killed under him. What glorious deeds on that day! Frederick had been defeated, but he had stayed on the stricken field until, some Cossacks approaching, Prittwitz had seized the King's bridle and galloped with him to safety. The Russians, though victory was theirs, had been too dazed to follow it up. Kunersdorf—and this was its anniversary, 12th August, and here William was sitting, while the Russians were again advancing, at a small table on his palace lawn, gazing down into the placid waters of the Spree with two plump dachshunds at his feet.

Some days later, the news from the East was even worse. The Germans were retreating behind the Vistula. For an hour and a half William walked with his aides in the blackest of moods. Finally he sat down on a garden seat and invited them to rest. They fetched another bench. "Do you despise me so much," said William, "that none of you will even sit down beside me?"

But there were other worries in these days, bright though they were with the swift advance. The word "England" still ground in William's mind like a knife, the treachery of his kinsmen, that utterly unwarrantable declaration of war.

He was worried, too, about his fleet. The British were ranging the North Sea. Ingenohl, the commander of the German High Seas Fleet, was burning to have at them. That would never do. Sixteen German heavy units were opposed to twenty-four British. In each one of his battleships William had a special cabin perpetually reserved for him with the walls covered with pictures of his loved ones and toilet articles laid out ready for use. To risk these ships would be like risking a part of himself. Anxiously he conferred with Tirpitz. The Grand Admiral was in two minds. His warrior's soul was aflame. It was difficult to persuade him that the German fleet must be kept intact as a counter at the coming peace negotiations. But finally the Admiral agreed. And a week later the justification for William's caution was there: British warships penetrated the Heligoland Bight, sank three small cruisers without loss. At once, William was bristling with reproaches: the German ships had been badly handled, Tirpitz had designed them wrongly, Ingenohl had been asleep. What would the German people think of him, William, the Admiral of the Atlantic?

At an early stage—to be precise, in the first week of war—the members of William's household watched him swing between gloom and euphoria and decided that his spirits must be kept up at all costs. There was only one way to achieve this: feed him with favourable news and dilute or suppress the rest. For the moment this was not difficult and the process seemed justified. But it was alarming to see how William seized on any hopeful information, however unreliable, from whatever source, with the trembling eagerness of a drug-addict and horrifying to hear him wallowing in gory details: piles of corpses six feet high, the N.C.O. who had killed twenty-seven of the enemy with forty-five rounds, and a hillside blue with the képis of fallen Frenchmen. The blood-bath became a regular feature of his day, the moment when he would launch off into horror-stories to ease the tension of his mind. Where did he get these tales? No one knew. In all, the Kaiser was not only agitated—which could be excused—but his mind swam far below the level of events. He lacked the stamina even for a short, six weeks' sprint.

The sprint ended in early September. In the East, the sixty-seven-year-old Hindenburg had been fetched from retirement and with Colonel Ludendorff as his chief of staff had won two brilliant victories over the Russians at Tannenberg and near the Masurian Lakes. For the moment, East Prussia was safe. But in the West, for reasons which will never be entirely analysed, the Germans drew back over the Marne and the Aisne. There was a gap between the first and second armies. Both had come a long way, the troops were exhausted, supplies were running short. They were under attack from the French. General Headquarters were too far back, nearly 200 miles away in Luxembourg, and this before the days when wireless or field telephones were efficient. Moltke did not possess the clear and forceful temperament of a great commander. Moreover, he was a sick man. Finally, when the dislocation of his forces was reported to him, he did not go to the front himself, but sent a subordinate with full powers to order advance or retreat. This man, Colonel Hentsch, is also said to have been sick, suffering from kidney trouble. Exploring the twenty-five-mile gap on the right wing he is said to have come across a German cavalry patrol which he took for Frenchmen. At any rate, he ordered a withdrawal—a temporary one for regrouping—and at the time this was believed to be merely a check before final victory. But it was, in fact, the turning-point of the war. Ahead stretched a vista of mud and blood in the trenches, four years of mortal combat ending in the collapse of Imperial Germany.

The champagne was over. From now on, Germany was to drink a bitter cup. In France, the rival armies raced for the Channel coast, each trying to outflank the other. Neither succeeded. Then they dug in, a mass of artillery was brought up and they awoke to the fact that modern weapons favoured the defence more than the attack. The lines solidified, the troops dug deeper into the earth and the long process of mutual attrition started. In the East, in Poland, Galicia and the Carpathians, the Austro-Hungarian army composed of seven nationalities, among them Slavs whose spiritual home was with the enemy, failed to hold the Russian tide. Reinforcements had to be sent and a steady drain began on German manpower. Italy, which Count Schlieffen had expected to be an ally, declared her neutrality and actually withdrew troops from the frontier with France, releasing French forces for employment further north. Japan declared war on Germany and occupied Kiau-chau. Britain commanded the seas and enforced a stringent blockade. The German merchant fleet was swept from the oceans of the world. One by one, her colonies in two hemispheres fell like ripe plums to the British, the French and the Japanese. Worst of all, the United States, deeply shocked by the rape of Belgium and stories of German frightfulness against the conquered population, suspicious of Teutonic militarism and fearful for her overseas markets, was supplying material and moral support to the Allies. It would be a long and bitter struggle. How was Germany placed to sustain it?

The first flush of victory had obscured some uncomfortable facts. The French and the British knew precisely why they were fighting, but what were Germany's war aims? What was the great prize which warranted the onslaught and could outweigh the moral censure of the whole world? Inept diplomacy had put Germany in the wrong and however sincerely her leaders believed that the Fatherland was threatened, to neighbouring countries the reverse seemed to be the case. It was they who were threatened, they who were the victims of the *Furor Teutonicus*. It was impossible, perhaps, to explain to the German people what they were fighting for because the Government and the military were not agreed on their war aims. Security was a colourless word, conquest was too brutal, yet perhaps security could not be achieved without it. The fact remained that except temporarily in the East foreign troops stood nowhere on German soil. The threat was not apparent. Was the war then being fought merely for the Hohenzollerns, for the glory and perpetuation of the Imperial dynasty?

This was a teasing suspicion and touched another thorny problem. Basically the German people were not united. The war had struck them at a time of political unrest. Among the working population and the left-wing parties in the Reichstag demand for democratic reform was growing. There were no signs yet of parliamentary government, but the pressure was strong. The people of a modern industrial State could not permanently be excluded from an effective voice in their affairs. But this whole process of change was blocked by the war. The lid was clamped down on political aspirations and the people were left with hopes and vague promises to be fulfilled after a victory which each year seemed more remote.

Only the Germans' innate discipline, their patriotism and their military tradition sustained them. They were in a war, so they would have to fight it and, once in, the threat to their national existence was plain enough if they lost. But they had to believe that they were going somewhere, that the sacrifice and suffering were worthwhile. An inspiration was needed, a star to cling to, a rallying point for their idealism and fervour. This only the Kaiser could supply. This was the moment, if ever, when he should sink himself in the national cause. Boundless wells of devotion were waiting to be tapped. He enjoyed the limelight, why did he not make use of it to spur, encourage and show his people that he was one with them in their trial? But William was a broken reed.

There were three men who guarded William from the outside world, the chiefs of his naval, military and civil cabinets. They were the last link in the chain of government, political and military, which on paper still culminated in him. Here the final weakness in war-time Germany arose. In all countries, the organization of the war effort in such unprecedented circumstances was clumsy and inefficient. But in Germany a War Lord who did not command and an ultimate arbiter who could not make up his mind wrecked all cohesion from the start. There was no proper co-ordination anywhere. Military and naval plans were never concerted, the politicians and the soldiers seldom sat at the same table, there was no commanding mind in charge of affairs, all this because the fiction was maintained that the Kaiser held the reins in his hands.

But where was the Kaiser, where could he be found? Immense

journeys were made by the Chancellor, the admirals and by Moltke's successor, Falkenhayn, to William on the West front, William on the East, and William, finally, in the snuggest of hide-outs at an immense castle in Upper Silesia only to find the faithful male nurses, the cabinet chiefs, with long faces and whispered advice: "Let us solve the problems amongst ourselves and then we need not disturb His Majesty."

The lack of central direction was most apparent in the U-boat war. In the early months, astonishing successes had been scored against British warships. Tirpitz, who at first had underestimated the new weapon, now became an ardent supporter of all-out submarine war. The British blockade of Germany seemed to justify this. If Germans were to be starved into surrender, why not England? In February, 1915, Germany declared the waters round the British Isles and Ireland to be a war zone in which merchant ships would be destroyed "without it always being possible to ensure the safety of the crew and passengers" or to distinguish between belligerent and neutral vessels. In the following months a number of American ships were sunk. Then, on 7th May, the 31,000-ton *Lusitania* in passage from New York to England was torpedoed without warning off the south coast of Ireland, 1,200 passengers, including 100 Americans, losing their lives. America protested sharply against this and the previous sinkings, claiming the right to send her ships where she chose without molestation and to protect American citizens on the high seas. Obviously, if Germany did not modify her submarine policy, this might lead to dangerous incidents and ultimately to war. The Germans were faced with a fateful decision in which political and military considerations overlapped. How did they cope with the problem?

Tirpitz and the admirals were already at loggerheads with the Chancellor over what they considered to be his feeble policy. Bethmann wanted to stop the war spreading and if possible achieve a negotiated peace. Falkenhayn favoured any means of preventing American munitions reaching Britain, and William's Chief of Naval Cabinet, a key figure, was mainly concerned to patch over the incipient quarrel and spare his master the necessity of intervening. In fact, it was a week before William even heard of the American note and a further ten days before a reply, over which he was not consulted, was sent, contending that the *Lusitania* had been carrying troops and munitions.

On 11th June, a second American note was received rejecting the principle of sink-at-sight on which some U-boats were operating. Meanwhile, U-boat policy was being acrimoniously discussed. The Kaiser was at Pless in Upper Silesia, the Chancellor 300 miles away in Berlin. Bethmann wanted to stop the sinking of neutral ships to placate America. From Berlin, Tirpitz and Bachmann, the naval Chief of Staff, hastened to Pless to enlist William's support against Bethmann. They arrived in the evening when the Kaiser was playing cards and he refused to interrupt the game. Next day, a heated discussion took place, William utterly unrealistic and suddenly declaring that his "conscience" forbade him to spare neutral ships. Result: the admirals were to go back to Berlin and sort out the problem with Bethmann. They need never have come.

For a whole month the argument continued. Neither the politicians nor the admirals would give way. Falkenhayn, who had enough to do directing the German armies, was brought in as mediator so that the Kaiser should not be faced with having to make a decision. This was in vain. As the naval men would not listen to him, Bethmann asked Müller, the Chief of Naval Cabinet, to draft a reply to the second American note. Bethmann liked the draft, Tirpitz did not. Again he descended on Pless—"not very tactful", noted Müller in his diary. Again he was sent back to Berlin to seek a compromise solution with the Chancellor, and at the end of his tether, William besought the faithful Müller to follow after to ensure that the sailors and politicians did not again "get in each other's hair". In Berlin, Müller campaigned for the Chancellor. A new reply was drafted—which all approved except the Foreign Secretary. Then the issue was raised whether Germany should concede free passage for certain British ships in return for an equal number of German. The sailors liked this, the politicians did not, thinking that the *quid pro quo* should be dropped. Müller urged the Chancellor to put his foot down; this after all was primarily a political matter. Bethmann said he would try.

Meanwhile, a telegram had come from a German banker in New York warning that the Americans were in ugly mood. This was reinforced by shipowner Albert Ballin who had been talking to an American journalist. He suggested a more conciliatory reply. The sailors would have none of it—and now it was 3rd July, three weeks after the American note had been received: deadlock. It was finally broken by the American Ambassador himself who helped the Foreign Under-Secretary to draft the reply to his own Government suggesting free passage for specially marked ships sailing under the American flag. With sombre thoughts, Müller, who had been too long away from his patient, hastened back to Pless. At last a reply to America had been sent and he reported the fact. But the Kaiser was quite uninterested, except to find a scapegoat. He seemed to think the delay and ineptitude in dealing with the matter was the fault of Bachmann, the naval Chief of Staff. The fellow must be dropped.

"In that position," he said, "I must have a man who is personally devoted to me."

So William excluded himself from the most crucial decisions and worse, in this bloodiest of wars, the position of father-figure, so vital to the nation's morale, fell vacant. In the peaceful glades and tapestried chambers of Pless he sought, but could find no rest. The days passed in dreadful monotony, sawing wood in the mornings, in the evenings playing cards or gazing abstractedly into the fire. And this was the Imperial Headquarters, the focus, supposedly, of the entire war effort. His officers felt sorry for him and tried to cheer him with praise. What splendid work he had done developing the army in those pre-war days! Yes, replied William, and he felt deeply hurt that the army had forgotten all he had taught it—hence the present high losses. No, he was too clever to fall for this flattery. No one really appreciated him. He had visited the West front and the East, but the visits had not been a success. The commanders, he sensed, had felt he was in the way and the troops, for some reason, had become restless when he had told them to take no prisoners, but grind the enemy in the dust, *"Schlagt möglichst viele von den Schweinen tot"*. Sometimes he felt there was a conspiracy to ignore him. "The General Staff," he complained to his cousin Max von Baden, "tells me nothing and asks me nothing. If people in Germany imagine that I lead the army they greatly deceive themselves. I drink tea, saw wood, go for walks and from time to time hear this or that has been done, just as the gentlemen choose."

But behind this pique lay a deeper fear. William's whole *Weltanschauung* was collapsing. For a quarter of a century he had danced in the limelight with the German people as a back-cloth to his performance. Now the cloth with its painted figures was lifting. Behind were creatures of flesh and blood, locked in mortal combat with a dynamism and a destiny of their own. A great drama was unfolding. The stage was filled with clamour and to his horror William found himself edged into the wings as a figure not essential to the plot, not synonymous with Germany, a character, in fact, that could be cut from the story altogether without altering the essential outline of victory or defeat. His feelings were those of a humiliated actor. He was no longer interested in the play, except perhaps in its denouement when the triumphant, sweaty warriors would move forward, grasping their defeated enemies by the hair, and cast the victory at their Emperor's feet, chanting in chorus: Belgium—Flanders—Lithuania—Malta—the Falkland Islands—the Azores—Dakar—Valona shall be German!

Meanwhile the drama had to be endured. The military men were glad to give their War Lord credit for their victories and he was delighted to steal their thunder. The Imperial train shuttled between East and West. Hindenburg had finally driven the Russians from German soil. The Kaiser prolonged his stay: "I wish to be the liberator of East Prussia, otherwise it will be seen as just another feat of Hindenburg's." In the West, he lectured troops about the Eastern campaign, telling them how at critical moments in the battle he had given direct orders to the Field-Marshal.

Falkenhayn, during this summer of 1915, was directing his main effort against Russia, believing that in France, where the Allies now had superiority in men and material, no decision could be reached until Russia was decisively weakened. Italy had declared war on Austria in May, Turkey had joined the Central Powers at the end of 1914. By defeating the Russians, Falkenhayn could relieve the Austrian ally and then finally crush Serbia, thereby opening a direct land-route through Bulgaria to Constantinople.

These plans were brilliantly fulfilled. The Germans under Mackensen broke through the Russian front in Poland and advanced towards Warsaw. In Pless, where the Empress had just arrived to ensure that William was not over-exerting himself, news was received that Modlin, north-west of Warsaw, was about to fall. The place was a formidable fortress. At once, William had visions of the keys being handed over to him by the governor—scene for an historical painting. He would visit Modlin. At 9 p.m. the royal train set off on its twelve-hour journey. William sat down to cards. He was always happy in railway trains, the movement soothed him. This evening, too, he was winning and to win at cards always put him in an excellent mood. In the middle of the game, Falkenhayn entered the compartment: "Just reported that Modlin is in Your Majesty's hands." Splendid, and the game continued. Next day the royal party alighted at the railway terminus north of Modlin and transferred to waiting motor-cars. Hindenburg was there to greet his Sovereign, but was not invited to accompany him. On through deserted villages and abandoned enemy positions William roared towards his historic moment. The fortress came in view, nearby an exhausted, dust-caked body of German troops. William addressed them: "The Great King"—Frederick, of course—"is gazing down through a gap in the clouds. . . ." Onward then, before the troops could recover from their surprise, to the fortress itself. Unfortunately it was still in enemy hands. . . .

The year 1915 ended with Germany's position considerably improved. Bulgaria was now an ally. The Serbs had been defeated. Austria had held the Italians, the British had tried and failed to seize the Dardanelles, and it was believed that Russia was now incapable of taking the offensive. But in the West, the decisive theatre, the war was no nearer a decision and a ferocious Franco-British onslaught had taught Falkenhayn an important lesson. Despite massed artillery which had flattened the German positions the Allies had made little progress and it was clear that to achieve a breakthrough in 1916 the Germans would have to use men and materials in quantities they did not possess. Instead, Falkenhayn decided to attack Verdun, attracting the flower of the French army there and bleeding it to death at smaller cost. This, he hoped, would knock "England's sword" from her hand and, combined with an intensified U-boat campaign, make her ripe for peace.

This plan was clearly a gamble, but it seemed the only way of ending the war in 1916 and Falkenhayn feared that Austria and Turkey would fall out by the autumn. The attack was launched in February but on too narrow a front and this, combined with heavy snow and the resolution of the French, brought it to a halt after three days. A slogging match then started, both sides suffering fearful losses, the ghastly drama mounting to a tragedy in which national honour and pride were thrown on both sides into the scale.

The U-boat question now became acute. Falkenhayn backed by the admirals wanted a sink-at-sight policy, hoping to destroy four million tons of shipping a year and starve Britain into surrender. Germany, they said, could not stand a long war and they added that not only the nation but the dynasty was at stake. This was a new and to William's ears an ominous note. But he did not argue the point. He knew well enough that the monarchy and the constitution allied to it would not survive defeat. Bethmann, on the other hand, viewed an all-out U-boat campaign as a desperate measure not required by the circumstances and certain to bring America and perhaps the smaller European neutrals into the war with the result that it would be prolonged into a struggle of mutual exhaustion. He, too, said that Germany's position as a great power and the fate of the Hohenzollerns were at stake.

Here was a conflict of opinion that only the War Lord could resolve. But this was the very kind of situation which William could not face. He knew it and his advisers knew it. Forced to choose between Bethmann and Falkenhayn he would have had a nervous collapse. That might mean a regency and in war-time particularly young Crown Prince William holding the reins would be a disaster. So the conflict was never fought out. Anxious intermediaries canvassed the rival parties and a compromise was reached before they were received by the Kaiser. On the eve of the meeting he was given to understand that he would be spared the necessity of choosing between his Chief of Staff and his Chancellor. With great relief, we are told, "he withdrew to his bomb-proof bedroom" and at the meeting next day he was calm and factual—because he already knew what the upshot would be: U-boat war against armed merchant ships for a month after which the position would be reviewed.

But despite the best efforts of soldiers and politicians, William did not escape from this situation unscathed. He was left now with Falkenhayn's warning ringing in his ears and a few days later it was repeated, reinforced by proffered resignation. This was refused. Tirpitz, on the other hand, who also asked to resign when U-boat policy was again modified under pressure from the United States, was allowed to go. William now felt abandoned. Everyone, he complained, was turning against him—everyone that is, who was a free agent. That did not include the German people. He took their support for granted. He was their Kaiser. They were clay in his hands and nothing enraged him more than to be told that the people would like to hear he was in Berlin at the centre of affairs, or that he was taking an interest in their food problems, receiving members of the Reichstag or visiting hospitals. "What do I care," he said, "what the people think?"

Dangerous words! But the Kaiser had found a new nest, Homburg, where he felt happier even than at Pless. To this retreat he grappled with the desperation of growing hysteria. Ailments of every kind—colds, tonsilitis, stiff neck, stomach upsets—came to his aid. Until he was completely better he could not move, whether to Berlin or elsewhere, and the ailments proved curiously tenacious. There was comfort of a kind beside his wife within the walls of the massive castle, but war business dogged him even there and his aides seemed to go out of their way to annoy him by retailing rumours circulating in the country, the one, for instance, that he had become a pietist and was spending hours each day on his knees in a chapel. They knew these stories were not true, therefore why repeat them? They knew he did not spend his days in a chapel, but taking motor trips in the countryside, shooting stags and studying the language of the Hittites—that, he had told them when they protested, was just as important as the whole war.

There were other signs in these months that William's mind was collapsing into confusion. The swing between apathy and unwarranted elation became more violent. Newspaper reports of war-weariness in France or political difficulties in England were enough to release foaming boasts about the German eagle striking its claws into enemy territory and a dictated peace. "If the English will not clear out voluntarily from German South West Africa we will send an expedition there and throw them out!" To ex-Chancellor Bülow, invited for the last time in his life to dine with

His Majesty, William revealed his plans for Belgium. He would not depose the King, he was a legitimist. Albert too was a monarch by the Grace of God. But of course he would have to dance to William's tune. "I picture the future relationship," he said, "like that of the Khedive of Egypt to the King of England." With barely a transition William then switched the conversation to the castle at Pless. He felt very happy there. The owner had fitted the wash-stands with fringed oil-cloth, a delightful touch which he meant to introduce in the royal residences.

Throughout this time, royalist feeling was steadily declining in Germany. In July, Falkenhayn called off the Verdun offensive after a loss of 240,000 men. In the previous week, the British army, now of 600,000 supported by twenty-five French divisions, had begun a deadly onslaught on the Somme, battering the German positions for a week with massed artillery before launching an assault supported with tanks. In East Galicia in June the Russian tide—so confidently thought to be broken—had flowed forward again, over-whelmed the weak Austrian defences and swallowed 200,000 prisoners. On both fronts the situation was critical. Resources were strained to the utmost and it became clear that time was not on Germany's side. The Allies' industrial potential was greater, they had larger reserves of manpower and, unlike blockaded Germany, they had access to the raw materials of the world.

All this could not be concealed from thinking Germans and they began to wonder how even a tolerable peace could be achieved. Defeat on one front was enough to bring disaster, but success on two fronts was necessary to victory. Meanwhile, Germany was barely holding her own. To do more than this would require not only tenacity, but a ruthless determination to mobilize the country's moral and material resources, devise new tactics and weapons, improve the training of the troops—and this in a Germany already suffering from food shortage, crass profiteering, industrial unrest and political divisions. A new spirit was needed. In these circum-stances thoughts turned from the Kaiser and began to rove com-pulsively in search of a national leader.

William was very upset when the appointment was urged of Hindenburg as supreme commander in the East. A sixth sense told him that this massive figure would overshadow the monarchy. The way in which men spoke of Hindenburg, the light in their eyes, the confidence in their voices filled him with jealous foreboding. And when they said that the *people* wanted this leader, that was the last straw. What did he care about the mood in Berlin? If he appointed Hindenburg he might as well abdicate at once. Hindenburg was inseparable from Ludendorff, the dinosaur and the dynamo, and

Ludendorff's plebeian face, his uncourtly manners, his implacable energy filled William with fear and disgust. Forceful men always frightened him and it offended him profoundly to sense that Ludendorff would be fighting not for the monarchy but for the German people. On the other hand, Hindenburg's very presence was an affront: his natural dignity, his imposing features, his Olympian calm. This man was the born father-figure, a statue of monolithic proportions, bronze brought to life. He was a challenge to the whole act which William had been playing for thirty years: nature's monarch confronting the monarch by primogeniture. And he had no withered arm.

But protest was futile. William went for long walks alone, retired to bed with stiff neck and queasy stomach, but the issue dogged him and when the Austrians actually asked for Hindenburg as supreme commander William caved in—and then felt happier. The monarchy, he had been told, could not survive a lost war unless Hindenburg was called to the helm.

When the nation's heroes had stemmed the Russian tide, the next step, their appointment to the supreme command in the West, was inevitable. In August, 1916, Rumania declared war on Austria and prepared to invade the rich cornlands of Hungary. The threat was serious. Two days later, Hindenburg was made Chief of the General Staff as successor to Falkenhayn with Ludendorff as Quartermaster-General and Falkenhayn was dispatched to deal with the Rumanians. He succeeded brilliantly, and a sigh of relief went up from the German people as Father Hindenburg with his familiar spirit took the reins in his powerful hands.

But nothing could conceal the fact that the military prospects were gloomy. In the Supreme Command it was realized that an outright victory in the West was most improbable. The only factors that could break the stalemate were the collapse of Russia and a successful U-boat campaign against England. But these were imponderables.

Meanwhile, though seeing no gleam at the end of the tunnel, Hindenburg and Ludendorff felt it their duty to equip Germany by every means for an indefinite continuance of the war and strengthen her forces to strike a decisive blow *if* the opportunity occurred. The "if" depended as much on the Allies as on Germany. Thus the catchword was "hope—and fight on". With their strong masochistic streak, this slogan appealed to the German people, moreover there were historical precedents. It was not only William who lived with the ghost of Frederick the Great. In time of trial all thoughts turned to Old Fritz, the heroic skeleton who had triumphed over a continent in arms.

At army headquarters on the Western front Ludendorff first studied the tactical situation. He found that front-line commanders were clinging to outworn and dangerous methods. In enemy attacks the creeping barrage, the obliteration of German forward defences had obviously come to stay. Yet the theory still prevailed that these, often consisting of a single line of trenches, must be held to the last man. Commanders were being sacked for the smallest surrender of ground. In consequence, they packed the front line with troops regardless of losses. One more battle of the Somme and German manpower would be bled white. All this was now abolished. In future, defence would be in depth consisting of large numbers of strong-points sited for the best arcs of fire and constructed with careful attention to thickness of concrete, thus offering only small and scattered targets to the enemy guns. Special units were set up to experiment with new weapons, including improved versions of the flame-thrower and the trench-mortar. The division was now made the battle unit with its own artillery. Training was intensified.

On the home front, a "Hindenburg programme" was introduced setting colossal targets in every sphere of war production with a special board to supervise the nation-wide effort, including agricultural output and the allocation of steel and coal. A law was passed conscripting all male civilians between the ages of seventeen and sixty. A large increase in the army was planned for 1917. Belgian workers were brought in to swell the labour force. Scientists were spurred on to find synthetic substitutes for materials in short supply.

All this could not be achieved, of course, without drastic interference in the political sphere and in many cases only half-measures were possible because the Government resented the soldiers' dictatorship. In the Reichstag the Conscription Bill was watered down to a law that Ludendorff called "neither fish nor fowl". Workers were still free to change their jobs. Wages were allowed to sky-rocket. Profiteering was not stamped on. The food rationing system was not simplified with the result that the black market flourished and no one knew when he was breaking the law. Above all, despite their efforts, Hindenburg and Ludendorff were unable to rally the whole nation to their all-out effort. The reason was simple: neither the Government, headed by Bethmann, nor the Reichstag with its majority of left-wing deputies was behind them. So a rift gradually began to develop between the spirit of the soldiers who fought blindly on and the morale on the home front where the workers under the influence of their political leaders saw the war, not as a life-and-death struggle for Imperial Germany, but as a chance to free themselves of its shackles and acquire rights and liberties.

There was disgust with the Imperial destiny, that *Reichsverdros-senheit* which had so aggravated William in previous years and first among the disenchanted was the Chancellor himself. Bethmann, noted the soldiers, had no feeling for the "greatness of the times". He was a pessimist swamped with cares and infected with only one longing: peace. Already in August, 1916, he was telling his friends that Germany would have to seek a compromise before her conquests were wrested from her. He was flirting, too, with the left-wing Socialists whose cry was for peace without annexations and universal brotherhood. This filled Ludendorff with rage. No concessions, he claimed, should be made to democracy as long as the war lasted. The Reichstag was merely a talking-shop filled with egotistic nonentities who professed to represent the masses but in fact served only their own ambitions. The masses needed leadership. A strong hand—and then everything would be possible. Bethmann, said Ludendorff, would have to go.

The struggle against Bethmann was slow to develop. That it was brewing was common knowledge, except to William. But unconsciously he was already taking sides. Allied to Hindenburg he would have no chance to shine; with the harassed Bethmann, on the other hand, he never had difficulty in scoring at least those little conversational victories which gave him the illusion of power.

So Bethmann was a comfort and doubly so because he did not confront the Kaiser with those stark alternatives of victory or disaster for which Ludendorff was gearing the people. If there was a way out, Bethmann would find it, and then: a pleasant dream—William announcing to the bare-headed populace, still reeling from their efforts, that Germany had come to terms with England, the whole thing had been a mistake, they were to return to their homes, go down on their knees and thank God for the German Emperor. Meanwhile, it was pleasant to force Hindenburg or Ludendorff to take long journeys to report to him at Pless. They were trying to pocket him, he could see that. But he had no intention of joining them at their headquarters in the West where he would "only be Hindenburg's adjutant". And anyway, that was unnecessary. Hindenburg, as he told his astonished courtiers, took Ludendorff's advice and Ludendorff merely did what he, the Kaiser, told him.

From now on William was caught between two mill-stones: the soldiers on the one hand, the Reichstag on the other. Slowly they ground him to powder. His last free action as German Kaiser was a peace offer to the enemy Powers in December, 1916. It contained no mention of the restoration of Belgium and was doomed to rejection from the start. Copies of the German Note to the Allies were sent to all neutral countries and to the Pope. In a published letter full of childish vanity William had instructed Bethmann to prepare the wording: "A deed of this kind requires a Ruler who possesses a conscience, feels responsible to God, has compassion for his own and the enemy peoples and, caring nothing for misinterpretation, has the will to free the world from its sufferings. For this I have the courage! In God's name I will risk it! Quickly lay the Notes before me and make everything ready." Meanwhile, the last available reserves had been thrown in to stop the enemy on the Somme, two forts at Verdun which had cost a sea of blood to capture were lost again to the French.

In January, 1917, came an ultimatum from Ludendorff: the U-boats must sink without warning all ships, neutral or belligerent, approaching Great Britain. The soldiers, the sailors, the German people were demanding it. This time, William was quickly convinced. There was a solid phalanx opposing Bethmann and he had no energy to support him. "Good God, has the man still got objections?" was his attitude at the Crown Council when the fateful decision was reached. Soon after he was noting on a telegram from Washington which foretold war with America: "It's all the same to me."

Within a year or possibly six months Ludendorff believed that Britain would be forced to her knees. No American troops, he calculated, could reach France before 1918. Meanwhile, on land the German forces must be built up for the final blow. As the U-boat commanders round the British coasts opened their secret instructions, William retired to bed with a hernia. An operation was performed and he was very gay during this time: for a whole week he refused to discuss war business and for a month he never set eyes on Hindenburg. For convalescence he retired to Homburg where a large suite of ladies and gentlemen and forty horses in the stables gave the illusion of an active life. But nothing could conceal the fact that, for this most fateful decision of his reign, he had been used as a rubber stamp.

The U-boat gamble failed, but only by a hair's-breadth, and despite America's declaration of war in April, 1917, other events seemed to justify the military in their uncompromising policy. By August, the Russian revolution removed all danger from the East, releasing forty German divisions for use on the Western front. Ludendorff calculated that for a few months in 1918 he would have superiority there—long enough perhaps to snatch victory.

Meanwhile in March the German line had been shortened by a withdrawal to scientifically planned positions between Arras and Soissons. Their strength was proved in the summer and autumn when the British attacked without major success. Further south the

French under Joffre's successor, Nivelle, had also attacked—and met disaster. Mutiny had broken out and for some months the French army was crippled as a fighting force. Finally, the Italians had been routed at Caporetto.

But though the soldiers were still justified in hoping, the politicians had an equal right to claim that the people's privations now entitled them to control their own destinies. At home the food and coal shortage was acute. Everyone knew that Austria was tottering. Why should the German people troop like cattle into the fourth year of war in the name of a Kaiser who did not rule, for the sake of a system that had failed? The Russian revolution provided a theory and an example. In Germany the left wing of the moderate Socialists split off and pursued Communist aims. In the Reichstag demands were raised for a new democratic constitution. A constituent committee was set up and in April, 1917, as a sop to the political wolves, Bethmann persuaded William to promise reforms. This "Easter egg for the German people" as William fatuously called it, declared the Prussian franchise to be outmoded and held out vague hopes of "associating men who enjoy the respect of their fellow citizens" more closely with the Government. It satisfied no one. The constituent committee was now demanding that the Chancellor and his ministers be made responsible to the Reichstag and that army and navy appointments, hitherto the prerogative of the Kaiser, should require the approval of the minister concerned. These demands met with William's outraged refusal.

William's change of mood was duly noted by Ludendorff and he awaited his chance to secure the dismissal of Bethmann. It came in July when the Centrist deputy Matthias Erzberger made a sensational speech in the Reichstag in which he coupled the failure of the U-boat war and Germany's exhaustion with a demand for a peace resolution abjuring conquests and seeking a compromise peace. This move Ludendorff was determined to stifle and Hindenburg lumbered into action to support him. They threatened to resign if Bethmann was not dismissed and announced their intention of coming to Berlin to browbeat the Kaiser. William met them with a smile of petty triumph on his lips. He really did not know, he said, why they had bothered to come. The Chancellor had already offered to go and his resignation had been accepted.

So Bethmann faded out. William's staff fetched out the Almanach de Gotha and searched for a successor. Ludendorff wanted Tirpitz, alternatively Bülow, but William could not stomach the strong man or the "traitor". Finally, a modest little man was decided on, Georg Michaelis, a middle-class Prussian, an impeccable official totally ignorant of foreign affairs whom Ludendorff believed he could dominate and who William felt sure would steal none of his thunder. When approached, Michaelis clasped his hand to his head, thought for a moment, then said: "With God's help I will risk it." Soon he was struggling with the refractory Reichstag. He failed to stop the peace resolution, but William thought it very fine. It stated: "On the threshold of the fourth year of war the Reichstag steps out of its previous reserve and announces to the world its readiness for a peace honourable to all concerned. . . ." No offer of terms was made: that, it was stated, was a matter for the Government. But short of a revolution, no Government could satisfy the Allies' demands: the restoration of Belgium, the cession to France of Alsace and Lorraine, the abandonment of all occupied territory. Rather than cede these demands Ludendorff was prepared for Germany to go down in defeat.

CHAPTER FOURTEEN

IN A COLD, GREY DAWN

FROM the start, William's had been a truculent autocracy based on a claim of divine right in flagrant contradiction to the spirit of the age, a subject of mockery to some, of offence to others. In times of peace the joyous tyrant—tyrant in intention if not in fact—had ridden on the swelling tide of prosperity. His poses, his pageantry, his ceaseless self-advertisement had corresponded to similar exhibitionist urges in his people. Even so, Holstein had noted that William was living on royalist capital and it was a symptom of popular dissatisfaction that a booklet written towards the end of the century by a Munich professor drawing far-fetched analogies between William's temperament and Caligula's sold 150,000 copies in four weeks and earned its publishers 75,000 marks.

In war-time it was not surprising that after the first successes had congealed into bloody trench warfare William's popularity waned still further. In peace he had claimed the limelight as the embodiment of German power and now, though taking no share in military decisions, he inevitably incurred the odium for the increasing hardships and sacrifices. Worse, there was a dynamic element in the population which looked on him as its implacable enemy. From his accession William had faced the alternatives of allying herself with those sections of the Reichstag which sought a more genuine form of democracy or of ruthlessly opposing them. He did neither, neither attempting a coup such as Bismarck favoured nor a *Volkskaisertum*, a conservative democracy with monarchical head. He breathed fire at the opposition, but did not touch it. So it grew. From thirty-five Reichstag deputies in 1890, the Social Democrats increased their representation to eighty-one in 1903 and 110 in 1912. This meant that in the 1912 Reichstag which continued until the collapse only a left-wing coalition could command a majority.

Though condemned under the exigencies of war and the existing constitution to a life of speechifying without power, the Social

Democrats were conscious of growing popular support. Dissatisfaction at home, the example of the Russian revolution abroad, stalemate in the field and the increasing pressure of Allied propaganda against German militarism convinced them that the dawn of their opportunity was near. Only the dogged resistance of German troops in the field sustained the military dictatorship. Once the heavy hand of Ludendorff acting through Hindenburg was lifted, the explosive mixture so long held in check would burst out, sweep the constitution aside and turn the whole country into fire and flame.

The political ferment steadily increased. After less than four months in office Michaelis resigned to be replaced by the seventy-four-year-old Graf Hertling, a former professor of philosophy whose ability to cope with the Reichstag was compromised from the start by his Conservative past. The majority parties had demanded to be consulted before the appointment of the new Chancellor and asked that he should draft his programme in consultation with their leaders. But William considered this as evidence of "left-wing politics" which Ludendorff assured him "did not belong in the supreme conduct of affairs" and he thought the vague promise of post-war electoral reform which he had made at Easter a perfectly adequate concession to the mushroom of democracy.

Meanwhile, acting on the well-worn principle "*Majestät muss Sonne haben*", his staff continued to shield him from harsh realities and gave in to his doctor's warning that he was on the verge of nervous collapse. So William continued in isolation while a remorseless feud was fought out between the army command and the politicians. As long as the remotest chance of victory remained, the military held, of course, the upper hand and in January, 1918, William was compelled to dismiss his Chief of Civil Cabinet, Valentini, because Ludendorff alleged he was responsible for "the left-wing course of the Government". At Hindenburg, acting as Ludendorff's mouthpiece, William shouted: "I don't want your fatherly advice!" But then he gave in and soon after was rejoicing to be rid of Valentini who, he said, had been pressing him step by step to surrender the rights of the Crown.

With the German spring offensive in 1918 which led to the defeat of the British Fifth Army and an advance to within striking distance of Amiens there was a chance of victory in the West. The good news from the front swung William's mood from gloom to dizzy euphoria. In Spa he now ordered his bags to be packed at the shortest notice and set off for the front. Reaching Avesnes on 21st March, he showed himself to the troops, swallowed the champagne of their plaudits and returned, his head full of stars, calling out to the military guard on the royal train: "The battle is won, the English are totally defeated!" Three days later the therapy was repeated, William once more returned with splendid news and declared over a bubbling glass that if an English emissary arrived to ask for peace he would be made to kneel before the Imperial standard, for this was "a victory of monarchy over democracy".

These initial victories were described in the official bulletins as being won "under the personal command of His Majesty". William accepted this as a delicate compliment, or perhaps as the truth, for some days later he was questioning the phrase as suggesting that previous victories had *not* been gained under his command. But the point was academic, for July saw William listening pale-faced to Hindenburg who, with the unvarnished truth at last, told him that the great gamble had failed. That evening, William was warning his staff that he was a defeated War Lord and they must treat him gently. Next day, he complained that he had not slept at all. During the night all his English and Russian relatives and the Ministers and Generals from the whole period of his reign had trooped past him like a vision, some of them mocking him.

But thanks to the power of self-deception William recovered quickly and in less than a fortnight he was calling the German failure on the Marne, where a renewed attack had been defeated and the Anglo-French had resumed the offensive, one of the greatest defeats which the enemy had ever suffered.

But the new Allied assault was, in fact, decisive. German reserves were exhausted. Victory was now impossible. The line had to be shortened and at best it might be held for a while until it caved in under the sheer weight of numbers. This was the last chance for an armistice on equal terms and at a conference at Supreme Command headquarters in Spa on 13th August, the military urged the Chancellor to negotiate. But the aged Hertling had been appointed merely to keep the seat warm in the expectation of final victory and time was now wasted in unrealistic discussions as to conquered territory that might still be retained.

So, without any decisive approach to the Allies, September came and with it a series of hammer-blows. On the 8th, fearing that the Western front might collapse at any moment, Ludendorff in a state of nervous prostration demanded an immediate armistice. Bulgaria collapsed. Rumania re-entered the war on the side of the Allies. Austria appealed for peace and an Allied offensive in Macedonia made rapid progress.

In the midst of these cataclysmic events, William got the wander-lust again. Powerless to influence events, he sped nervously from Berlin to Essen and from Essen to Kiel on a programme of inspections and speeches. The Krupp workers he harangued for a good twenty minutes, to his satisfaction but not to theirs, calling for loyalty and a last effort. At Kiel he inspected the U-boat training school, then addressed 400 officers in the mess, starting on a factual theme, but ending in a process of auto-intoxication with the old cry of "forcing them to their knees" and with a neat little rhyme, coined apparently on the spur of the moment: *"Das Ziel erkannt, die Muskete gespannt, Flaumacher an die Wand"*—"Fix the goal, train the guns and defeatists to the wall". In late September, perceiving that the Reichstag was getting restive with the doddering Chancellor, William decided that it was Hertling's fault for being too feeble and declared: "The Chancellor should call a thunderous halt to the movement for parliamentary government. That means revolution, pure and simple, particularly after I have bound the Essen workers to me by oath. . . ."

But the movement for parliamentary government which William chose to treat as an exhibition of dangerous cussedness reflected, in fact, the basic problem of his reign, one which he had never tackled and was never to understand: how to reconcile a monarchical State according to Prussian tradition with a democratic constitution in keeping with modern social and intellectual needs. It was a problem of adaptation, of keeping pace in the political sphere with the enormous changes that had taken place in the daily lives and thoughts of the people and no sooner had William spoken than the Reichstag raised it again, demanding the resignation of the Hertling government. This was unconstitutional, but William, on advice, gave in for the sake of appearing to retain some freedom of action, promising at the same time to associate the people increasingly with the task of government. How and when? These questions were not answered.

On 3rd October, while the military situation rapidly deteriorated, Prince Max von Baden, a cousin of William's and heir to the Duchy, became Chancellor. On that same day, at the insistence of the Supreme Command, the Allies were contacted with a request for an armistice. The Chancellor had only one illusion. He knew that William must go, but he hoped to save the dynasty, in spite of the facts. These were simple: the monarchy could not continue to exist except on the basis of moderate constitutional change. But in the Reichstag there were too few moderates. Thus there were only two possibilities, reaction or revolution, and in fact—as the existing régime was discredited—only one: an upheaval, bloody or otherwise.

In raising the question of William's abdication, the Chancellor was not breaking new ground. Throughout the war, Allied propaganda had concentrated on the "War-Lord" as the symbol of all they were fighting against. At home, the people were disenchanted with theatricals, and the Press—never inclined to spare the person of the Kaiser—was making heavy innuendos. Many high-placed observers were recording in their diaries: the Kaiser must go. The only person who was seemingly unaware of these trends was the Kaiser himself. When Max von Baden raised the question of voluntary abdication on 6th October, he reacted with his usual braggadocio: "A successor of Frederick the Great does not abdicate!" Returning to his palace, however, William became thoughtful. Next day, his Chief of Civil Cabinet asked the Chancellor to treat the Kaiser gently: "he was considering abdication". Max replied: "In such serious times, no one can be treated gently, least of all the Kaiser."

Then, on 8th October, a new and dreaded factor arose. In reply to the German overtures, President Wilson inquired with whom he was dealing: the military autocrats or the representatives of the people? William saw the import at once. "The object of this," he said, "is to bring down my House!" From now on, his fevered mind barely distinguished between his cousin and the enemy. After 6th October he never saw his Chancellor face-to-face again. But while he stayed on in Berlin, sulking and unconsulted, fresh warnings were coming from Washington. The President now made it clear that negotiations could only be conducted with a new representative government. With Germany's "militaristic rulers and monarchical autocrats" only surrender could be discussed. Thus the enemy encouraged the extremists at home. Max von Baden began to fear an internal explosion. A typical newspaper comment came from the *Deutsche Zeitung*: "No one is too highly placed for us to bring him before the judgement-seat of history or to take upon himself the responsibility for recent cataclysmic events." The Kaiser had now become a scapegoat. Seeking an explanation of their plight, Germans fixed on William: to him they ascribed the disastrous war and the prospect of a savage peace. All who had failed were ripe for the axe. Ludendorff, too, was a stumbling-block. The Chancellor, seeking to open a safety valve for revolutionary pressure, threatened to resign if Ludendorff stayed. So the Quartermaster-General, the brain behind Germany's staggering military achievement, went, unmourned by William who, still seeing himself as a permanency, declared: "Let him go. It will ease my position."

But the Chancellor, for the sake of the dynasty, was bent on easing him out of it. He still hoped that, where personal persuasion had failed, the logic of facts would penetrate William's mind. He strove to bring home to him that among German royalists the monarchy was still respected, but not the monarch. Throughout his reign

William had been an insatiable talker. Now, nothing that he could say would make any impression. Late in October, when William issued a decree accepting a new order "transferring basic rights from the Kaiser to the people", the Chancellor suppressed it. A declaration to the Parliamentary Secretaries of State welcoming "a new order" was also withheld from the Press. The new order, as Prince Max but not the Kaiser realized, would have no place in it for William and from 24th October, when a third Note arrived from President Wilson refusing outright to negotiate with a monarchical Germany, he repeatedly sent intermediaries to the Kaiser urging immediate abdication.

Their pleas fell on deaf ears and on 29th October, without informing the Chancellor, William suddenly left for Supreme Headquarters at Spa. For six weeks he had been in Berlin, unconsulted, as he complained, "sitting there completely useless". Now he succumbed to a tropistic urge to cling to the one pillar of the régime which offered him security, the army. But even to Spa, where his arrival took his officers completely by surprise, the Chancellor's emissaries followed him. On 1st November, the Prussian Minister of the Interior arrived, proceeded—well aware of the probable reaction—to sound the Imperial feelings about abdication, tried to describe the situation, internal, external, the Press demanding the sacrifice, the Chancellor insistent, and now mutiny in the fleet at Wilhelmshaven. "I know it all!" William interrupted. "You don't need to tell me"— and proceeded to dress the Minister down, the "Prussian official", the "subject". The army was faithful, he said, "and if the slightest thing happens, I will write my answer to them with machine-guns, even if I have to shoot up my own palace. *Order there must be!!*" Very well, then, said the Minister, I take it that my visit is unnecessary and that I may leave? No, said the Kaiser. No, there is no harm in a talk. Let us go into the garden. So they paced in the garden, the Minister talked and, true to habit, William's mind began to perceive sunbeams where there was none. He seemed to think that this was not a discussion about objective reality, but a personal issue between him and the Minister. The Minister seemed to have worries. William with his charm would soothe them away. Finally, after half an hour, he smiled benevolently, clapped the fellow on the shoulder and invited him to lunch, saying that their little talk had been very beneficial and had cleared the air.

On 3rd November, the naval mutiny spread to Kiel and Hamburg. The sailors set up revolutionary councils and soon, supported it was said by Russian funds, were roving the whole of North Germany in bands, spreading revolt like wildfire. On the same day, William visited his troops in the field: decorations, speeches, cigarettes. . . .

In Berlin, meanwhile, the Chancellor was parleying under increasing pressure with the Social Democrats, trying to salvage the monarchy from the wreckage. They agreed that, once William had abdicated, he should act as regent for the eldest of his grandsons, but, no abdication forthcoming, they threatened on 8th November to abandon the Government and join the revolution. Max von Baden countered with a "democratic solution": William should appoint a regent immediately and agree to abdicate as soon as elections for a constituent assembly could be held. This was telephoned to William at Spa: he refused. That same morning, in fact, being assured by Hindenburg and Groener—Ludendorff's successor as Quarter-master-General—that the army was still loyal, he had proposed a hectic plan for crushing the internal enemy. An immediate armistice should be concluded with the Allies, the field army should then turn right about, advance over the Rhine to Berlin and there, if necessary, "shoot the place to pieces".

But now even the bulwarks of the Prussian tradition, Hindenburg and his senior officers, William's aides, his military advisers—all men with their spiritual home in the Prussia of Frederick the Great—had to bow their heads before the gale. Bismarck's cement was crumbling. Germany was quite literally falling apart. Brunswick and Bavaria had declared the Republic. On the coast, in the west and the south, workers' and soldiers' councils were seizing power. Revolutionaries were occupying the main railway junctions and supply depots which had been withdrawn behind the Rhine in view of the coming armistice. Home troops had almost everywhere gone over to the revolution. So-called "reliable" forces had succumbed to their influence. Food and ammunition for the front were blocked in Cologne and Munich. Even the army in the field was disaffected. Deserters in their thousands were storming the railways in Liège and Namur. Worst of all, the revolutionaries were acquiring a sense of purpose. Insurgents were reported advancing from Cologne, destination: Supreme Headquarters. Between them and the Kaiser stood a division thought to be particularly reliable. News now came that it had dissolved, refused to obey its officers and the men were straggling off, each for himself, towards home.

In the light of these ugly facts, Hindenburg, Groener and their senior officers discussed the Kaiser's plan on the afternoon of the 8th. Only Groener—a Württemberg General, say Prussian historians, and therefore insensitive to its drastic and pleasant simplicity —seems to have objected to the plan on principle. Hindenburg was all for it, so were Plessen, the Commandant of the Imperial Head-quarters, and von Schulenburg, Chief of Staff to the Army Group "Deutscher Kronprinz". They considered it impossible for the

German Emperor to capitulate to a "handful of insurgents". But were they just a handful? No, indeed. Serious battles might develop. Allied troops might attack the army in the rear while it fought the revolutionaries in front. Hindenburg saw the tactical and logistic difficulties. Reluctantly he came to the view that the Kaiser's plan was impracticable.

Next day, 9th November, 1918, was a fateful one for the House of Hohenzollern. It began with a conference at 10 a.m. between William and his military advisers. William still stuck to his plan. Plessen supported it. The atmosphere was tense with the struggle of men who were being forced to abandon their last illusions. No one thought of abdication. The bed-rock of Prussian tradition was laid bare: the bond, hitherto believed indissoluble, between the King of Prussia and his army. This, surely, was the granite against which the revolutionary tide would beat in vain. All present, about a dozen officers, seemed agreed—despite the facts—that the army was overwhelmingly loyal. But William, they said, was the linch-pin. The morale of the troops depended on his presence. Given that, nothing would be impossible. "The army will be true to the oath which it swore to you," said Schulenburg to the Emperor. "It will collapse if its War Lord abandons it." This was the very gospel of Hindenburg's faith. At this fateful juncture he could not bring himself to deny it. Yet it was contradicted by the facts. Torn, he kept silent. But then, another voice was raised, Groener's, the Württemberger's. "Oath! War Lord!" he said. "Those are mere words, nothing more, in times of revolutionary upheaval!"

William glared. There was a painful silence. Then at last Hindenburg spoke. Carefully skirting the question of the army's loyalty, he pointed out that there was no transport and the soldiers would have to march to Berlin. That would take two or three weeks. To assemble the troops at all would be difficult. To turn their back on the Allies would be dangerous. To make a dash for Berlin and reclaim the Imperial Crown would be impossible.

Inch by inch now the Kaiser and his advisers fought their retreat. An alternative, less ambitious plan was suggested. Loyal troops should seize Aachen and Cologne. William enthusiastically agreed. But again the Field-Marshal vetoed on practical grounds. Very well, then, said William, he would return home peacefully after the armistice at the head of the army. Remorseless for the truth, Groener now spoke. That would not be possible, either, for the whole revolution had turned against the person of the Kaiser. Then he threw a red rag into the bull-ring: "The army will march home in an orderly and peaceful manner under its own generals and commanders—but not under Your Majesty's command, for it no longer stands behind Your Majesty." This cut away the ground under William's feet. Where could he be safe if not with his army? There were gasps of protest and, topping them, the Kaiser's strident voice: "I demand that in writing, from you and from the Field-Marshal, but not until my army commanders have been consulted!" At this moment, an officer burst into the room. Berlin was on the telephone. The Reich Chancellor was demanding immediate abdication.

So the distracted group was pushed an inch further down the slippery slope, from discussing William's safety to the question whether he could stay at all. As though to escape the Chancellor's prodding, the Kaiser with his officers now left the villa where Supreme Headquarters was housed and went out into the adjoining park. There, under the dripping trees, the discussion was continued, little knots of men forming and re-forming, William as pale as death. It was lunch-time, but that was forgotten. There was a sense of impending doom and of the need for some supreme gesture on William's part to assert his authority as German Emperor and free himself in one splendid act from the insidious glue of events. Death in battle? A last forlorn attack on the Western front? The men looked at their Emperor and some hoped, perhaps, that the idea would come to him. But William was now in converse with the Crown Prince who had just arrived. His army group, he said, was completely loyal. William could march home with them.

But then, just after 1 p.m., a General Staff officer, Colonel Heye, appeared. William's wish had been anticipated and from three army groups, including the Crown Prince's, senior officers had been summoned to Spa to answer the questions, could the Kaiser reconquer the homeland at the head of his troops, would the troops fight the Bolshevists? *One* out of thirty-nine officers had said "Yes". Twenty-three had said "No". Fifteen were dubious. This Colonel Heye reported, though wrapping the truth in professions of loyalty. Hoping for a negative answer, William asked whether the armies would march home in good order without him. Implacable, Groener broke in with a "Yes". Heye said "Yes", but added, to soften the blow, "If Your Majesty cares to march with them, they will be happy for you to do so."

Was this the nadir? Not yet. The retreat in the park was being matched by a frenzied rearguard in the villa where abdication was being repeatedly pressed by telephone from Berlin. The capital was said to be running with blood. The troops had gone over to the revolution. Abdication must be announced to prevent civil war. It was a matter of minutes, not of hours.

In vain William's civil advisers in the villa demanded to speak to the Chancellor, demanded confirmation of the bloodshed in Berlin, protested against the ultimatum. Hearing of this, William hurried back to the villa. He was at the end of his tether. He was ready to abdicate. But Plessen and Schulenburg caught their sagging Emperor under the arms. Let him abdicate as German Emperor, they said. But he could and should remain King of Prussia. Thus the essentials would be preserved: the monarchical tradition, the nucleus of the army, the Prussian state. William clutched at this straw, ordered a declaration to this effect to be drawn up for transmission to the Chancellor. This time, Spa called Berlin on the telephone: the Chancellor was to wait for an important announcement from the Emperor.

At last the initiative seemed to have passed to William. The world should know that he could act. Max von Baden was now waiting for *his* instructions. In a mood of relief, William and the Crown Prince withdrew to the drawing-room of the villa. Then, at about two o'clock, a head suddenly appeared round the door and a strangled voice said: "Would Your Majesty be pleased to come out for a moment." William and his son jumped up, went into the dining-room where General von Gontard, a faithful aide, was standing, tears rolling down his cheeks, with a piece of paper in his hand. "Your Majesty and the Crown Prince have been deposed," he said.

William seized the paper. It was a wireless message put out by the German news agency: "The Kaiser has abdicated as German Emperor and as King of Prussia. The Crown Prince has renounced his rights to the throne. Ebert has been appointed Reich Chancellor." Ebert, a moderate Socialist and the son of a saddler.

"Treason! Shameless, outrageous treason!" For a moment William was transfixed, then talking fast he began to pace the room. He would issue a denial, he said. Free himself from this act of violence. The Crown Prince, who was ready for the road, was to go at once to his Army Group, tell them what had happened and prepare for their Emperor to join them. Schulenburg, also present, was to find the Field-Marshal, discuss immediate steps to hold the army together. "I can rely on it that Your Majesty will see it through with the army?" "You know my decision, Graf!" Then William turned, strode to the garden room, seized paper, pencil, feverishly began to write, covering sheet after sheet with his protest, to be telegraphed at once to Berlin. . . .

No one at Spa was in any doubt that the Chancellor, Max von Baden, must have announced William's abdication. But why had he done it, why betray his royal cousin? There was no answer to this question, though plenty of wild surmise. Telephone calls to Berlin secured a garbled picture. The Chancellor was unobtainable. It appeared that the announcement had been made about one o'clock. Yet frantic appeals from the capital for William to abdicate had continued to come after that time. Their intention was clear: to legalize the *fait accompli*. All at Spa were outraged by this deception. Their every instinct, from William downwards, was to reverse the betrayal. But how could it be done? They did not know that earlier in the day the Social Democrats had repeated their demand for immediate abdication, that military suppression of the revolution by the troops available in Berlin was now impossible and that the Chancellor had felt obliged to fulfil the Socialist demand as Ebert was the only man who could control the masses. Nor did they know that, even as William was scribbling his protest in the garden-room, the Socialists were proclaiming the Republic in Berlin.

All they knew was that the physical threat to the Emperor was increasing. It did not find him a coward. At 3 p.m. he gave orders for the small villa, the Villa Fraineuse, to be put in a state of siege. The royal train was in the station. His military staff were to leave it and join him and his adjutants in the house. Mattresses were to be found, arms and ammunition. The guard battalion was to be brought in closer and lodged in neighbouring houses. William was now keyed for a final, ghastly drama: William Imperator Rex besieged by his own people, shooting it out with tipsy deserters, men who still bore on their belts the inscription: "*Gott mit uns*".

But even this supreme gesture was to be denied him. At 3.30 p.m., news came that the picked troops of the guard battalion were beginning to waver. They would not shoot, they said, on German citizens unless the Kaiser personally was attacked. This made them useless for ensuring his safety. Hindenburg, Groener, Plessen, Schulenburg—all the military and civilian advisers—now met again in agonized discussion. Most of them were Prussians. The monarchy was their life-blood. They were conscious of a terrible responsibility. First, the abdication announced from Berlin. Could it be reversed by military means? Hindenburg said "No", and his word was final. Second, should the Kaiser's protest be published and his declaration retaining the Prussian throne? This was a difficult decision. Publication without military backing would be an empty gesture. It would certainly be a dangerous one, sowing further chaos, inviting revolutionary aggression, and insurgents were already said to be marching on Spa. The Kaiser's safety was paramount: publication would have to wait. And now—the most terrible question of all: Hindenburg broached it, supported by Groener. They could no longer accept responsibility for William's safety, they said, even during the coming night, whether in Spa, or in the royal train, or in the villa, or in the whole of Germany.

Holland, said Hindenburg, was only thirty miles away. The roads were all good, even the minor ones were paved. The Kaiser could be quickly there before the insurgents knew what had happened. "But he is safest here," said someone. "Suppose shooting breaks out in front of the villa?" "Then he could leave by the back," replied Hindenburg.

At this, general argument broke out. Some were for postponing a decision. Schulenburg raised a lone voice, pleading for William to join his troops in the field. But Hindenburg was adamant. The situation brooked no delay, and on his own responsibility he ordered one of those present to "take preparatory steps", without saying, apparently, what these should be.

At 4 p.m. the distracted counsellors returned to William. He understood that Berlin could not be reconquered at the point of the bayonet. He agreed to defer publication of his protest and of the declaration promised to Max von Baden three hours before. He listened tensely while Hindenburg tried to convince him of his personal danger. He seemed to appreciate that, but he drew an unexpected conclusion. Before the word Holland was spoken, he broke in, saying he would remain King of Prussia and would join his troops at the front.

Baulked, Hindenburg returned to his theme from this new angle. It would be impossible, he said, to go to the front. The armistice commission had crossed the French lines two days ago. A cease-fire was imminent. Even if William reached the troops he would find them on the point of returning home. "The army flooding back might take Your Majesty prisoner, transport you to Berlin and hand you over to the revolutionaries. There is a serious danger that sooner or later Your Majesty might be seized by the insurgents and delivered over to the internal or external enemy. The Fatherland must be spared that humiliation at all costs." Moreover, in view of their attitude to him, if the Kaiser joined the troops it was possible that the Allies might break off negotiations altogether. But not only would it be dangerous to go to the front. Conditions at home, even here in Spa, were becoming more threatening every hour. The guard battalion for instance.... "What of it?" said the Kaiser. The guard battalion would defend the Kaiser, of course, but only, so the men said, if he was personally attacked. That meant that if insurgents surrounded the villa they might refuse to fire.

One can imagine a pause. Then the Kaiser saying: "Well, what do you advise?" At any rate, Hindenburg, the faithful vassal, now broached the dread subject at last. There was only one thing to do,

he said. His Majesty should go abroad. But that, of course, was for
His Majesty to decide. He, Hindenburg, was merely putting the facts
before him.

William was in great agitation, pacing up and down, flinging
questions to right and left, asking again and again: "What can I do
in a situation like this? I am not usually at a loss, but I don't know
what to do." His dilemma is easy to understand. All his life he had
preached and believed the doctrine that the King of Prussia and his
army were blood brothers sworn to eternal loyalty. The military
virtues of discipline, courage and obedience were the bed-rock of the
German Empire. To go now, to leave his army at this crisis in its
fate would seem like a betrayal of all he had stood for. And it would
look remarkably like cowardice. As long as there was one division,
one battalion, one company still faithful to him he would rather place
himself in their midst and go down fighting. At least it would be a
glorious end. But where were these men to be found, even this
handful? Perhaps he was looking at them now: Hindenburg, Plessen,
Schulenburg, his aides and adjutants. Perhaps they were the only
soldiers within reach whose total fidelity could still be relied on.

The men were waiting for William's decision. But he could not
make up his mind. He would inform them later, he said. For the
moment he would stay. "But . . ." Hindenburg protested. Time
was getting desperately short. At any moment William might be
compelled to leave. Preparations must be made now in case that
became necessary. Had he His Majesty's permission to contact
German representatives in Belgium and Holland, purely as a
preparatory measure? This provoked an outburst of anger from the
Kaiser, but at last, pressed from all sides, he agreed. But this did not
mean, he said, that he had decided to go. That decision he expressly
reserved to himself. He would inform the gentlemen. As the villa
was said to be dangerous, he would be spending the night in the
royal train.

It was five o'clock. The conference was closed. William shook
each man by the hand. But not Groener. He had not forgotten
Groener's advice: ". . . the army no longer behind Your Majesty",
and now William took his revenge. "I have ceased to be German
Kaiser," he said, "and you are a Württemberg General. I have
nothing more to do with you."

The officers dispersed. William stayed on in the villa with a
handful of aides. Without the massive, comforting presence of
Hindenburg, his thoughts took a different turn. He began to feel
lonely and afraid. Suddenly he turned to one of his adjutants. "You
no longer have a War Lord," he said. "I have just agreed to abdicate.
I am going to Holland. I have no desire to be strung up by the mob."

But he made no move and at 7 p.m. Plessen and a recent Foreign Secretary, Admiral von Hintze, anxious for their master's safety, came to the villa and found him still there. In ten minutes' talk they managed to convince him that delay was no longer possible. He must leave immediately for Holland that night. They held, said William later, a "pistol to his chest". At 7.15 his staff were suddenly ordered to pack everything: His Majesty would leave for the royal train at 8. Satisfied, Plessen and von Hintze left, Plessen to tell Hindenburg that the Kaiser was setting out under cover of darkness for Holland. Hindenburg ought to have been pleased. He had been pressing for this all day. But at 5 p.m. he had taken his leave believing he would see William next morning. Now he was distraught, fearing that the Kaiser would go before he could take a last farewell.

The fear was unnecessary, for on the way to the station William was changing his mind again. "I am supposed to go to Holland tonight," he told an officer sitting beside him in the car. "But I cannot agree. I call more troops here, I tell the army I am staying with it as King of Prussia, and then I am advised to desert them before they even arrive! Suppose they do remain faithful to me, and fight for me? Just a handful, that's all I need. I'll fight with them to the last. And if we all get killed, so be it: I am not afraid of dying. And there's my wife and children. I can't leave them in the lurch. No. *I will stay*."

This seemed like a final resolve, the authentic voice of heroism. In the train, still stationary in its siding at Spa, William kept up the theme. His suite, told of the advice he had received, heard him say: "I feel so ashamed. I can't go. I'll stay even if one battalion stands by me." And to a General: "I refuse to follow the advice of the Supreme Command. It is monstrous to suggest I should abandon the army and leave the country. They would think I was afraid." Two senior officers now came to him as spokesmen for a large group who wished to resign their commissions rather than serve under a republican government. "No," said William. "Tell the gentlemen I expect them to remain at their posts so that order and discipline can be restored. I, too, am staying here."

But, meanwhile, all except William had their eyes on the world of reality and were watching the situation deteriorate still further with dread in their hearts. A revolutionist attack was developing from Aachen. The chief of the military railway authorities had just reported that the line to Holland could not be kept open much longer. In Spa, at their headquarters in the Hotel Britannique, the staff officers of the Supreme Command were preparing for a siege, issuing arms and ammunition, ready to spend the night at their

desks. They, too, were convinced of the imminent danger and were
sending messages to William, urging immediate departure, at the
same time assuring him of their loyalty: "Their hearts were bleeding
at the fate of their beloved Kaiser. Their thoughts were with him."

Thus William was alone in his resolve to stay. With his whole
world collapsing around him, he was not afraid to die. Indeed, he
was demanding death—but on his terms. Ever fertile in imaginative
pictures, his fevered mind was now conjuring a vision of William
and the faithful few braving the forces of darkness, a kind of morality
tale, God versus the Devil, with Germany for stage and the world
for audience. What an end! What applause! What a mighty vindica-
tion of the whole theme of his reign!

But the facts of the situation were different. Germany was not a
stage, but a raging sea swept by the revolutionary tide. There were
no spotlights, there was no curtain, no expectant audience waiting
for it to rise on the last soul-stirring, sanguinary act of the Hohenzollern drama. There was simply a man sitting in a railway train in a
dirty siding, surrounded by a hungry, vengeful and despairing
people who at any moment might break in and slit his throat. This
at all costs Hindenburg and his colleagues were determined to
prevent.

Von Hintze had contacted the Dutch authorities and arranged for
William to be met at the frontier. Now, at 8.30 p.m., he was told that
the Kaiser had changed his mind again and was refusing to leave.
In despair, Hintze telephoned the royal train and spoke to a member
of the suite. The Kaiser was to be told that every member of the
Supreme Command, including Hindenburg, all his advisers, military and civilian, were unanimously of the opinion that he must
leave at once. The situation was desperate. They could no longer
accept responsibility for his safety. And there was the Kaiserin to
think of. She was in Berlin. What would be her fate if the Kaiser
was captured or killed by the Bolshevists? From Holland, with
Dutch backing, he could arrange for her safety. But not from here,
not from Spa. Finally, if he stayed the Kaiser would plunge the
country into civil war—a war that could have only one possible
outcome: the triumph of chaos.

William was just sitting down to a meal when this message was
brought to him. Time and again during his reign harsh reality had
broken into and shattered his dreams. Now this last vision of a
heroic stand collapsed, leaving him cold and bewildered. "Very
well," he said, "if it must be, I will go—but not before tomorrow
morning."

This was William's last decision on German soil—not a free one
because he had no alternative. Now, in the last hours that remained

to him, in the vacuum between Kaiserdom and life as an exile in Holland, while crowds in Paris were baying "*A bas Guillaume!*" and red flags were waving over his proud fleet, he sat down and composed his apologia: "Today I have fought a terrible inner struggle. I did not want to expose myself to the reproach of cowardice and abandon any part of my army that still remained loyal to me, but would rather fight and die with it. But as all responsible military authorities, including the General Staff, have declared that the troops will not and cannot physically fight any more—either against the enemy or their own people, so—the Reich Chancellor Prince Max von Baden having betrayed me behind my back with the Social Democrats—there remains nothing for me but to resolve with a bleeding heart to leave my army. For almost thirty years I have lived and worked for it and now, after four and a half years of brilliant victories, it collapses shamefully through the youth at home poisoned and blinded by Jews and Social Democrats—at the very moment when peace is within our grasp. . . ."

At five o'clock next morning in rain and total darkness, by car as being less conspicuous, William set out for Holland. The Hohenzollerns had been rulers in Brandenburg for over five hundred years.

CHAPTER FIFTEEN

EXILE

IT was still raining when the cars reached the frontier at Eysden. The Dutch Government knew that the Kaiser was coming, but thought it would be by train and there was no one to meet him. Suspicious guards eyed the German party and refused to let him pass. Finally, a telephone call to The Hague gave William the privilege of waiting for several hours on the dripping railway station until the royal train arrived from Germany. He then vanished inside and remained invisible for the rest of that day and the following night.

Count Godard Bentinck who owned a large house at Amerongen agreed to shelter the royal party. Next morning he motored to the station at Maarn where he was due to pick up his guest. Little traffic had passed that way during the war. Grass grew between the sleepers. The paintwork was peeling, footsteps echoed on the empty platform. Outside, beyond the barrier, a silent crowd of local people had gathered. It was still raining. When the royal train drew in a solitary figure emerged, walked quickly up to the Count and said: "Well, what do you think of this?" Then, as William was led to the car, his suite of thirty persons began to unload luggage, an assorted refugees' pile, including several crates of champagne.

On the journey to Amerongen the Kaiser spoke barely a word, but in the large house behind a double moat the nightmare began to lift. Here was at least a temporary resting-place, quiet, comfortable and secluded. The fear of a violent end dissolved. Everyone was very considerate. Soon the suite arrived. There was bustle, much bowing and scraping and William had the happy feeling that he was still the centre of interest. That night at his first meal he was very talkative, but too stunned as yet to think of reproaches. Pinning the blame, clearing his conscience would come later.

For some weeks, while the Dutch authorities wondered what to do with the uninvited guest, chaos reigned at Amerongen. Aircraft

circled overhead, journalists besieged the house now guarded by
Dutch troops, lorries laden with the Kaiser's personal possessions
began to arrive, the suite settled down in hastily converted stables.
William himself went to ground. Already he was becoming the
model exile. Caution was the key-note: no explosive utterances, no
fireworks with the Press. Even with his host he avoided politics. He
still felt at the centre of a whirlwind. Six secretaries could barely
cope with the mail. Letters of devotion or the coarsest abuse poured
in by every post. The mood of the Allies was ugly. "Hang the Kaiser"
was on many lips. There was nothing that William could do but
lie low and hope that the storm would blow over. Meanwhile, he
laid dignity around him like a cloak. The moustache was allowed to
droop, a pointed beard was grown. Subtly the War Lord was transformed into the venerable *grand seigneur*, sniffing roses in the
garden, felling trees, dispensing little gifts which he had thoughtfully
brought with him and, when those ran out, signing his name with a
big W on logs which he had chopped with his strong right arm.

But two things were difficult to bear: the restrictions on his
liberty and the knowledge that a large part of mankind was heaping
the odium for the war, the deaths of ten million men, the ravaged
countryside of France on his solitary head. Pacing alone for hours in
the picture gallery at Amerongen he excised the most painful sting
of all, his rejection by his own people. They had not really rejected
him at all, he decided. Prince Max had betrayed him by announcing
his abdication. That had confused the public mind and he had had
to leave. It was natural that Germans should now be accusing him
of desertion and the violence of their language was an expression
merely of their deep affection for him. Love and hate were notoriously close together. It was only indifference that he could not bear.
Events in the Republic would surely disgust Germans with their
new form of government. Some day, perhaps quite soon, there
would be a swing of the pendulum, the monarchy would be
restored and they would come back to him, cap in hand. Meanwhile,
he was quite content to wait. He was in no hurry. The stage would
have to be a very firm one before he would step back on it. There
must be no trapdoors.

But world opinion was a different matter. That was harder to
shrug off. A flood of accusing books, pamphlets and articles were
being published. With fascinated horror he read them all. Was he
to be stamped for the rest of his life as the bloodthirsty butcher of
war-time cartoons, with stained apron and dripping knife? With all
sincerity William could say that he had not wanted the war. He
totally failed to recognize this image of the ruthless monster as himself. Had the world gone mad? It was impossible for him to answer

all the charges, innuendos, half-truths and untruths in detail. Of course, war hysteria accounted for a lot of them. That he could understand. It was foolish, but it was human. All the same, this unanimity of rejection had a virulence which left him baffled and frightened to the depths of his soul. Fortunately, he was innocent. He could only wait for the world to come to its senses.

Meanwhile, Amerongen was certainly the safest place, and he would start compiling some "Comparative Historical Tables", a sort of potted record of pre-war events to show how Germany was encircled. He already had some telling entries: "March, 1908. *England*. Lord Fisher, the First Sea Lord, proposes that Germany's unpreparedness should be exploited to fall upon the German Fleet in time of peace" . . . "March, 1909. *England*. During the Bosnian crisis France and England make secret preparations for mobilization against Germany" . . . "July, 1911. *England*. Threatening speech by Lloyd George in the House of Commons" . . . "July, 1914. *Russia*. The Grand Duchesses Anastasia and Militza tell the French ambassador that their father, the King of Montenegro, had informed them in a cipher telegram that 'we shall have war before the end of the month'. . . ."

While William was compiling this ammunition, felling trees, sniffing roses, the Empress arrived from Berlin, a broken woman. Rioters had thrust into the palace, only her courage had quelled them. Her family was scattered. The greatness of Germany, the Imperial destiny, the high hopes for her husband's reign—all lay in the dust. Five hundred years of Hohenzollern rule had come to an end. Was this not enough to break anyone's heart? That William's energy was undiminished, that the flow of talk, the press of activity still continued, that he seemed incapable of grasping the tragedy made it truly unbearable. She felt utterly alone. She longed to make contact with him now—now or never—so that they could comfort each other. Then she realized that even this profound upheaval had not stirred William to the depths. There were no depths. On that mighty throne he had lived like one in a dream and he was wondering now why the world had robbed him of his toys. On the very day that she reached him, he had signed his abdication, renouncing the throne for ever. He seemed to think that the document would one day prove the Republic's undoing.

Soon Augusta was living in a nightmare. The Allies were demanding William's extradition for trial as a criminal. They had inserted a guilt clause in the Treaty of Versailles. He was to be "publicly arraigned for a supreme offence against international morality and the sanctity of treaties". A cartoon was published showing him strung on a wire between the Eiffel Tower and the opposite bank of the Seine. The poor lady withdrew to her room with ailing heart tended by two faithful ladies-in-waiting who in earlier days had been known as the "Halleluja aunts" because of their piety. This was no longer a joke. She needed all the comfort that faith could give her.

William, at this time, was screwed to the highest pitch of tension, felling immense numbers of trees (over a thousand during the eighteen months he was at Amerongen), taking long walks in the woods, excitedly retracing war battles with the aid of staff maps and talking into the early hours of the morning with that fabulous memory of his, chain-smoking all the time, about the crowded events of his reign. He had no doubt of his ability to defend himself if it came to a trial and he even considered surrendering himself voluntarily: black limelight would perhaps be better than none. But the Allies were out for blood. The trial, if it took place, would be a grisly and undignified farce. There was no reason why William should acknowledge the competence of an enemy tribunal set up in Paris as a concession to vengeful hysteria. So he waited, and the Dutch Government came to his aid, very properly refusing to surrender him.

With this last danger removed, William could think of becoming a professional exile. To all prisoners with an indefinite sentence the moment comes when they cease to rebel and realize that a life can be built even in captivity, and to William, Holland had the supreme attraction of being safe from a hostile world. The home government had left him many of his properties in Germany and he was still rich enough to lead a life of elegance and comfort. An adequate suite was allowed him. It only remained to find a permanent home where selected pilgrims could be received and a somewhat muted, though still imperial, state could be enjoyed.

In June, 1920, the ex-Kaiser moved to a large and attractive house which he had bought with sixty acres at Doorn. Soon further convoys were trundling across the frontier with an entire marble staircase from his palace in Potsdam, furniture, pictures and ancestral bric-à-brac. Central heating and electric light were installed, modern cooking arrangements, and several rooms were built on to the already stately pile. In this place William was by no means a mournful recluse. He had to be careful what he said and he dared not venture too far in one of his nine motor-cars in case of hostile encounters. He was painfully aware that some people's feelings towards him were, to put it mildly, ambivalent. But there was no restriction on his movements and to his household or selected guests he still seemed extremely lively. Assisted by faithful friends who applied their litmus paper—not too acid, not too alkali—he was engaged on a new project now, his memoirs. He had no picture of

his behaviour in pre-war years, or of his own personality, no aware-
ness of the impact it had made on the world. All he knew was that
his personality had aroused disapproval, therefore on paper it would
now be changed. In place of the gadfly there would be a bumble bee,
purposeful, single-minded, busily industrious for the welfare of the
Germans. But the effort involved in writing of himself as though
he had been his grandfather exhausted even William's tempestuous
vitality. The narrative flagged, the colour drained away as, for page
after page, he attempted the impossible feat of standing truth on
its head.

In any case, writing for an invisible audience was a dreary task,
he much preferred a live one. This was soon forthcoming. Count
Bentinck's daughter was to be married to the young man doing
service as William's adjutant, Captain Ilsemann. The wedding, with
hundreds of guests, including Bentinck relatives from Germany,
England and Holland, was to be at Amerongen. William was
invited. This would be his first semi-public appearance since the
exile. He looked forward to it with tremulous joy. The day dawned
clear and sunny. From Doorn he motored to the big house through
the village of Amerongen already decked with flowers, flags and
greenery for the bride. The villagers in holiday mood waved to him
as he passed. This was quite like old times.

Meanwhile at the house, where a civil ceremony was first to take
place, the guests were drawn up in the big salon in a ceremonial
half-circle, ladies on the left, gentlemen on the right, awaiting
William's arrival. Suddenly, the double doors were flung open, two
servants in long blue coats and three-cornered hats announced:
"The Kaiser!"

In the silence which fell like a knife, a small erect figure took two
quick steps into the room, stopped, clicked heels, nodded jerkily to
left and right—then stood, apparently unsure of his welcome. The
guests saw a symphony in grey: grey hair, grey skin, grey beard, grey
Field-Marshal's uniform, clanking with medals, one hand holding
his helmet, the other clasping his sword. Very slim, but rather old,
a nice old man, but with curiously staring eyes. He bore no simi-
larity whatever with the former War Lord. Perhaps to underline the
fact that this was only a dress affair he was wearing brown shoes.

But, in Doorn, the Empress Augusta was fast declining. She died
in April, 1921, and was buried in Potsdam. In the following year
William married the thirty-four-year-old Princess Hermine of
Reuss, a capable widow with five children. The marriage was
strongly resented by German monarchists, but their cause, though
Hermine by no means despaired of it, was already doomed. For a
year after the armistice the imperial régime had been too discredited

for the monarchists to raise even a timid voice. Then slowly a restoration came to be seen as the only alternative to a republican government fulfilling none of the high hopes originally pinned to it. Amid continuing hardships and mounting inflation, numbers of ex-officers formed action-groups ostensibly to support the Government against red revolution, but in fact to destroy it if opportunity offered. In the early 'twenties the reactionary tide slowly grew until Hitler's abortive *putsch* taught monarchists that the Government could not easily be overthrown from no matter what quarter. Thereafter they turned to constitutional methods. But Hindenburg's election to the Presidency in 1925 brought another blow. The old man yearned for a restoration, but guilt at his part in William's abdication made him insist that only William should be restored. But few people now wanted the ex-Kaiser and in any case the slow economic revival, the entry of Germany into the League of Nations coupled with prospects of finally settling the reparations question offered a brighter future under the existing régime.

Finally, the social basis on which the monarchy had rested was disappearing and a new generation was growing up which could only read of William in history books; what these young people read did not encourage them. The last spasm of monarchist hopes took place with the rise of Hitler. With the unerring insight of a fellow-sufferer he had made a veiled reference in *Mein Kampf* to William as *ersichtlich geisteskrank*, "obviously mental". But his deeds, it was believed, would be different from his words. These hopes were finally dashed when Hitler became Chancellor, set up the monolithic State with sole allegiance to himself and completely rejected the Hohenzollern tradition.

No doubt all this was a relief to the old man at Doorn. He much preferred the small band of the faithful to the seething masses of renascent Germany. At last the world was beginning to forget him, and that was a comfort, too. To talk of old times, to invite selected guests to listen to his monologues, to smile benevolently on his grandchildren—that was the proper treatment for ageing nerves. One lesson he had now thoroughly learnt: the world of action was no place for him. To live and die quietly was his only aim. Discussion of current politics was banned at Doorn. What news trickled through to the outside world gave a picture of astonishing calm: William's birthdays when old generals quaintly kissed his hand, the opening of the study season at Doorn with the first lecture given by William on the origin and use of the baldacchino, a charity bazaar opened by Hermine, and only very occasionally some acid remark about the ex-corporal swiftly retracted when a bark of rage came from Berlin.

The years passed like a slow river without ripple or fuss. For the world his story was over. As for him, he may even have found contentment.

He died on 4th June, 1941, after twenty-two years in exile without seeing his native land again. In the previous year, when Holland was invaded, the British Government had offered him asylum in England. But England was a book of memories with every page already filled. It was better not to disturb them, or reopen old wounds. So he stayed, to gaze from his window at the guard of honour which Nazi Germany placed at his gate, and then withdraw when the groups of army sightseers became too large. He had arranged his funeral with meticulous care. A dignified mausoleum had been built in the grounds. There was to be no funeral oration with the risk of equivocal words, but only selected passages from the Bible.

So, while Europe was convulsed with new horror, William was laid to rest, with his family in attendance and the aged Field-Marshal Mackensen in tears—weeping for Imperial Germany.

INDEX

Aachen, 171, 177
Abbazia, 70
Abdul Hamid, Sultan of Turkey, 79
Abyssinia, 69
Adrianople, 132
Aehrenthal, Austrian Foreign Minister, 109, 123–4
Agadir, 128
Albania, 132, 133, 135
Albert, King of the Belgians, 157
Albert of Saxe-Coburg, Prince Consort, 11–12
Albrecht, Archduke of Austria, 13
Aldershot, 42, 55
Alexander II, Tsar of Russia, 100
Alexander III, Tsar of Russia, 47, 53
  death of, 56
Algeciras, Act of, 128
  conference at, 107
Alix of Hesse, Princess (later Tsarina of Russia), 55
Alsace-Lorraine, 41, 53, 95, 127, 163
America, United States of, 77, 78, 149, 151–2, 155, 156
Amerongen, 180, 181, 183, 184
Amoy, 65
Anhalt-Dessau, Duke of, 43
Anti-Socialist Law, 40, 44, 45, 46
Armenia, 67
Arnim, Count von, 51
Athens, 43
Augusta, German Empress and Queen of Prussia (wife of William I), 43
Augusta Victoria, German Empress and Queen of Prussia, 80, 92, 154, 178, 182

marriage to William II, 19
  her personality and relationship with William, 82–5
  death of, 184
Austria-Hungary, 17, 53, 62, 77, 91, 95, 107, 109, 149, 155, 158, 166
  and the Serbian problem, 121
  and the Balkan wars, 131–4
  and the outbreak of World War I, 135–43
Avesnes, 165
Aymé, François (William's French tutor), 18

Bachmann, Chief of Naval Staff, 152
Baden, 50
Baden, Prince Max von (Reich Chancellor, 1918), 167, 168, 169, 170, 173, 175, 179, 181
Bad Gastein, 21
Balfour, Arthur, 87
Balkans, the, 62, 95, 107, 109, 122
  wars in the, 131–4
Ballin, Albert, 84, 152
Bavaria, 71, 170
Bear Island, 75
Bebel, August (Socialist leader), 40
Belgium, 98, 144, 157, 163, 176
Belgrade, 135, 139, 140
Bentinck, Count Godard, 180, 184
Berchtold, Count, Austrian Foreign Minister, 136, 151
Berlin, Treaty of, 123
Berlin-Baghdad railway, 135
Bethmann-Hollweg, Theobald von (Reich Chancellor, 1909–1917), 129–31, 133, 151, 152, 155, 159, 160, 161, 162

Bethmann-Hollweg, *cont.*
  personality of, 125
  negotiates with Britain, 127-8
  and the outbreak of World
    War I, 135-43
Bielefeld, 38
Bismarck, Herbert von, 41, 50
Bismarck, Otto von, 12, 13, 15, 17,
  20, 24, 25, 26, 27, 28, 30, 33, 51,
  56, 57, 58, 74, 77, 100, 108, 120,
  164
  becomes Prime Minister of
    Prussia, 11
  cultivates Prince William, 21
  goads him against his parents,
    22
  constitutional powers of, as
    Chancellor, 31
  his conflicts with William and
    dismissal, 36-48
  his Reinsurance Treaty with
    Russia, 52-3
  visits William, 59
  colonial policy of, 62
  death of, 80-81
Bismarck Archipelago, the, 62
Björkö, Treaty of, 96-100, 104
Black Eagle, Order of, 25, 30
Black Sea, the, 95, 131
Boer War, the, 85, 88-9, 100, 111
Bonn, University of, 19
Bornstedt, 29
Bosnia, Austrian annexation of,
  110, 123-4
Bosphorus, the, 95
Boxer Rebellion, the, 89-90
Brandenburg, 71, 179
Bremen, 34
Bremerhaven, 34, 38
Breslau, 43
Brown Islands, the, 62
Brunswick, 170
Bucharest, Peace of, 133
Bulgaria, 53, 131-3, 135, 154, 166
Bülow, Bernhard von (Foreign Sec-
  retary 1897-1900, Reich Chan-
  cellor 1900-1909), 66, 76, 77, 78,
  79, 81, 83, 85, 87, 88, 89, 90, 102,
  103, 104, 156, 162, 164

first meeting with William, 73-
  75
becomes Chancellor, 91
his terms for an alliance with
  Britain, 92
and the Treaty of Björkö, 96-
  100
Moroccan policy of, 105-108
and the *Daily Telegraph* affair,
  112-18
his Balkan policy, 122-4
resignation of, 124-5

Cambon, Paul, French Ambassador
  in London, 96
Cameroons, the, 62, 129
Canary Islands, 69
Caporetto, Battle of, 162
Caprivi, General von (Reich Chan-
  cellor 1890-1894), 50, 53, 59, 95,
  104
  internal policy and dismissal,
    56-8
Carnot (President of France), assas-
  sination of, 56
Caroline Islands, 77
Cassel, 18
Cassel, Sir Ernest, 130
Cavita, 77
Century Magazine, 115
Chamberlain, Joseph, 77, 78, 87,
  88, 91
Charlottenburg, 25, 27
China, 62, 112
  at war with Japan, 64, 65
  Boxer Rebellion in, 89-90
Clemenceau, Georges, 108
Cologne, 74, 170, 171
Colonies (German), 62-3, 75
Congo (French), 106, 128, 129
Connaught, Duke of, 78, 92
Conservatives (German), 46-7, 56-
  57, 71, 88, 90, 115, 116
Constantinople, 43, 123, 131, 154
Constitution of German Reich, 24,
  30-31, 46, 57, 86, 116
Corfu, 43, 120
Cowes, 55, 98
Cronberg, 110

Cronstadt, 32, 53
Crown Council, 25, 32, 44, 161
Cuba, 77
Czernin, Count, 117

Daily Telegraph Affair, the, 111–118, 123
Damascus, 79
Dardanelles, the, 67, 154
Darmstadt, 43
Delagoa Bay, 66, 88
Delcassé, French Foreign Minister, 96, 106–107
Denmark, 32, 51, 98
Dogger Bank Incident, the, 96, 104
Donaueschingen, 114, 116
Doorn, 58, 130, 183, 184, 185
Dreadnoughts, 109
Dresden, 40
Dreyfus Case, the, 101
Durazzo, 132, 133

East Prussia, 40, 57, 120, 128, 147, 148, 154
Ebert (first Chancellor of the German Republic), 173, 174
Edward, Prince of Wales (later Edward VII), 41–2, 54, 56, 84, 88, 89, 94, 98, 105, 107, 108, 110, 111, 112, 126, 130, 142
    accession of, 92
    visits Kiel, 103
Egypt, 67, 93
Elbing, 57
Employers' Liability Act, 40
Ems, 22
England (*with* Great Britain), 11, 12, 13, 14, 26, 41, 51, 63, 66, 68, 69, 76, 77, 78, 87, 95, 96, 98, 105, 106, 107, 109, 116, 123, 161, 182, 186
    reaches Entente with France, 93
    and the German Navy, 126–31
    and the outbreak of World War I, 141–4
Entente, Anglo-French, the, 93, 95, 104

strength tested over Morocco, 105–108, 109
Erzberger, Matthias, 162
Essen, 38
Eulenburg-Hertefeld, Count Philipp zu, 22, 23, 39, 47, 50, 51, 55, 58, 59, 69, 76, 80, 83, 86, 90, 115, 120
    his friendship with William, 34–6
    warns William of growing unpopularity, 70–71
    his pen-portrait of William, 73
Eysden, 180

Falkenhayn, General von (War Minister, later Chief of General Staff 1914–1916), 138, 143, 151, 154, 155, 156, 157
Fashoda, 78
Federal Council, the, 12, 30, 31, 115, 116
Federal Princes, the, 24, 57
Fisher, Lord, 182
Formosa, 64
France, 27, 51, 62, 64, 77, 78, 95, 96, 111, 133, 134, 182
    rapprochement with Russia, 53
    reaches Entente with England, 93
    clashes with Germany over Morocco, 105–108
    and outbreak of World War I, 136
    fighting in (1914), 146–9
Frankfurt-am-Main, 32, 43
Franz Ferdinand, Archduke of Austria, 84, 114, 136
Franz Josef, Emperor of Austria, 21, 41, 133, 137, 138
Frederick II (the Great), 16, 18, 19, 24, 30, 44, 48, 49, 50, 71, 77, 89, 110, 147, 154, 158, 168, 170
Frederick William III, King of Prussia, 22
Frederick William, Crown Prince of Prussia (later Frederick III): marriage of, 9, 17, 29, 31

Frederick William, *cont.*
  dominated by his wife, 11–14
  denounces William as imma-
    ture, 20
  jealousy of William, 21
  develops cancer of the throat,
    22–3
  becomes Emperor, 25
  his short rule, 26
  condition deteriorates, 27
  death of, 28
French Revolution (1848), 39
Friedrichskron, 28, 29
Friedrichsruh (home of Bismarck),
  32, 36, 44, 59, 80
Fürstenberg, Prince von, 114, 116

Galicia, 149, 157
George V, 141, 142
German East Africa, 62
Giesl, Freiherr von (Austrian Am-
  bassador in Belgrade), 139
Gontard, General von, 173
Great Britain, *see* England
Greece, 131–3
Grey, Sir Edward (British Foreign
  Secretary), 127, 141, 143, 144
Groener, General (successor to
  Ludendorff), 170, 171, 172, 174,
  176

Hague, the, 180
Haldane, Lord (British War Minis-
  ter), 130, 131
Hamburg, 38, 120, 169
Hanover, 43, 120
Hardinge, Sir Charles, 110
Hatzfeld (German Ambassador in
  London), 77, 78
Hauptmann, Gerhart, 57
Heinrich, Prince of Prussia (brother
  of William II), 66
  marriage of, 27
Heligoland, 56, 148
Hentsch, Colonel, 149
Hermine, Princess of Reuss (Wil-
  liam's second wife), 184, 185
Hertling, Count (Reich Chancellor
  1917–1918), 165, 166, 167

Herzegovina, Austrian annexation
  of, 110, 123
Heye, Colonel, 172
Hindenburg, General (later Field
  Marshal), 148, 154, 157–8, 160,
  161, 162, 165, 166, 170, 171,
  174–8, 185
Hintze, Admiral von, 177, 178
Hinzpeter, Georg (William's tutor),
  16–17, 19, 37, 38
  his characterization of William,
    18
Hitler, Adolf, 185
Hohenlohe-Schillingfürst, Prince
  (Reich Chancellor 1894–1900),
  63, 67–8, 88, 89, 104
Hohenzollern (royal yacht), 40–41,
  75, 86, 93, 96, 97, 98, 103, 124,
  137, 138
Holland, 98, 175, 176, 177, 178,
  179, 183, 186
Homburg, 92, 156
House of Correction Bill, the, 86–7

Ilsemann, Captain, 184
Ingenohl, Admiral von, 147, 148
Ireland, 151
Irene, Princess of Prussia, 27
Italy, 43, 70, 84, 93, 105, 107, 108,
  149, 154

Jagow (Foreign Secretary), 139
Jameson, Doctor, 67–8
Japan, 62, 78, 98, 105, 107, 109,
  112, 149
  Emperor of, 43
  war with China, 64–5
  at war with Russia, 93, 95–6

Kiau-chau:
  leased by Germany, 65, 75
  captured by Japanese, 149
Kiderlen-Wächter (Foreign Secre-
  tary), 126, 128–9, 131, 132, 133
Kiel, 32, 40, 90, 136, 166, 167, 169
  Canal, 56
  Kiel Week, 103, 115, 120, 126

Kitchener, General, 78
Kluck, General von, 146
Korea, 64, 95
Kruger (President of the Transvaal), 66, 68

Lassalle, Ferdinand, 39
Laurenzo-Marques, 66
League of Nations, 185
Leopold II, King of the Belgians, 101–102
Liaotung Peninsula, 64
Lichnovsky, Prince von (German Ambassador in London), 141, 144
Liège, 146, 170
Lloyd George, 129, 182
Ludendorff, General, 148, 157–8, 159, 160, 161, 162, 163, 165, 166, 168
Ludwig, King of Bavaria, 71
Lusitania, sinking of the, 151

Macedonia, 132, 166
Mackensen, General von (later Field Marshal), 154, 186
Mackenzie, Dr. Morell (Scottish laryngologist), 23
Malet (British Ambassador in Berlin), 66
Manchuria, 64, 65, 95, 96
Manila, 77
Mariana Islands, 77
Marne, Battle of the, 148–9
Marschall, Freiherr von Bieberstein (Foreign Secretary 1890–1897), 50, 53, 58, 59, 60, 67, 68, 75, 77.
Marshall Islands, 62
Marx, Karl, 39
Massawa, 69
Memel, 75
Meteor (William's racing yacht), 54, 103
Metternich, Count (German Ambassador in London), 110, 126, 129, 131
Michaelis, Georg (Reich Chancellor, July–Sept., 1917), 162–3, 165

Modlin, 154
Moltke, Field Marshal Count Helmuth von (Chief of General Staff 1858–1888), 24, 34–5, 144
  Colonel General Helmuth von (Chief of General Staff 1906–1914), 138, 142, 143, 144, 146, 148
Monaco, Prince of, 125
Montenegro, 109, 132
Morocco, 93, 104–108, 128–9
Müller, Admiral von, Chief of Naval Cabinet, 152
Munich, 71, 170
Muraviev (Russian Minister), 111

Namur, 146, 170
Naples, 90
Navy, the German, 32, 63
  expansion of, 74–6, 77, 88, 109, 126–8
Navy, the Royal, 42, 43, 61, 76, 88, 144
  builds Dreadnoughts, 109
Neues Palais, the, 27, 83
New Guinea, 62
Nicolas II, Tsar of Russia, 21, 55, 64, 65, 75, 77, 78, 89, 90, 94, 95, 136, 140, 141, 144
  coronation of, 56
  and the Treaty of Björkö, 96–8
Nivelle, General, 162
Norway, 98

Old Age and Sickness Insurance Act, 44
Oldenburg, 70
Omdurman, Battle of, 78

Palmerston, Lord, 13
Pan-Slavism, 121–2, 135, 137
Panther (German gunboat), sent to Agadir, 128–9
Peking, 89, 90
Persia, Shah of, 40
Philippines, the, 77
Pillau, 98
Piraeus, the, 43
Pless, 151, 152, 153, 157, 160

Plessen, Colonel General, 170, 171, 173, 174, 176, 177
Pola, 70
Poland, 149, 154
Port Arthur, 64, 65, 95
Portsmouth, 41, 53
    Peace of (between Russia and Japan), 107
Posen, 72
Potsdam, 18, 22, 25, 26, 27, 32, 183, 184
Pretoria, 66
Prinkenau, 82

Radziwill, Princess Marie, 115
Reinsurance Treaty (with Russia), 95
    allowed to lapse, 52–3
Reval, 110
Rhineland-Westphalia, 38
Roberts, Field-Marshal Lord, 93, 112
Rossbach (Frederick the Great's victory), 71
Rouvier, French Prime Minister, 106
Rudolf, Crown Prince of Austria, 41
Rumania, 53, 135, 158, 166
    King of, 41
Russia, 21, 22, 24, 52, 55–6, 62, 64, 67, 69, 77, 78, 95, 105, 108, 111
    rapprochement with France, 53
    and the Treaty of Björkö, 96–99
    ends war with Japan, 107
    and the Balkan situation, 122–124, 131–4
    and the outbreak of World War I, 135–44
    revolution in, 161
Russo-Japanese War, the, 93, 95–6

Sachsenwald, the, 44, 58
Salisbury, Lord, 41, 67, 69
Samoa, 85
San Remo, 23, 25
Sarajevo, 136
Saxony, 38

Scapa Flow, 130
Schleswig-Holstein, 17
Schlieffen, Count von (with Schlieffen Plan), 101, 104, 106, 146, 149
Schlitz, 70
Schoen, Freiherr von (Foreign Secretary), 114
Schulenburg, Lieutenant-General von, 170, 171, 173, 174, 176
Senden, Admiral Baron von, 34–5, 76
Serbia, 109, 121–4, 131–4, 135–40, 154
Sigismund, Prince of Prussia (brother of William II), death of, 18
Simplicissimus (comic periodical), 115
Sino-Japanese War, the, 64–5, 80
Social Democrats, the, 39–41, 44, 45, 46, 56–8, 116, 160, 162, 164–165, 170, 174, 179
Solomon Islands, 62
Somme, Battle of the, 157, 159
South West Africa (German), 62, 156
Spa, 165, 166, 169, 172, 174, 175, 177
Spain, at war with America, 77
    King of, 105
Spithead, 42
Stemrich, Foreign Under-Secretary, 112
Stockholm, 32
Stuart-Wortley, Colonel, 112, 118
Stuttgart, 40
Swaine, Colonel (British military attaché), 26–7
Sweden, King of, 32, 98
Switzerland, 46

Tangier, 93, 106
Tannenberg, Battle of, 148
Tirpitz (Secretary to the Navy, later Grand Admiral), 60, 77, 88, 103, 141, 143, 144, 151, 152, 154, 156, 162
    and expansion of the German Navy, 63, 74, 126–7, 129–31

Tirpitz, *cont.*
    his "Risk Theory", 76, 156, 162
Togoland, 62
Tokyo, 64, 65
Toulon, 53
Transvaal, the, 66, 67, 68
Treitschke, Heinrich von (German historian), 63
Triple Alliance, the, 66, 105, 107, 108, 135
Triple Entente, the, 121, 135
Tripoli, 105
Tsushima, Battle of, 96
Turkey, 62, 67, 79, 80, 122, 123, 135, 155
    and the Balkan war, 131–4

U-boat War, German policy in, 151–2, 155–6, 161
"Uitlanders", the, 66, 67
Upper Silesia, 38, 151

Valentini (Chief of Civil Cabinet), 165
Venice, 70
Verdun, 155, 157
Versailles, Treaty of, 182
Victoria, Princess Royal, Crown Princess of Prussia, later the Empress Frederick, 20, 22, 23, 24, 27, 28, 29, 49, 59, 80
    marriage, 9
    ambitions for a liberalized Prussia, 11–14
    attitude to William, 15–17
    complains of his disrespect, 21
    becomes Empress, 25
    her moral isolation, 26
    visits England, 42
    serious illness of, 92–3
    death of and last wishes, 103
Victoria, Queen of England, 12, 18, 20, 21, 22, 24, 49, 54, 55, 56, 85, 88, 89
    visits Germany, 27
    incensed with William, 41
    invites him to England, 42

and the Kruger Telegram, 68–69
    death of, 91
Vienna, 41, 59, 70
Vladivostock, 96

Waldersee, Count Alfred von, 24, 25, 27, 29, 34
    made C.-in-C. of China expedition, 89–90
Wei-hai-Wei, 65
Weser, River, 34
Wiesbaden, 120
Wight, Isle of, 54
Wilhelmshaven, 89
Wilhelmshöhe, 120
William I, King of Prussia, German Emperor from 1871, 11, 12, 16–17, 20, 26, 30, 40
    death of, 24–5
William II, King of Prussia and German Emperor:
    birth, 14
    his withered arm, 14–15
    schooling and personality, 16–18
    relationship with parents, 19
    marriage, 19
    cultivated by Bismarck, 21
    ambitions on his father's illness, 23, 24, 26, 27
    accession, 28–9
    opens the Reichstag, 30
    constitutional powers of, 30–31
    restlessness of, 32
    attends army manœuvres, 33, 34, 35
    conflicts with and dismisses Bismarck, 36–48
    first visit to England as Emperor, 41–2
    further travels of, 43
    his defects of temperament, 49
    his fear of Socialism, 51–2
    attitude to his uncle Edward and further visits to England, 54–5

threatens the "parties of revolution", 57
dismisses Caprivi, 58
reconciliation with Bismarck, 59–60
his aggressiveness, 61–2
and expansion of the German Navy, 60, 63, 74–6, 88, 103, 110, 126–8, 129–31
supports President Kruger, 66
and the Kruger Telegram, 68
attempts to embroil England with Russia, 69
tactless speeches of, 71
visits the Holy Land, 79–80
on his dismissal of Bismarck, 80–81
bored with domesticity, 83–4
visits Queen Victoria on her 80th birthday, 85–7
and relations with Britain, 78, 87, 88, 91, 103, 129–31
and the Boxer Rebellion, 89–90
at Queen Victoria's deathbed, 92
reaction to Anglo-French Entente, 93–4
and the Treaty of Björkö, 96–100
threatens Leopold II, 101–102
his interest in technology, 102
receives Edward VII at Kiel, 102–103
encourages sport of yachting, 103

his demonstration at Tangier, 106
alarmed at Bülow's Moroccan policy, 107–108
and the *Daily Telegraph* affair, 111–18
his loss of self-confidence, 119–20
attitude to Austria, 124
accepts Bülow's resignation, 124–5
his disinterest in Morocco, 129
and the Balkan Wars, 132–4
and the outbreak of World War I, 135–45
his failure as War Lord, 146–63
abdication of, 164–79
his life in exile, 180–86
second marriage of, 184
death of, 186
William, Crown Prince, 117, 155, 172, 173
Wilson, President, 168, 169
Windhorst, Ludwig, 46
Witwatersrand, the, 66
Worms, 43
Württemberg, King of, 125

"Yellow Peril", the, 64, 94
York, Duke of, 93

Zanzibar, 56
Zedlitz-Trützschler, Count, 84